POVERTY, RACISM, AND SEXISM

Exploring the structural causes and consequences of inequalities based on a person's race, class, and gender, *Poverty, Racism, and Sexism: The Reality of Oppression in America* concentrates on this formidable set of disadvantages, demonstrating how Americans are adversely affected by just one or a combination of three social factors.

Grounded in sociological thought, the text highlights unfolding stories about major social inequalities and relentless campaigns for people's rights. Weaving together such concepts as individualism, social reproduction, social class, and intersectionality, the book provides a framework for readers to understand the vast injustices these groups encounter, where and why they originated, and why they continue to endure.

Poverty, Racism, and Sexism is a compact, versatile volume which will prove an invaluable resource for those studying social inequality, social problems, social stratification, contemporary American society, social change, urban sociology, and poverty and inequality.

Christopher B. Doob is a sociologist, writer, researcher, and now Emeritus Professor of Southern Connecticut State University. He has written books on introductory sociology, social problems, race and ethnicity, social inequality and social stratification, and, most recently, sports.

POVERTY, RACISM, AND SEXISM

The Reality of Oppression in America

Christopher B. Doob

Routledge
Taylor & Francis Group

NEW YORK AND LONDON

First published 2021
by Routledge
605 Third Avenue, New York, NY 10158

and by Routledge
2 Park Square, Milton Park, Abingdon, Oxon OX14 4RN

Routledge is an imprint of the Taylor & Francis Group, an informa business

Library of Congress Cataloging-in-Publication Data
Names: Doob, Christopher Bates, author.
Title: Poverty, racism, & sexism : the reality of oppression in America /
Christopher B. Doob. Other titles: Poverty, racism, and sexism
Description: New York, NY : Routledge Books, 2021. |
Includes bibliographical references and index.
Identifiers: LCCN 2020051425 (print) | LCCN 2020051426 (ebook) |
ISBN 9780367672676 (hbk) | ISBN 9780367672683 (pbk) |
ISBN 9781003130550 (ebk)
Subjects: LCSH: Equality--United States. | Racism--United States. |
UnitedStates--Race relations. | Sexism--United States. |
Poverty--United States.
Classification: LCC HM821. D657 2021 (print) |
LCC HM821 (ebook) | DDC305--dc23
LC record available at https://lccn.loc.gov/2020051425
LC ebook record available at https://lccn.loc.gov/2020051426

ISBN: 978-0-367-67267-6 (hbk)
ISBN: 978-0-367-67268-3 (pbk)
ISBN: 978-1-003-13055-0 (ebk)

Typeset in Bembo
by Taylor & Francis Books

CONTENTS

ILLUSTRATIONS

Figures

Photos

Tables

PREFACE

I settled on this title, *Poverty, Racism, and Sexism: The Reality of Oppression in America*, early in the project and soon afterward went looking online for a resemblance to its combination of issues. In 1949 journalist Claudia Jones wrote what became a celebrated essay entitled "An End to the Neglect of the Problems of the Negro Woman," stating that there had been a "growth in the militant participation of Negro women … [in the] present-day struggles of the Negro people" (Jones 1949, 3). Jones's article highlighted three issues—social class, race, and gender—examining what became known as "the triple oppression" Black women suffered. Like Jones's approach the present book concentrates on a similar set of issues, indicating how poverty, racism and/or sexism become major injustices undermining or even ruining their lives.

Jones's article provided a powerful voice from the past. For me it was the first of many new voices, both from the past and present, that have illuminated this work and made its creation a constantly stimulating experience.

This is a compact, versatile volume that can prove useful for an array of courses on such subjects as social inequality, social problems, social stratification, contemporary American society, social change, urban sociology, and poverty and inequality. It is a fairly short work, focusing on what are indisputably core issues in the discipline.

The book uses a conflict perspective to examine the injustices that three large categories of Americans encounter in daily living. Throughout the chapters I provide extensive detail including quotes and concepts linked to people's disadvantaged lives in order to convey a clear sense of both the sources of their troubles and how actual individuals feel and react to the formidable stresses and dangers they must endure.

This is the second book in which I have focused on what appear to be central elements of a complex subject matter. In my *Racism: An American Cauldron*, internal colonialism, a version of conflict theory, examined four sources of oppression which the theory emphasized. In the present work, concentration on three important subject areas permits readers to develop a detailed sense of the scourges inflicted on millions of Americans' lives, with studies and reports testifying to their salience and often displaying provocative interrelationships between or among the three categories of people involved.

The discussion in this book focuses on poor people, racial minorities, and girls/women at various major phases in their lives—during both childhood and adolescence, at school, and on the job. In addition, the text examines critical quality-of-life issues and possible solutions to some of the major problems that the destructive conditions produce. A number of central concepts and ideas appear in the opening chapter and often return in the following ones—an approach producing more continuity in content than textbooks often provide and potentially making the material both more interesting and easier to grasp and retain.

I have written this book with the following motto in mind: Keep learning about the past and present while committing to a better future.

Bibliography

Jones, Claudia. 1949. "An End to the Neglect of the Problems of the Negro Woman." *Political Affairs* 28 (June): 1–19.

ACKNOWLEDGMENTS

Cliff Brown at the University of New Hampshire, Ruth Hernández at Skidmore College, Celeste Lee at Spelman College, Rhonda Levine at Colgate University, and David J. Maume at the University of Cincinnati provided very useful reviews.

I am grateful to Tyler Bay for his many editorial contributions. During the production process, Sarah M. Hall, Emma Harder, and Charlotte Taylor added significantly to the project's advancement. In addition, Jim DeLucia's observations have been helpful. Teresa Carballal has shared her singular perception, offering valuable insights and ideas.

1

LIVING AT RISK

Sociologist Alexis McCurn was starting a research project in Central East Oakland, a poor, largely Black city. One morning the bus in which she rode passed a small park, and McCurn saw women and men asleep on benches or on the grass and others talking while drinking from bottles in paper bags. As the bus proceeded along a thoroughfare, she noticed a number of Black women in their late twenties to mid-thirties, stationing themselves on this busy street with at least a block separating them. These were likely to be sex workers.

Not long after McCurn had started her ride, a Black man, probably in his late thirties, approached where she was sitting and slid into the seat behind her. Grasping the safety bar on the top of her seat, the man leaned forward and in a low voice asked, "How much do you charge for an hour?" Quickly McCurn turned around and said, "That's not my business." The man, however, was not convinced and indicated that he would "make it worth … [her] while." Fed up, McCurn replied loudly, "I am not a prostitute." The man was irritated. He said, "You don't have to get loud with me" (McCurn 2017, 52).

McCurn concluded that because she was a fairly young Black woman who found herself in a poor area where prostitution was prevalent, the man felt confident that she was a sex worker. In McCurn's study this was one of her first encounters with the local people, and she soon concluded that it was fairly typical of the assaults on their self-image that young Black women living in poor urban communities often suffer (McCurn 2017, 52–53).

Such assaults are known as **microaggressions**—disrespectful behavior, whether intended or not, that indicates the person initiating the action considers the other individual an inferior (Krivkovich et al. 2018). Clearly the microaggressions involved the three central issues featured in this work. To begin, the residents were all poor, living in a city "that has long struggled with drug activity, poverty, and violence" (McCurn 2017, 52).

Racism and sexism also played prominent roles. McCurn noted that in Central East Oakland, Black men encountered "a routinely denied mainstream masculine status." To compensate for this denial, they frequently sought to dominate Black women, inflicting verbal and physical sexual harassment and even assault while struggling to build a satisfactory sense of male identity. Living in a disadvantaged community containing many poor Black men, young Black women could often find themselves "targets of sexually predatory male behavior." Furthermore, McCurn noted, extensive mass-media representations of Black women have "reinforce[d] the widespread internalized view of them as subordinate and worthy of oppression and assault" (McCurn 2017, 54).

Like the women featured in McCurn's research, the people discussed in the upcoming chapters frequently must endure a variety of painful, debilitating conditions. Sometimes the situation involves one disadvantaged status they possess, and sometimes as in the McCurn study more than one. Certain fundamental ideas discussed in the upcoming section will generally guide the discussion.

A Conceptual Framework for Analyzing At-Risk Groups

A **risk** is the probability of an unwanted outcome involving exposure to loss or injury. In this work what one might consider the most obviously powerful groups—the wealthy, whites, and men—have created risks for historically oppressed groups—the poor, racial minorities, and women. However, risks result from additional sources, including self-destructive behavior. People take risks frequently—driving without a seat belt, drinking too much, forsaking dietary restrictions a doctor advocated, and so forth (Clearwatch Security 2020; Protection Circle 2017). "Disadvantaged" can serve as an alternative designation for the three at-risk categories of people represented in this work.

The original researchers examining risks were epidemiologists, who dealt with the incidence, location, and control of diseases. A **risk factor** is an element in a situation that increases the probability of a certain outcome, usually an unpleasant one such as a disease or some other negative condition (Creavey et al. 2018, 483–84; Offord and Kraemer 2000). While extensive attention to risk factors focuses on susceptibility to diseases, the conditions exacerbating psychological, economic, political, and social problems the members of the three categories of people featured in this book suffer can also be risk factors.

The pervasive risks poor individuals, racial minorities, and women face bring to mind **conflict theory**, which is a perspective contending that the struggle for wealth, power, and prestige in society should be the central concern of sociology. It certainly is a central concern throughout this book. The young Black women living in the poor area that McCurn described are almost certain to suffer the adverse effects of that struggle.

Conflict theory has benefited from Karl Marx's insightful, economically grounded analysis, which originated in the nineteenth century but continues to provide insight into the workings of modern society. Within the capitalist system, Marx focused on two social classes, which differ in their relationship to the means of production—the factories, farms, and businesses where goods and services are developed and dispersed. The bourgeoisie is the class with ownership of the various means of production. That ownership provides wide-ranging power and control over business activity as well as other major sectors of society. The proletariat comprises the workers who do not own the means of production. They must labor for wages because they have no other source of income (Marx and Engels 1959, 4).

Marx described capitalism as a brutal system, driven by the bourgeoisie's unrelenting pressure for ever-expanding profits. The value of a product is largely based on the monetary worth of a worker's labor. However, Marx emphasized, workers only receive a small, subsistence portion of the value of their labor. Marx strongly condemned the capitalist system when he wrote, "The bourgeoisie ... has pitilessly torn asunder the motley feudalities that bound man to ... [others in the work world] and has left remaining no other nexus between man and man than naked self-interest, than callous 'cash payment'" (Marx and Engels 2005, 43).

Marx observed that to keep control of capitalism, the bourgeoisie has powerful tools available. One is ideology, which involves the complex of values and beliefs that support a society's social-stratification systems and their distribution of wealth, income, and power (Cole 2019; Doob 2019, 34). Clearly support for capitalism has been a major contributor to American ideology.

In his well-known *The Protestant Ethic and the Spirit of Capitalism*, sociologist Max Weber commented on how religion seemed to promote Americans' commitment to capitalism. He noted that the early Puritan settlers believed in the Calvinist doctrine of predestination, which stated that before birth God selected people either for salvation or damnation. While individuals could not influence that outcome, they could get an indication which it would be by examining the evidence. In actuality, Weber emphasized, Calvinism "gave ... groups of religiously inclined people a positive incentive to asceticism" (Weber 1958, 121)—specifically, a powerful reason to work hard, to save, and to invest what they had saved to become wealthy and manifest the certainty that they were heading toward salvation. Eventually the doctrine of predestination no longer held sway, but the practical measures promoting capitalist activity involving working hard and seeking wealth remained highly influential throughout the society (Weber 1958).

While widespread support for capitalist activity persists, it appears that a unified American ideology is problematic, with survey data suggesting that party membership provides a clear indication of a split in shared values and beliefs. For example, a nationally representative sample of American residents 18 and older

Dems → too much inequality

found that Democrats and Democratic leaners are almost twice as likely as their Republican counterparts to say that the country has too much inequality—78 percent vs. 41 percent—and an even greater disparity between the two parties' supporters exists on whether or not the government should make the reduction of economic inequality a priority, with 61 percent of Democrats and just 20 percent of Republicans agreeing with that course of action (Horowitz et al. 2020).

Another influential concept used in this work has its groundwork in Marxist theory and its unrelenting criticism of capitalism (Bhattacharya and Ferguson 2018). Social reproduction is the process by which people belonging to certain categories, such as social classes, have differing access to the valuable resources that influence the transmission of inequality from one generation to the next (Bourdieu 1977; Bourdieu and Passeron 1990). Research on the topic has tended to reach a distinct conclusion—which, according to sociologist Jay MacLeod, "attempts to show how and why the United States can be depicted more accurately as the place where 'the rich get richer and the poor stay poor' than as 'the land of opportunity'" (MacLeod 2009, 7–8). Historically, however, "the land of opportunity" idea has received extensive support.

In the late nineteenth century, Horatio Alger, Jr. wrote over 100 stories about poor boys who moved to a big city and through hard work, perseverance, and good fortune eventually became wealthy—"rags to riches" was the theme (Encyclopedia Britannica 2020). It was a popular idea, embraced by many Americans for decades. On the other hand, as MacLeod suggested, the concept of social reproduction takes an opposing position, emphasizing the persistent sources supporting social inequality that remain prominent and influential in the society.

Some of the benefits associated with social reproduction are obvious, such as a family's economic status, which permits parents in the more affluent social classes to obtain the various goods and services that can support their children's success in school and elsewhere while the poor and others in lower-income classes cannot afford to do so and as a result have less access to those benefits.

During the social-reproduction process, children in more affluent classes receive additional, less obvious advantages. For instance, compared to their poor counterparts, middle-class parents are more inclined to provide a planned socialization experience for their children—to use extensive dialogue to give them knowledge and support that both supplies useful information leading to a successful life and encourages them to be confident and self-content and, in addition, increases the likelihood that as parents themselves the children will transmit that same advantages to their offspring (Talbot 2015).

All in all, one might consider that the concept of social reproduction suggests that life resembles a competitive race without a conventional common starting point for all participants; instead they are strewn out at the start, with the family into which they are born determining the location they receive.

PHOTO 1.1 While the material advantages parents in more affluent social classes can transmit to their children are significant, they are also more likely than the poor to provide their offspring nonmaterial assistance, which can help them learn ways of becoming more effective in interaction with others. In this instance the father and mother are somewhat critical of their teenage son's behavior and are trying to explain how he might have handled a perplexing situation more effectively.

Source: Shutterstock/ Iakov Filimonov

Growing up, children, especially when they are very young, are often unaware of the benefits they receive, simply acquiring them as a standard part of daily living. Seemingly minor encounters can produce major impacts. With a parent or a teacher, a child engages in a provocative dialogue and might begin to sense the invaluable contribution to his or her understanding and growth such exchanges can impart.

In fact, among adults, too, the advantages that occur in the course of social reproduction, while often significant, are likely to go largely unexamined, making it probable or even inevitable that following the American tradition, the beneficiaries will simply celebrate their individual achievements and be critical of the more modest outcomes that disadvantaged groups attain.

Parents' failure to examine and adjust their socialization impact can be damaging for children. Growing up, I had a middle-class friend, whose father incessantly preached a sink-or-swim, individualistic ideology. My friend was confused and also intimidated, needing pointers on how to advance his own interests and goals but feeling intimidated about broaching the subject at home. Once after receiving an especially trying parental lecture, he told me, "Dad doesn't seem to realize that what he asks sounds easy, but I haven't the slightest idea about where to start." Meanwhile he began to realize over time that some of his age peers were receiving detailed parental assistance on similar challenges. As a result, probably unbeknownst to the father in this instance, his sink-or-swim approach put his son at a decided disadvantage when compared to others his age. One point of emphasis, however, is that while middle-class children can lose out during social reproduction, their less affluent peers generally tend to be more disadvantaged.

The issue just examined suggests the possibility that once people understand how the process of social reproduction works, they might start appreciating that many situations where historically selected groups have been considered innately inferior turn out to be simply instances where their members were deprived of material or nonmaterial resources that could have helped them be successful.

Consider, for instance, US public-schools, where poor people generally receive an inferior education, increasing the likelihood that they express themselves less effectively and have fewer basic skills for success in most better-paying jobs.

An awareness of social reproduction and the role schooling plays in affecting it encourages an examination of how public-schools are financed. It turns out that the United States is one of very few nations with a heavy reliance on local funding. Around the country, school districts use property tax to provide about 45 percent of the total cost. Schools in wealthier areas receive more local funding because the properties in their districts are more valuable, generating more property tax, especially compared to impoverished areas. In most other wealthy countries, the contribution from the federal and regional governments provides the dominant share (Leachman and Figueroa 2019).

As a result of the American system of public-school funding, high-poverty schools generally suffer significant deficiencies in such critical areas as early childhood education, quality teaching, and the provision of a top-level curriculum (Martin et al. 2018).

Besides deficient local funding, children in less affluent districts have additional educational disadvantages. A significant issue is that tutoring for the Scholastic Assessment Test (SAT) or the American College Testing (ACT) is expensive. Social reproduction comes into play, with well-off families much more readily able to afford purchasing the service for their children and obtaining the significant educational benefits provided. Even though some colleges have made these tests optional, the College Board, which produces the SAT, continues to emphasize that the test is an important factor in influencing college-admissions decisions. Many American parents agree. In affluent neighborhoods as many as three quarters of the students receive tutoring in preparing for these tests. The estimate is that students working with a private tutor will spend between 20 and 30 hours, costing parents as much as $10,000 (Wellemeyer 2019).

It is hardly surprising that when the SAT results for 2016 were divided into eight categories based on family income, students' composite scores were higher with each increasingly affluent category. Thus test takers from families that earned less than $20,000 a year averaged a total of 1,314 points for the three sections, those in the $20,001-$40,000 category increased to 1,394 points, and those at the top in the over $200,000 bracket obtained 1,717 points (CollegeBoard 2016). As the concept social reproduction emphasizes, social inequality is likely to perpetuate in this situation, with the more affluent the parents, the greater the likelihood that they can purchase the tutoring that will increase the likelihood that their children will score high on the SAT or ACT and enter the college of their choice. That educational experience, in turn, is likely to serve as the gateway to an economically and occupationally elevated existence that probably is similar to their parents'.

The discussion of social reproduction suggests the importance of the issue of **social class**—a large category of similarly ranked people located in a hierarchy and distinguished from the other categories by such traits as education, occupation, income, and wealth. Throughout the book it will be clear that the concept of social class is a basic building block for sociological analysis.

Social reproduction emphasizes that certain groups possess advantages that promote greater success than their less well situated peers, and the three categories of people examined in this book are prominent victims of such unequal outcomes.

The American Context Featuring Poverty, Race, and Gender

The renowned sociologist C. Wright Mills distinguished between what he called "personal troubles" and "public issues." Personal troubles are an individual's private matters that they recognize, and when difficulties arise involving them it is their responsibility to find a resolution. In contrast, public issues are matters that transcend individuals, involving situations in which the structures, values, and beliefs of a society interrelate and affect outcomes. Unlike personal troubles, public issues are just that—public, subjects that can readily lead to discussion and debate and perhaps organized activities where various individuals and groups seek to improve the public setting for disadvantaged people's benefit (Mills 1959, 8–9).

In many instances, however, the members of those groups can find the situations they face pose painful difficulties, and they are left to their own devices in dealing with them. Consider the following example. A 12-year-old child is failing in school and is unhappy, viewing the situation as a private trouble that is something he or she must face alone. In this instance parents and teachers are consistent, berating the youngster for not taking school seriously and persistently getting low grades. However, like many situations, an unexplored public issue exists. The school is in a poor district, and as the previous discussion indicated, the American public-school system generally underfunds facilities in such areas, increasing the likelihood of inferior schooling and putting a high percentage of children at risk for doing badly.

Historically topics like the unequal funding of schools have received limited public attention. In recent years that has sometimes changed, and a useful concept addresses that altering reality. **Intersectionality** is the recognition that an individual's oppressions, limitations, and opportunities often result from the combined impact of two or more influential statuses—in particular, gender, race, social class, age, job, parent role, and sexual preference (Castro and Holvino 2016, 329–30; Chan and Erby 2018, 1250–51; Gearity and Metzger 2017, 161; Gordon 2016, 340–45; Harris and Ford 2017, 43–44). As when using the concept social reproduction, individuals analyzing intersectionality must make a determination of the relevant causal factors and their interaction in the process at hand.

The following illustration involving race and social class indicates that historical connections among intersectional statuses are often apparent. The first Black arrivals in this country were slaves, denied their freedom and compelled to engage in forced labor until slavery ended. At that time they might have been technically free, but because of their earlier lives in slavery, the vast majority of African Americans were poor and deficient in the skills and education that would have provided them a chance to make a decent living. As upcoming chapters indicate, the severe, combined disadvantages of being both Black and poor have disproportionately hampered numerous African Americans' economic and social progress from post-slavery days to the current era. In addition to the risks accompanying race and poverty, Black girls and women have often faced additional challenges as females.

The concept of intersectionality can be reminiscent of C. Wright Mills's distinction between private troubles and public issues. Sometimes when the members of selected groups suffer significant disadvantages, they undoubtedly visualize the issues as private troubles, with little possibility of any collective action to overcome the adverse conditions. Advocates of intersectionality, in contrast, firmly believe that people possessing two or more at-risk statuses should view their challenges as public issues, examining how the statuses combine to produce greater disadvantage and then forcing change in the oppressed conditions that their members suffer.

The intersectional perspective emphasizes that when traditional analyses focused on a single factor—say gender or race—the dominant tendency has been to dichotomize the factor into a privileged category and a degraded one—man vs. woman, white vs. Black person, straight vs. lesbian or gay individual. Instead the intersectional strategy involves an appreciation of a broad social context, where investigation involves a thorough, dispassionate evaluation of the key statuses impacting people's lives as well as an assessment of how those factors interact with each other and a plan about the reduction of current inequalities. In the course of these activities, an appreciation of the reality of social reproduction, if not the use of the concept itself, becomes an imperative.

Addressing women of color, questioners often assume that one of the two traits dominates—that they either consider that belonging to a racial minority or being a woman is more significant. Ancella Livers, a journalist and a management specialist, disagreed, contending that "the experiences of women of color belie these assumptions. They are 'both/and' not 'either/or'" (Livers 2006, 205).

Detail about the following event supports Livers's position, with the failure to address intersectionality readily proving detrimental for victimized groups. In 1976 Emma DeGraffenreid and several other Black female co-workers sued General Motors for discrimination, contending that the automaker segregated its workforce by both gender and race, and Black women lost out on both counts. For instance, they could not get a job on the factory floor because those positions were only for men, and while women could qualify for office jobs, they were usually reserved for whites.

As a result Black women were doubly deprived, shut out from both types of jobs because of their combination of gender and race. However, the court refused to consider that intersectionality was a valid reality, ruling that the plaintiffs needed to focus on either gender or racial discrimination.

Kimberlé Crenshaw, a young law professor, considered the DeGraffenreid suit "a big miss"—an overlooked chance to win an important case that indicated clearly how Black women lost out because of the combined discriminatory

PHOTO 1.2 Supporters of women's rights are likely to grasp the reality of intersectionality, with not only gender but also race and social class often influencing their sense of its effect.

Source: Shutterstock/ Drazen Zigic

impact of both gender and race. That realization motivated Crenshaw to develop the concept of intersectionality, believing it could help reveal the "profound invisibility [Black women suffered] in relation to the law." Originally, Crenshaw noted, she applied the concept to Black women, but later on she and others discovered its relevance for people belonging to various groups with two or more disadvantaged statuses (Crenshaw 2019). Throughout these chapters it becomes apparent that both historic restrictions and current discriminations can combine to limit intersectional individuals' outlooks and goals.

Intersectionality and social reproduction are important concepts involving the broad social context affecting people. While intersectionality examines the effect upon disadvantaged individuals or groups of various statuses they possess, social reproduction focuses on resources likely to perpetuate intergenerational inequality. Both concepts can be useful in examining poor people's lives.

The American Outlook on Poverty

In our society poverty is a controversial topic, starting with its measurement. The United States Census Bureau establishes poverty thresholds based on federal government estimates of the cash incomes below which a household has insufficient money to obtain food and other primary necessities. Government personnel update the numbers annually using the inflation figures which the Consumer Price Index provides. For example, in 2019 the Census Bureau established the following estimates of poverty thresholds—below $13,011 for a single individual and below $31,021 for a five-person household (United States Census Bureau 2020). In 2019 the nation contained about 34 million poor people, with a poverty rate of 10.5 percent (Semega et al. 2020).

For many Americans the conditions promoting disadvantages for vulnerable groups have seldom been a major concern or interest. Their focus has been elsewhere, finding the American ideology exciting, offering a romanticized view of the fame and fortune people can achieve. In 1931 in *The Epic of America*, historian James Truslow Adams spoke of what he considered "the American dream" in glowing terms, indicating that the country was

> that dream of a land … in which each man and each woman shall be able to attain to the fullest stature of which they are innately capable, and be recognized by others for what they are, regardless of the fortuitous circumstances of birth or position.
>
> *(Adams 1931, 214–15)*

People's innate capability, which Adams cited, has been a point of emphasis for many Americans, whose ideology unreservedly honors individual achievement, believing that groups' and individuals' inborn capacity for accomplishment ranges widely and strongly influences, even determines their success in society.

Sharing a similar point of view, nineteenth-century sociologist Herbert Spencer wrote about "the survival of the fittest," indicating that its meaning was much like Charles Darwin's concept of "natural selection, or the preservation of … favoured … [species] in the struggle for life." Darwin focused on animals and plants, contending that those making the best adaptations to their environment over time are more likely to survive and thrive. Spencer believed that the same process applied to human beings, and he enthusiastically asserted that "[i]ndeed, when once enunciated, the … [application of Darwin's concept to human beings] is so obvious to scarcely need proof" (Spencer 1864, Vol. I, 445). A convenient claim since he offered no plausibly supportive evidence.

Nonetheless over time many Americans, particularly those who are economically, politically, and socially well situated, have applauded Spencer's conclusion, declaring that it is in people's best interest that the alleged fittest of human beings—namely affluent individuals and one racial group, namely whites—control the society, engaging in activities that supposedly would be most productive for all people. Since that era the prevailing national policy has been to follow the fiercely evolutionary course Spencer outlined, with minimal intervention by government or other organizations to support the supposedly "less fit" groups (Breslin 2010; Crossman 2017; Khan Academy 2019).

References throughout the book indicate that in the US, the federal government spends less money for poor people's health care, education, and other basic needs than its affluent European peers. Widespread ideological support for Spencer's position would appear to promote that long-term trend.

It appears, however, that Spencer's doctrine possesses a major omission: Yes, it can be true that disadvantaged groups like those examined in this work are less prepared for success, but he ignored the reality that such people have lacked crucial resources and opportunities to be successful, simply asserting the unsubstantiated claim that they are inherently inferior.

A popular, fairly similar ideological position involves the so-called "meritocracy myth." This idea first appeared in the English-speaking world when in 1956 Alan Fox, a socialist scholar, sharply criticized what he characterized as a merit system that emphasized successful people's alleged superior traits but in fact simply rewarded individuals whose education and other advantages already made them privileged (Rottenberg 2018).

In citing this viewpoint, contemporary economist Robert Reich wrote, "Most Americans still cling to the meritocratic notion that people are rewarded according to their efforts and abilities. But meritocracy is becoming a cruel joke" (Reich 2019). Sociologist Stephen J. McNamee has taken a similar position. Writing four editions of a book entitled *The Meritocracy Myth*, McNamee indicated that while he acknowledged that an individual's contribution has merit, it is far from being the only factor influencing a person's success. Other possible contributors, he noted, include inheritance, helpful social contacts, knowledge of the behavioral standards for key groups, the appropriate education, and protection from such dangers as significant discrimination and growing economic inequality (McNamee 2014; McNamee 2018; McNamee and Miller 2014).

Meanwhile in recent years as Table 1.1 indicates, the ostensibly "fittest" people received a distinct financial boost with the passage of the Tax Cuts and Job Acts of 2017. A feature of such legislation is that much of its content is technical, often obscuring the fact that privileged groups receive special advantages.

During the COVID-19 pandemic, Congress passed The Coronavirus Aid, Relief, and Economic Security Act, better known as the CARES Act, to assist both financially vulnerable families dealing with stay-at-home orders and economically at-risk businesses that with aid would survive and be able to employ workers when it was safe to return to jobs. In short, the act's stated intention was to help employees and organizations in serious financial need during a major crisis.

However, Jesse Drucker, an investigative reporter, indicated that "if you spend a little time digging into some of the [law's] provisions," it becomes apparent that wealthy companies and individuals were the chief beneficiaries, including some businesses unaffected by the pandemic.

TABLE 1.1 Wealthy Individuals' Tax Cuts and Loopholes

Officially the Tax Cuts and Jobs Act of 2017 cut corporate tax rates from 35 to 21 percent. That reduction, however, is only corporations' most obvious current tax benefit. In addition, through their extensive influence in the political process, these powerful entities have obtained substantial loopholes, greatly reducing their tax payments. While corporations received various taxation advantages long before the 2017 tax law, that act has sharply increased the impact of new tax breaks—to the extent that the Congressional Budget Office estimated that in the course of the decade after the law was passed, it will drain an additional $1.9 trillion from federal revenues.

Some specifics regarding corporate taxes include:

Decline of corporate tax revenues over time	From 32 percent of the total in 1950 to 10 percent in 2013
The 258 Fortune 500 companies that were profitable every year between 2008 and 2015	Averaged a tax rate of 21.2 percent, slightly over half the 35 percent rate required at the time
Between 2008 and 2015, some corporations paying no federal income tax and others under 10 percent	Eighteen major corporations including General Electric and Priceline.com paid no federal income tax and 48 less than 10 percent
One hundred or 39 percent of 258 corporations that were profitable every year between 2008 and 2015	Paid no income tax for one or more years during that time period
Means by which US corporations avoid paying $90 billion a year	By sending profits to their subsidies, which are often located in foreign tax havens

Source: Policy 2017; Thornton 2018.

Drucker indicated that the most prominent example of his claim involved businesses that documented losses on their tax returns. In many instances these companies were very profitable, but the losses allowed them to offset taxes they might owe elsewhere, such as gains made in the stock market. Before the CARES Act, that benefit existed but only for people making less than half a million dollars a year. Following its passage, however, Congress temporarily removed the cap, helping only wealthy people and over 10 years depriving the government of about $135 billion. In summary Drucker stated, "the government, in the CARES [A]ct, is going to give out $135 billion in tax relief only to people that make at least half a million dollars, only to the top 1% of taxpayers in this country" (Gross 2020).

Survey evidence indicates that the American public generally opposes such Congressional largesse. For instance, a national Reuters/Ipsos poll of over 4,000 respondents indicated that 64 percent of the sample either strongly or somewhat agreed that the very rich need to pay a wealth tax—specifically an extra share of their wealth each year to support important public programs. While 77 percent of Democrats supported the idea, a majority of Republicans (at 53 percent) did too (Schneider and Kahn 2020). These findings suggest widespread recognition that the huge amount of potential tax money wealthy citizens avoid paying represents a significant loss for disadvantaged groups, which sorely need the benefits those tax revenues could generate.

As far as poor people are concerned, the one-time cash benefits they received from the CARES Act, sometimes accompanied by increased unemployment payments, provided only a brief respite, and as two major studies indicated, the number of poverty-stricken people sharply increased in the months that followed, particularly among Blacks, Hispanics, and children. The two investigations differed somewhat in their representation of poverty and in the time period covered. One of them, which the University of Chicago and Notre Dame conducted, found that three months after the CARES emergency package ended, 6 million more American residents experienced poverty (Han et al. 2020; Parolin et al. 2020). Bruce D. Meyer, an economist at the University of Chicago and an author of the aforementioned study, regretted the findings. "These numbers are very concerning ... They tell us people are having a lot more trouble paying their bills, paying their rent, putting food on the table" (DeParle 2020).

The overall reality is that the United States does a mediocre job of alleviating poverty. In 2016 when compared to 34 other affluent nations, the US and Israel tied for the highest relative poverty rate, measured as people possessing less than half the median disposable income, which is the money people retain after the removal of all taxes. The US and Israel both had nearly 18 percent of their residents qualifying as poor (OECD Social Indicators 2019).

It turns out that the United States spends far less on programs assisting the poor than virtually all its affluent peers. Most European nations and Canada have developed forms of assistance that often keep families out of poverty, providing generous cash assistance to children, extensive unemployment payments, and universal or nearly universal health coverage. In contrast, the American poor, traditionally regarded as less fit, lose out. Economist Rebecca Blank concluded, "While low-income families in the United States work more than in many other countries, they are not able to make up for lower governmental income support relative to their European counterparts" (Confronting Poverty 2019).

Throughout these chapters discussions involving income tend to focus on poor people, but sometimes additional Americans can find themselves in dire financial situations. Using data from several surveys conducted by the Federal Reserve, researchers learned that adult members of middle-income households located between the fortieth and seventieth percentiles of the national income distribution and possessing incomes between $40,000 and $70,000 a year indicated that even modest expenses they suddenly encountered could prove a major challenge for them. One third of these middle-income adults said that faced with a sudden $400 expense, they would either need to borrow money, sell something, or simply be unable to pay the amount (Brainard 2019).

Just as proponents of the American ideology have harshly addressed poor people's needs and interests, they have historically mistreated racial minorities.

Race, Racism, and Racial Groups

The first prominent arrival to the New World anticipated the potential for exploiting its original inhabitants. Writing to the King and Queen of Spain about the Indians he met, Christopher Columbus indicated that they were peaceful toward their neighbors and that "their discourse is ever sweet and gentle, and accompanied with a smile; and though it is true they are naked, yet their manners are decorous and praiseworthy" (Brown 1972, 1). To Columbus and the millions who followed, these seemingly positive qualities were signs of weakness. The Indians were sweet, pliable, but definitely savage people, who, Columbus believed, should be "made to work, sow, and do all that is necessary and to *adopt our ways* [the author's italics] (Brown 1972, 2). The European invaders provided religion and schooling but also ruthlessly appropriated most of the land and imposed an alien and alienating way of life.

Besides his exploration of the New World, Columbus, unbeknownst to him, appears to have had another historical impact. Supposedly he was the first person to call the people he encountered Indians, mistakenly thinking he had ended up in India. In ensuing centuries some of the so-called Indians became critical of the term, noting its pejorative use in such common phrases as "drunken Indian" or "rotten Indian." For these critics Native American became the preferred designation (Giago 2011).

That usage, however, hardly resolved the issue. A writer on the topic noted,

> The term [Indian] remains in use because there are still many people who have been called, and have called themselves, Indians all their lives. Who is

going to argue with an elder or a veteran who served their people and this country as an Indian and still wants to be known as that?

(Marks 2018)

At the moment both terms are in use and are likely to remain so. Dr. Andrew Jolivétte, the former chairman of the American Indian Studies Department at San Francisco State University, indicated that no single term is appropriate for referring to the indigenous peoples of the Americas. He added,

> On some days I might say Indian, other days I might say Native [American] … And that's okay, we have to be comfortable in this society with the fact that identities are malleable—they move, they change as we evolve and get older.

(Ling 2016)

So that's that, and I will adhere to Jolivétte's standard.

Like Native Americans, African Americans were brutally exploited. Kept in slavery, they were at the mercy of a system where as a result of the intersectional combination of poverty and racism, the social reproduction they encountered provided almost no access to resources and opportunities to improve either their own lives or their children's. Inevitably racist outlooks and rationalizations prevailed during slavery times.

Southern whites often argued in favor of the system by contending that Blacks were inferior, representing an irreversible deterioration from what was supposedly the original white race. Whites' domination, they believed, was the inevitable outcome of that process (Fredrickson 2002, 79–80). During slavery some intellectuals asserted that not only were Blacks inferior, fated to be a subservient class, but that such an arrangement assured a productive, stable society, where, to be sure, whites were decidedly the major beneficiaries. In the 1850s George Fitzhugh's *Sociology for the South* and *Cannibals All!* emphasized that the abolition of slavery would create a brutal society in which employers would mercilessly exploit Black workers. Slavery, Fitzhugh enthusiastically claimed, was actually a fairly benign system that protected them (Bailyn et al. 1977, 581).

It turns out that most modern Americans know little about slavery, either details about the horrors it inflicted or about its major role in the rise of the American economy to world prominence. With this recognition of the limited extent to which early Blacks' lives mattered, *The New York Times* initiated "The 1619 Project" with the intention of "telling the unvarnished truth" and in the process providing guidance for a more honest, informative way of teaching history (New York Times Magazine 2019, 1). If that initiative proves successful, then other investigators could extend the project onward, ultimately spelling out in detail the uninterrupted oppression and vast loss of opportunity Blacks have suffered from slavery times to the present.

As historical examples illustrate, racism has been a harsh reality since Europeans first came to the New World. **Racism** is the belief that real or imagined traits of one race establish its superiority over another or others. People committed to racism do not assess circumstances affecting the group in question but simply assume that it is innate racial traits producing their limitations. Racism is often quite subtle, toned down, but like other "isms," those who engage in it inevitably feel superior to the individuals in the target group.

A progression toward equal rights for racial minorities has been a slow, painful process. Nonetheless distinct racial progress has occurred. One advancement has featured **affirmative action**, which is a policy that seeks to improve the educational or occupational opportunities for candidates historically limited by their race, gender, religion, disability, age, or national origin. Businesses and government agencies have often established programs to implement the policy. In some instances government programs require that organizations achieve certain hiring quotas, denying funding if they are not obtained. Critics of affirmative action are likely to emphasize the cost of the programs and the danger of hiring less qualified candidates (Kenton 2019).

A national sample of adult Americans indicated that 61 percent of the respondents supported affirmative action for racial minorities, with 72 percent of Blacks, 66 percent of Hispanics, and 57 percent of whites responding positively. In addition, individuals who described themselves as liberals were distinctly more likely to take a supportive position—83 percent, compared to 50 percent for conservatives (Norman 2019).

Presently extensive racial discrimination persists, with many people pessimistic about race relations. A national survey conducted by Gallup Poll in 2001 indicated that 44 percent of the respondents were very or somewhat satisfied with the state of race relations while 48 percent were very or somewhat dissatisfied. In 2020 the respective figures were 36 and 58 percent—a distinct turn toward the dissatisfied options. Furthermore Blacks and whites had differing opinions on such issues. In 2020 when asked about relations between those two racial groups, 46 percent of whites chose very good or somewhat good while just 36 percent of Blacks picked those two options (Gallup Poll 2020).

Another national survey indicated that the Trump administration contributed to the growing sense that race relations are bad. Fifty-six percent of the interviewees believed that Trump had made race relations worse while 15 percent stated that he had produced an improvement. In addition, about two thirds of the respondents declared that since Trump became president, it has become more common for people to make racist statements (Horowitz et al. 2019).

In fact, the issue involves more than simply racist statements and requires detailed commentary. Evidence indicates that in recent years the number of white supremacist groups has been increasing. While the precise numbers are difficult to determine, prominent sources agree about an increase and make roughly similar assessments. For example, the Center for Homeland Defense and Security concluded that in 2020 there were 199 white supremacist groups divided into two categories—first, neo-Nazis who claimed that except for Jews who are deemed inferior, white racial groups are superior to others and second, white nationalists who are committed to protecting white culture and interests from allegedly destructive immigrants and minorities (Bruza 2020). Focusing on the second type of white supremacists, the well-known Southern Poverty Law Center indicated that in 2019 the nation contained 155 white nationalist organizations, a 55 percent increase from 2017 (Southern Poverty Law Center 2020).

Research conducted by the 2016 American National Election Survey during Trump's first campaign for the presidency included about 3,000 non-Hispanic whites, who ranged widely in their political and social views. About 6 percent of them supported a set of three convictions—a strong sense of white identity, an uncompromising desire to share other whites' interests and goals, and a sense that as whites they suffered at least a moderate degree of discrimination. This segment of the white population felt that in recent years with a steady influx of immigrants and increased rights and privileges for minorities, including the election of a Black president, they had experienced an erosion of whites' previous dominance (Clark 2020; Hawley 2018; Jardina 2019).

During Trump's presidency two major factors seemed to support the rapid growth of white supremacy movements. The administration contained a persistent concentration of individuals who have been strong supporters of white nationalism, including White House senior advisor Steven Miller, White House strategist and campaign manager Steve Bannon, and former Attorney General Jeff Sessions, whose influence continued to permeate the administration after his departure. In addition, Trump readily took racist positions and engaged in racist rhetoric, tweeting that Black Lives Matter is "a symbol of hate" and declaring that he preferred immigrants from majority-white nations like Norway and not from "s***hole countries" in Africa and the Caribbean (Collins 2020).

During Trump's presidency the administration often received support from conservative TV programming, which would constantly emphasize the danger facing whites' interests—for instance, shortly before the 2018 mid-term election Fox News commenter Tucker Carlson warning that Mexico was trying to "change the demographics" of the country to alter election results and Laura Ingraham asserting that Democrats "want to replace you, the American voters, with newly amnestied citizens and an ever increasing number of chain migrants" (Serwer 2019).

In early 2020 the FBI became aware that what its officials referred to as a "Michigan-based militia group" was seeking to mobilize a large force of supporters to storm the capitol building and take hostages, including Governor Whitmer. Meanwhile President Trump and Governor Whitmer were openly feuding about the coronavirus, particularly the governor's stay-at-home order to reduce the surging number of cases. During the first presidential debate, Trump refused to condemn white supremacist groups, calling on them to "[s]tand back and stand by" (Carrega et al. 2020; Jones and Waldrop 2020). It was a clear call for the white supremacist groups' mobilization. Several months earlier in response to the governor's stay-at-home order, Trump had tweeted, "LIBERATE MICHIGAN" (Wise 2020).

Then in October 2020 federal and state officials, confident that their undercover informants had gathered enough information for an indictment, announced the arrest of 14 individuals charged with the intentions of kidnapping Governor Whitmer and also overthrowing several other state governments the suspects believed were violating the US Constitution (Carrega et al. 2020). While President Trump did not actually meet and plan with the militia group, the events that occurred pointedly suggest the decisive impact on such democracy-threatening schemes that a major political figure can help ignite.

Finally, it seems useful to make several observations about the racial designations used for the categories of people featured in this book. The terms "racial minority" and "people of color" are used interchangeably. In addition, in referring to racial groups, sources often mention Hispanics (Latinos) as a separate category, suggesting that they represent an ethnic group and not an actual race. While that is an accurate conclusion, it seems to make the subsequent reference cumbersome, and so my designation will be "racial groups" with the understanding going forward that at times the use of the term represents an oversimplification of reality. One more point that is gaining public support but remains debatable: When referring to the two largest racial groups in our society, "Blacks" will be capitalized because like other capitalized racial groups—Asians, Hispanics, and Native Americans—a shared sense of history and identity exists while "whites" remains lowercase because a common tradition among the members is less evident (Coleman 2020; Laws 2020). Throughout the text the terms Blacks and African Americans are used interchangeably, and so are the designations Hispanics and Latinos even though the latter pair are not fully synonymous. Like racial minorities, women have had a lengthy struggle to achieve equality.

Girls, Women, and Sexism

In the pre-industrial life of early America, work was usually home-centered, with family members dependent on each other for basic sustenance. While fathers and sons were farmers, shopkeepers, laborers, and other job holders, wives and daughters cooked, cleaned, engaged in child care, spun and wove, and made clothes, candles, soap, and shoes.

Women, however, were not always restricted to household tasks. Some, primarily widows of businessmen, replaced their deceased husbands, serving as innkeepers, merchants, printers, craft workers, physicians, tavern owners, and shopkeepers (Hesse-Biber and Carter 2005, 21–22; Padavic and Reskin 2002, 60).

In his autobiography Benjamin Franklin described a printer's widow who took over her husband's business and proved more successful than he had been. A reason for her success was that in her native Holland a woman's education included bookkeeping. Always practical, Franklin suggested that if widowed, women would find this work "of more use to them and their children ... than either music or dancing, ... enabling them to continue, perhaps, a profitable mercantile house" (Franklin 1962, 95).

Franklin's recommendation had little impact, and so such self-employed women were more the exception than the rule. What became fairly common during the early industrial era was that some women worked on average about 12 hours a day for low wages in mills, factories, sweatshops, or as household servants (Padavic and Reskin 2002, 61).

Over time, however, some occupational advances for women began to appear. The following list includes some of the changes in women's rights and activities that occurred in the wake of legally established gender discrimination in the eighteenth century:

- 1769: The colonies adopted the British system depriving women of the right to own property and to possess their own earnings.
- 1777: The 13 original states passed laws preventing women from voting.
- 1839: The state of Mississippi granted women the right to possess property in their own names as long as their husbands agreed.
- 1848: At the first women's rights convention, 100 women and men (out of 300 attendees) signed a document demanding the end of discrimination against women.
- 1869: Granted the right to practice law in Iowa, Arabella Mansfield became the first female lawyer.
- 1883: Ida B. Wells, the daughter of slaves, sued the Chesapeake, Ohio, and Southwestern Railroad after she was dragged from her seat for refusing to sit in a segregated railcar. This incident influenced her becoming a journalist and eventually leading a four-decades-long anti-lynching campaign during which she traveled internationally speaking to foreign audiences about the horrors of lynching.
- 1887: In Argonia, Kansas, Susanna Medora Salter was the first woman elected mayor of a town or city.
- 1890: When Wyoming became a state, it permitted women to vote in all elections, a right that Wyoming Territory originally provided its female residents in 1869.
- 1916: In Montana Jeanette Rankin was the first woman elected to the U.S. House of Representatives.
- 1918: Two years after starting a birth-control clinic in Brooklyn, Margaret Sanger won a suit permitting doctors to advise their patients about birth control in support of health. This clinic was the forerunner of what in 1942 became Planned Parenthood.
- 1920: The Nineteenth Amendment was ratified, ensuring women's right to vote throughout the country.

- 1964: The U.S. Senate passed the Civil Rights Act, which included Title VII prohibiting gender discrimination in employment and creating the U.S. Equal Employment Opportunity Commission (EEOC) seeking the elimination of all employment discrimination.
- 1964: Patsy Mink, a Japanese American, was the first woman of color elected to Congress.
- 1968: Shirley Chisholm became the first Black woman elected to Congress, and four years later she was the first African American from one of the major parties to seek the presidency.
- 1972: Congress approved Title IX, a law declaring that girls and women in organizations receiving federal funds would not encounter discriminatory treatment.
- 1980: Paula Hawkins of Florida was the first woman elected to the U.S. Senate without succeeding either her father or husband.
- 1997: Madeleine Albright became the first secretary of state.
- 2016: Hillary Rodham Clinton received the Democratic nomination for president, becoming the first woman to head a major party's ticket, and while she lost in the Electoral College, she received nearly 3 million more votes than Donald Trump.
- 2018: Congress contained a record number of women, with 102 female House members and 25 Senators (Albrecht and Strand 2010; Blancaflor 2019; Desilver 2018; Michals 2015; Mulligan 2017; Norwood 2017; United States Census Bureau 2019).
- 2018: A Gallup Poll conducted for nearly two decades found that a national sample's backing of affirmative action for women had reached 65 percent, the highest figure since its inception (Norman 2019).
- 2020: Kamala Harris became the first woman and also the first person of color elected to the vice presidency. Her mother was Indian (from India) and her father Black.

If asked to guess which states were the first to provide women important political or economic rights, many Americans would probably suggest various eastern ones. After all, many of those states are currently known to be relatively liberal, supporting equality-promoting reforms. However, some of the information just provided suggests a different outcome, with females first obtaining important rights in central or western states—which were less established and as a result were likely to be more flexible about reformed rights.

Most of the women previously listed were white and middle-class. Historically an intersectional reality for women of color has been that they have had few if any opportunities to succeed in mainstream economic and political organizations where both their gender and race have been counts against them. Table 1.2 lists some of the consequences suffered by people in the three disadvantaged groups.

TABLE 1.2 Some Highlighted Issues Involving the Three At-Risk Groups

Poverty	Ideological backing for poor people's minimal governmental support; in an assessment of the relative poverty rate in 35 affluent nations, US tied for the highest
Race and racism	Racist outlooks and rationalizations dating back to Columbus and the slavery days; survey data obtained between 2001 and 2020 indicating that over time Americans increasingly dissatisfied with the state of race relations; a majority of respondents indicated the Trump administration made race relations worse
The gender struggle	In the preindustrial era, women heavily but not exclusively involved in household tasks; gradually changes occurring in female political and economic opportunities, with midwestern and western states leading the way

Sources: Horowitz et al. 2019; Mulligan 2017; Norman 2019; OECD Social Indicators 2019.

Regardless of their race, girls and women over time have been the victims of **sexism**—beliefs asserting that real or imagined differences between women and men establish the superiority of men. Real differences would involve such physical traits as distinctive sexual organs while widespread claims that men are more intelligent, more capable of leadership, and more stable emotionally illustrate alleged male advantages. Besides girls and women, victims of sexual discrimination involve people who are lesbian, gay, bisexual, or transgender (LGBT), sexual minorities discussed in later chapters.

Although women's rights and opportunities have increased over time, the results of national surveys are instructive, suggesting that Americans' views about women's place in modern society involves more than simply economic and political advancement and, that as Figure 1.1 indicates, Americans' satisfaction with the treatment of women has sharply declined over time. The Gallup Poll found that in 2001 70 percent of the respondents interviewed indicated that they were very or somewhat satisfied with the treatment of women in society; 61 percent of women and 80 percent of men reached that conclusion. In 2018 the overall figure had fallen to 53 percent, with 46 percent of women and 61 percent of men opting for very or somewhat satisfied. The sharp drop in satisfaction coincided with highly publicized accounts involving the mobilization of the Me Too initiative, with a host of accusers asserting that more than 400 prominent men engaged in misconduct ranging from sexual harassment to sexual assault (Brenan 2019). As discussion in Chapter 7 indicates, the women's rights movement has a lengthy history and is currently very active.

Harsh, sometimes measurable conditions limiting their lives are standard outcomes for the people discussed in this book, and many studies in upcoming chapters support that conclusion. Because of the significant impact that risks have on them, a brief quantitative and qualitative look at some of the types of risks they experience seems a useful issue to include at this introductory stage.

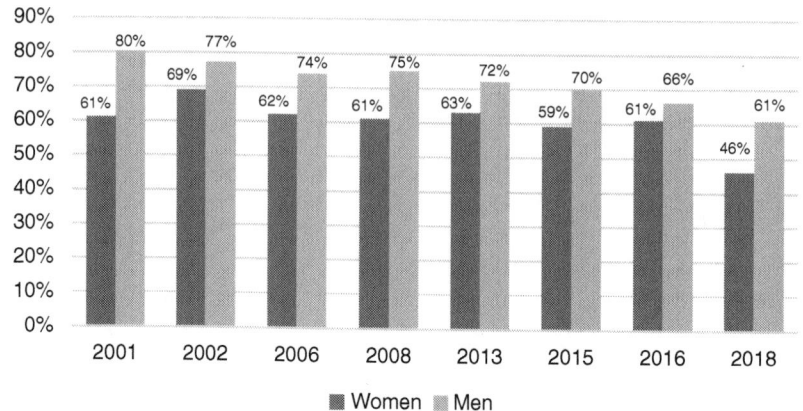

FIGURE 1.1 Percentage of Adult Americans Satisfied with How Women Are Treated[1]
[1]About 6,500 randomly chosen adult respondents roughly divided between women and men answered the question about their satisfaction with how women are treated.
Note: The percentage of Americans very or somewhat satisfied with women's treatment has declined over time, with 5 to 19 percent of women consistently less satisfied than men in a given year.

Risks and Their Impact

Using age, race, marital status, and educational level, researchers Mark A. Rank and Thomas A. Hirschi developed a poverty risk calculator based on hundreds of thousands case records obtained from a longitudinal study that started in 1968 (Rank 2017). The research provided data highlighting the magnitude of US economic inequities. The investigators wrote,

> For example, the five-year risk of poverty is 5 percent for an American who is 45 to 49, white and married, with an education beyond high school. In contrast, the five-year risk for an individual who is 25 to 29, nonwhite and unmarried, with an education of high school or less is a whopping 72 percent.
>
> *(Rank and Hirschi 2016)*

In the upcoming chapters, various risk factors will play a significant role. It will become apparent that people who are poor, minority-group members, or women are more likely than others to encounter such risk factors as deficient family socialization and support, limited and inferior schooling, unemployment or poverty-level jobs, and lowered quality of life involving such issues as diet, health, and longevity.

The African American residents mentioned in the chapter's opening would be prime candidates for such risks. Riding on a local bus in a poor district, sociologist Alexis McCurn was propositioned, with the man readily assuming that any young Black woman traveling alone in that area was a prostitute. For McCurn that was a novel experience, but for local Black female residents such verbal and even physical microaggressions could be a common reality.

During the nearly two years in which McCurn conducted her study, she found that the youthful female members of this poor, largely Black city were often vigilant and defensive-minded, developing survival techniques to protect themselves both psychologically and physically as they moved through neighborhoods where local men were likely to harass them. An effective approach for countering such abusive treatment was what McCurn called "buffering," using certain tactics for reducing or eliminating the potential harassment.

Twenty-year-old Amaya, a respondent in the study, indicated that one of her means of protection was the presence of companions when passing through potentially dangerous areas. She explained,

> When I walk down 3rd Avenue, I try to always be with somebody else. During the day it's not too bad. The guys hanging outside do say nasty stuff and try to be slick and touch you when you go by, but at night or really early in the morning, that's when it's rough out here. That's when girls get snatched up.
>
> *(McCurn 2017, 62)*

For Amaya "snatched up" meant a female being assaulted, even kidnapped or forced into prostitution.

Another means of buffering Amaya employed involved a careful assessment of neighborhoods she considered passing through based on experience and information she obtained from others. She received a certain amount of psychological buffering by knowing that the areas through which she walked regularly were considerably safer during the day than at night. While it is generally sensible for people to stay away from places where they are threatened, residents like Amaya often have no option but to encounter such dangerous places in the course of shopping, working, and daily living (McCurn 2017, 62).

What emerges as a positive reality about Amaya and others like her is that in spite of a high-risk life they keep battling, continuing to show an unrelenting commitment to maintaining as safe and pleasant an existence as possible. As the upcoming chapters indicate, many individuals faced with the risks highlighted in this volume display a similar determined, even courageous commitment in spite of difficult, often dangerous circumstances.

Finally, throughout the book, the significance of C. Wright Mills's emphasis on the importance of public issues is apparent, indicating that in context after context the three sets of people being examined are at risk, sometimes extreme risk for unfortunate, even dire outcomes. As a rule individuals accept personal responsibility for those outcomes, but they seem to be much better prepared to maximize the results when they have an awareness of and knowledge about the immediate social issues and, in particular, when they connect with individuals and groups supporting basic improvements.

Key Terms in the Glossary

affirmative action
conflict theory
ideology
intersectionality
microaggressions
racism
risk
risk factor
sexism
social class
social reproduction

Discussion Topics*

1. Define social reproduction. Then discuss a personal history, your own or someone else's, which provides clear, thought-provoking illustrations of how the process works.

2. Discuss the tendency of the US government to do less to help the poor than its counterparts in other affluent nations. How does ideology contribute to this outcome?

3. Is intersectionality a useful concept? Provide an example, pointing out important influences different statuses are likely to provide.

4. Is it reasonable to conclude that US race relations have steadily improved over time?

5. Discuss the increasing tendency to use the racial designations "Blacks" and "whites."

6. Do you believe that the treatment of women is improving or worsening? Explain.

7. List and discuss the risk factors that seem most closely associated with people who are poor, people of color, or women.

8. A possible class project might involve a paper written about members of one of the three at-risk groups, providing information about the extent to which the individuals in question cope with the difficult conditions they encounter. It might prove helpful to make some use of C. Wright Mills's terminology: Do the individuals covered in the paper recognize the relevance of public issues or are they simply preoccupied with their personal troubles?

9. Comment on the following statement: While a majority of Americans believe that very rich people should pay a wealth tax, the Senate and the House of Representatives passed the Tax Cuts and Job Acts that drastically reduced the amount of federal taxes wealthy individuals must pay. Can you find any source material that sheds light on this pair of outcomes? Explain.

*Each discussion section will contain one suggestion for a research paper.

Bibliography

Adams, James Truslow. 1931. *The Epic of America*. Boston, MA: Little, Brown and Company.

Albrecht, Jay, and Bradford Strand. 2010. "A Review of Organized Youth Sport in the United States." *YouthFirst: The Journal of Youth Sports* 5 (Spring): 16–20.

Americans for Tax Fairness. 2019. "Fact Sheet: Corporate Tax Rates." https://america nsfortaxfairness.org/tax-fairness-briefing-booklet/fact-sheet-corporate-tax-rates/.

Bailyn, Bernard, David Brion Davis, David Herbert Donald, John L. Thomas, Robert H. Wiebe, and Gordon S. Wood. 1977. *The Great Republic*. Lexington, MA: D.C. Heath.

Bhattacharya, Tithi, and Susan Ferguson. 2018. "Deepening Our Understanding of Social Reproduction Theory." *Krytyka Polityczna & European Alternatives*. (September 12). http://politicalcritique.org/world/2018/understanding-social-reproduction-theory/.

Blair, Hunter. 2017. "Corporations Pay between 13 and 19 Percent in Federal Taxes—Far Less than the 35 Percent Statutory Tax Rate." Economic Policy Institute. (August 10). https://www.epi.org/publication/corporations-pay-between-13-and-19-percent-in-federal-taxes-far-less-than-the-35-percent-statutory-tax-rate/.

Blancaflor, Saleah. 2019. "5 Asian American Trailblazers Who Changed the United States." NBC News. (May 6). https://www.nbcnews.com/news/asian-america/5-asian-american-political-trailblazers-who-changed-united-states-n994606.

Bourdieu, Pierre. 1977. "Cultural Reproduction and Social Reproduction," pp. 487–510 in Jerome Karabel and A.H. Halsey (eds.), *Power and Ideology in Education*. New York: Oxford University Press.

Bourdieu, Pierre, and Jean-Claude Passeron. 1990. *Reproduction in Education, Society and Culture*, 2nd ed. London: Sage.

Brainard, Lael. 2019. "Is the Middle Class within Reach for Middle-Income Families?" Board of Governors of the Federal Reserve System. (May 10). https://www.federalreserve. gov/newsevents/speech/brainard20190510a.htm.

Brenan, Megan. 2019. "Record-Low 46 Percent of Women Pleased with Society's Treatment." Gallup Poll. (January 17). https://news.gallup.com/poll/246056/record-low-women-pleased-society-treatment.aspx.

Breslin, Dermot. 2010. "Generalising Darwinism to Study Socio-Cultural Change." *International Journal of Sociology and Social Policy* 30 (July/August): 427–439.

Brown, Dee. 1972. *Bury My Heart at Wounded Knee*. New York: Bantam Books.

Bruza, Emily. 2020. "American Extremism: White Supremacists." Center for Homeland Defense and Security. (May 26). https://www.hsdl.org/c/american-extremism/.

Carrega, Christina, Veronica Stracqualursi, and Josh Campbell. 2020. "13 Charged in Plot to Kidnap Michigan Governor Gretchen Witmer." CNN Politics. (October 8). https://www.cnn.com/2020/10/08/politics/fbi-plot-michigan-governor-gretchen-whitmer/index. html.

Castro, Mayra Ruiz, and Evangelina Holvino. 2016. "Applying Intersectionality in Organizations: Inequality Markers, Cultural Scripts and Advancement Practices in a Professional Service Firm." *Gender, Work & Organization* 23 (May): 328–347.

Chan, Christian D., and Adrienne N.Erby. 2018. "A Critical Analysis and Applied Intersectionality Framework with Intercultural Queer Couples." *Journal of Homosexuality* 65: 1249–1274.

Clark, Simon. 2020. "How White Supremacy Returned to Right Wing Politics." American Progress. (July 1). https://www.americanprogress.org/issues/security/reports/2020/07/01/482414/white-supremacy-returned-mainstream-politics/.

Clearwatch Security. 2020. "The Difference between Threat and Risk." https://www. clearwatchsecurity.co.uk/the-difference-between-threat-and-risk/.

Cole, Nicki Lisa. 2019. "Theories of Ideology." ThoughtCo. (July 3). https://www. thoughtco.com/ideology-definition-3026356.

Coleman, Nancy. 2020. "Why We're Capitalizing Black." *The New York Times*. (July 5). https://www.nytimes.com/2020/07/05/insider/capitalized-black.html.

CollegeBoard. 2016. "2016 College-Bound Seniors: Total Group Profile Report." Table 10: "Student Background Information and Characteristics," p. 4. https://secure-media. collegeboard.org/digitalServices/pdf/sat/total-group-2016.pdf.

Collins, Sean. 2020. "Trump Once Flirted with White Nationalism. Now It's a Centerpiece of His White House." *Vox*. (July 21). https://www.vox.com/21313021/trump-white-nationalism-supremacy-miller-bannon-immigration.

Confronting Poverty. 2019. "Why Is Poverty Higher in the U.S. than in Other Countries?" https://confrontingpoverty.org/poverty-discussion-guide/why-is-poverty-higher-in-the-u-s-than-in-other-countries/.

Creavey, Kristine L., Lisa M. Gatzke-Kopp, and Gregory M. Fosco. 2018. "Differential Effects of Family Stress Exposure and Harsh Parental Discipline on Child Social Competence." *Journal of Child & Family Studies* 27: 483–493.

Crenshaw, Kimberlé. 2019. "Why Intersectionality Can't Wait." Gunda Werner Institute. (May 20). https://www.gwi-boell.de/en/2019/05/20/why-intersectionality-cant-wait.

Crossman, Ashley. 2017. "Social Darwinism." ThoughtCo. https://www.thoughtco.com/social-darwinism-3026588.

DeParle, Jason. 2020. "8 Million Have Slipped Into Poverty Since May as Federal Aid Has Dried Up." *The New York Times*. (October 15). https://www.nytimes.com/2020/10/15/us/politics/federal-aid-poverty-levels.html.

Desilver, Drew. 2018. "A Record Number of Women Will Be Serving in the New Congress." Pew Research Center. (December 18). https://www.pewresearch.org/fact-tank/2018/12/18/record-number-women-in-congress/.

Doob, Christopher B. 2019. *Social Inequality and Social Stratification in US Society*, 2nd ed. New York: Routledge.

Encyclopedia Britannica. 2020. "Horatio Alger." https://www.britannica.com/biography/Horatio-Alger.

Franklin, Benjamin. 1962. *The Autobiography of Benjamin Franklin*. New York: Collier Books. Originally published in 1791.

Fredrickson, George M. 2002. *Racism: A Short History*. Princeton, NJ: Princeton University Press.

Gallup Poll. 2020. "Race Relations." https://news.gallup.com/poll/1687/race-relations.aspx.

Gearity, Brian T., and Lynett Henderson Metzger. 2017. "Intersectionality, Microaggressions, and Microaffirmations: Toward a Cultural Praxis of Sport Coaching." *Sociology of Sport Journal* 34: 160–175.

Giago, Tim. 2011. "The Name 'Indian' and Political Correctness." *HuffPost* (May 25). https://www.huffpost.com/entry/the-name-indian-and-polit_1_b_67593.

Gordon, Linda. 2016. "'Intersectionality', Socialist Feminism and Contemporary Activism: Musings by a Second-Wave Socialist Feminist." *Gender & History* 28 (August): 340–357.

Gross, Terry. 2020. "How The CARES Act Became A Tax-Break Bonanza For The Rich, Explained." *npr*. (April 30). https://www.npr.org/2020/04/30/848321204/how-the-cares-act-became-a-tax-break-bonanza-for-the-rich-explained.

Han, Jeehoon, Bruce D. Meyer, and James X. Sullivan. 2020. "Income and Poverty in the Covid-19 Pandemic." National Bureau of Economic Research. (August). https://www.nber.org/papers/w27729.pdf.

Harris, Cherise A., and Kristie A. Ford. 2017. "'Where's Your Man?': Intersectionality in the Adoption Stories of Two, Black, Single, Female Sociologists." *Michigan Family Review*. https://quod.lib.umich.edu/m/mfr/4919087.0021.103/?rgn=main;view=fulltex.

Hawley, George. 2018. "The Demography of the Alt-Right." Institute for Family Studies. (August 9). https://ifstudies.org/blog/the-demography-of-the-alt-right.

Hesse-Biber, Sharlene, and Gregg Lee Carter. 2005. *Working Women in America: Split Dreams*. New York: Oxford University Press.

Horowitz, Juliana Manasce, Anna Brown, and Kiana Cox. 2019. "Race in America 2019." Pew Research Center. (April 9). https://www.pewsocialtrends.org/2019/04/09/race-in-america-2019/.

Horowitz, Juliana Manasce, Ruth Igielnik, and Rakesh Kochhar. 2020. "Most Americans Say There Is Too Much Economic Inequality in the U.S., but Fewer than Half Call It a Top Priority." Pew Research Center. (January 9). https://www.pewsocialtrends.org/2020/01/09/most-americans-say-there-is-too-much-economic-inequality-in-the-u-s-but-fewer-than-half-call-it-a-top-priority/.

Institute on Taxation and Economic Policy. 2017. "The 35 Percent Corporate Myth." (March 9). https://itep.org/the-35-percent-corporate-tax-myth.

Jardina, Ashley E. 2019. *White Identity Politics*. New York: Cambridge University Press.

Jones, Sheena, and Theresa Waldrop. 2020. "14th Person Charged in Alleged Plot to Kidnap Governor." CNN. (October 16). https://www.cnn.com/2020/10/15/us/michigan-governor-plot-charge/index.html.

Kenton, Will. 2019. "Affirmative Action." Investopedia. (October 6). https://www.investopedia.com/terms/a/affirmative-action.asp.

Khan Academy. 2019. "Social Darwinism in the Gilded Age." https://www.khanacademy.org/humanities/us-history/the-gilded-age/gilded-age/a/social-darwinism-in-the-gilded-age.

Krivkovich, Alexis, Marie-Claude Nadeau, Kelsey Robinson, Nicole Robinson, Irina Starikova, and Lareina Yee. 2018. "Women in the Workplace 2018." McKinsey & Company. (October). https://www.mckinsey.com/featured-insights/gender-equality/women-in-the-workplace-2018.

Laws, Mike. 2020. "Why We Capitalize 'Black' (and Not 'white')." *Columbia Journalism Review*. (June 16). https://www.cjr.org/analysis/capital-b-black-styleguide.php.

Leachman, Michael, and Eric Figueroa. 2019. "K-12 School Funding Up in Most 2018 Teacher-Protest States, but Still Well Below Decade Ago." Center on Budget and Policy Priorities." (March 6). https://www.cbpp.org/research/state-budget-and-tax/k-12-school-funding-up-in-most-2018-teacher-protest-states-but-still.

Ling, Laura. 2016. "Should You Say Native American or American Indian?" *Seeker*. (September 14). https://www.seeker.com/should-you-say-native-american-or-american-indian-2004656587.html.

Livers, Ancella. 2006. "Black Women in Management," pp. 205–221 in Margaret Foren Karsten (ed.), *Gender, Race, and Ethnicity in the Workplace: Issues and Challenges for Today's Organizations*. Vol. 1, Management, Gender, and Ethnicity in the United States. Westport, CT: Praeger.

McCurn, Alexis. 2017. "'I Am Not a Prostitute:' How Young Black Women Challenge Street-Based Micro-Interactional Assaults." *Sociological Focus* 50: 52–65.

MacLeod, Jay. 2009. *Ain't No Makin' It: Aspirations and Attainment in a Low-Income Neighborhood*, 3rd ed. Boulder, CO: Westview Press.

McNamee, Stephen J. 2014. "The Meritocracy Myth Revisited." *Sociation Today* 12 (Fall/Winter): 1–10.

McNamee, Stephen J. 2018. *The Meritocracy Myth*, 4th ed. Lanham, MD: Rowman & Littlefield.

McNamee, Stephen J., and Robert K.Miller, Jr. 2014. *The Meritocracy Myth*, 3rd ed. Lanham, MD: Rowman & Littlefield.

Marks, Don. 2018. "What's in a Name? Indian, Native, Aboriginal, or Indigenous?" CBC News. (February 22). https://www.cbc.ca/news/canada/manitoba/what-s-in-a-name-indian-native-aboriginal-or-indigenous-1.2784518.

Martin, Carmel, Ulrich Boser, MegBenner, and Perpetual Baffour. 2018. "A Quality Approach to School Funding." Center for American Progress. (November 13). https://www.americanprogress.org/issues/education-k-12/reports/2018/11/13/460397/quality-approach-school-funding/.

Marx, Karl, and Friedrich Engels. 1959. "Manifesto of the Communist Party," pp. 1–41 in Lewis S. Feuer (ed.), *Marx & Engels: Basic Writings on Politics & Philosophy*. Garden City, NY: Basic Books.

Marx, Karl, and Friedrich Engels. 2005. "The Annotated Communist Manifesto," pp. 37–90 in Phil Gasper (ed.), *The Communist Manifesto: A Road Map to History's Most Important Document*. Chicago: Haymarket Books.

Michals, Debra. 2015. "Shirley Chisholm." National Women's History Museum. https://www.womenshistory.org/education-resources/biographies/shirley-chisholm.

Mills, C. Wright. 1959. *The Sociological Imagination*. London: Oxford University Press.

Mulligan, Susan. 2017. "Stepping through History: A Timeline of Women's Rights from 1769 to the 2017 March on Washington." U.S. News & World Report. (January 20). https://www.usnews.com/news/the-report/articles/2017-01-20/timeline-the-womens-rights-movement-in-the-us.

New York Times Magazine. 2019. "We've Got to Tell the Unvarnished Truth." (August 18): 1–18.

Norman, Jim. 2019. "Americans' Support for Affirmative Action Programs Rises." Gallup Poll. (February 27). https://news.gallup.com/poll/247046/americans-support-affirmative-action-programs-rises.aspx.

Norwood, Arlisha R. 2017. "Ida B. Wells-Barnett." National Women's History Museum. https://www.womenshistory.org/education-resources/biographies/ida-b-wells-barnett.

OECD Social Indicators. 2019. "Poverty." https://www.oecd-ilibrary.org/sites/8483c82f-en/index.html?itemId=/content/component/8483c82f-en#Fig6.4.

Offord, David R., and Helena Chmura Kraemer. 2000. "Risk Factors and Prevention." Evidence-based Mental Health. https://ebmh.bmj.com/content/3/3/70.

Padavic, Irene, and Barbara Reskin. 2002. *Women and Men at Work*, 2nd ed. Thousand Oaks, CA: Pine Forge Press.

Parolin, Zachary, Megan Curran, Jordan Matsudaira, Jane Waldfogel, and Christopher Wimer. 2020. "Monthly Poverty Rates in the United States during the COVID-19 Pandemic." Center on Poverty & Social Policy, School of Social Work, Columbia University. Teacher's College, Columbia University. (October 15). https://static1.squarespace.com/static/5743308460b5e922a25a6dc7/t/5f87c59e4cd0011fabd38973/1602733471158/COVID-Projecting-Poverty-Monthly-CPSP-2020.pdf.

Protection Circle. 2017. "Threats and Risks." (January 27). https://protectioncircle.org/.

Rank, Mark. 2017. "Changing the World, One Website at a Time." *Contexts*. (October 5). https://journals.sagepub.com/doi/full/10.1177/1536504217732061.

Rank, Mark A., and Thomas A. Hirschi. 2016. "Calculate Your Economic Risk." *The New York Times*. (March 18). https://www.nytimes.com/2016/03/20/opinion/sunday/calculate-your-economic-risk.html.

Reich, Robert. 2019. "The Myth of Meritocracy." *The American Prospect*. (April 9). https://prospect.org/education/myth-meritocracy/.

Rottenberg, Catharine. 2018. "Neoliberal Meritocracy." *Cultural Studies* 32 (November): 997–999.

Schneider, Howard, and Chris Kahn. 2020. "Majority of Americans Favor Wealth Tax on Very Rich: Reuter/Ipsos Poll." Reuters. (January 10). https://www.reuters.com/article/us-usa-election-inequality-poll/majority-of-americans-favor-wealth-tax-on-very-rich-reuters-ipsos-poll-idUSKBN1Z9141.

Semega, Jessica, Melissa Kollar, Emily A. Shrider, and John Creamer. 2020. "Income and Poverty in the US: 2019." Figure 7. Number in Poverty and Poverty Rate: 1959 to 2019. United States Census Bureau. (September 15). https://www.census.gov/library/publications/2020/demo/p60-270.html.

Serwer, Adam. 2019. "Conservatives Have a White Nationalism Problem." *The Atlantic*. (August 6). https://www.theatlantic.com/ideas/archive/2019/08/trump-white-nationalism/595555/.

Southern Poverty Law Center. 2020. "The Year in Hate 2019: White Nationalist Groups Rise for a Second Year in a Row—Up 55% since 2017." https://www.splcenter.org/presscenter/year-hate-2019-white-nationalist-groups-rise-second-year-row-55-2017.

Spencer, Herbert. 1864. *The Principles of Biology*. Vol. I. London: Williams and Norgate.

Talbot, Margaret. 2015. "The Talking Cure." *The New Yorker*. (January 5). https://www.newyorker.com/magazine/2015/01/12/talking-cure.

Thornton, Alexandra. 2018. "11 Ways the Wealthy and Corporations Will Game the New Tax Law." Center for American Progress. (July 25). https://www.americanprogress.org/issues/economy/reports/2018/07/25/453981/11-ways-wealthy-corporations-will-game-new-tax-law/.

United States Census Bureau. 2019. "Signatures to the 'Declaration of Sentiments." (August 27). https://www.census.gov/programs-surveys/sis/resources/historical-documents/declaration-sentiments.html.

United States Census Bureau. 2020. "How the Census Bureau Measures Poverty." (August 26). https://www.census.gov/topics/income-poverty/poverty/guidance/poverty-measures.html.

Weber, Max. 1958. *The Protestant Ethic and the Spirit of Capitalism*. Translator Talcott Parsons in 1930. New York: Charles Scribner's Sons.

Wellemeyer, James. 2019. "Wealthy Parents Spend Up to $10,000 on SAT Prep for Their Kids." *MarketWatch*. (July 7). https://www.marketwatch.com/story/some-wealthy-parents-are-dropping-up-to-10000-on-sat-test-prep-for-their-kids-2019-06-21.

Wise, Alana. 2020. "Democrats Blame Trump Rhetoric for Michigan Governor Kidnapping Plot." *npr*. (October 8). https://www.npr.org/2020/10/08/921824550/democrats-blame-trump-rhetoric-for-michigan-governor-kidnapping-plot.

2

YOUNG DISADVANTAGED CHILDREN

A study done by the Organisation for Economic Co-operation and Development found that American babies are less likely to reach their first birthday than those in 19 other affluent nations. In the second decade of the twenty-first century, the leading causes of those deaths have been premature births and Sudden Infant Death Syndrome. The issue here involves **mortality rate**, namely a measure of the number of deaths in a specific population over a designated time span. In this case the focus involves infants. Broad conditions contributing to the discrepancy between American infants and their foreign peers include higher poverty rates and a deficient government safety net (Thakrar et al. 2018). The high mortality rate was part of a larger picture about poor American children's health. On this issue Ashish Thakrar, the lead author, was blunt. "The poorer children are, the worse their health outcomes are" (Johnson 2018).

Racial minorities, whose members tend to have higher poverty rates than whites, suffer greater infant mortality. Compared to non-Hispanic whites, African American mothers are twice as likely to have a child dying in the first year. American Indian and some Latino communities also have high mortality rates, but "available data show that racial disparities between African Americans and non-Hispanic whites are the starkest" (Taylor et al. 2019).

While various factors contribute to the differences, a large study of discharged patients emphasized one particular finding—that compared to white females, women in all other major racial and ethnic groups displayed higher rates of medical complications during delivery (Admon et al. 2018). Lindsay Admon, the lead author, indicated that for the protection of both mothers and babies "[i]t's important that we identify racial and ethnic minority women with chronic conditions as a high-risk group." Referring to those disadvantaged groups' vulnerabilities during pregnancy, she added, "The trends we're seeing now are startling" (Carroll 2018). Table 2.1 provides information about American infants' mortality rate.

TABLE 2.1 Details about the High US Mortality Rate for Infants

The US, the highest infant mortality rate among 20 wealthy nations	The other nations: Australia, Austria, Belgium, Canada, Denmark, Finland, France, Germany, Iceland, Ireland, Italy, Japan, the Netherlands, New Zealand, Norway, Spain, Sweden, Switzerland and the United Kingdom

Infant mortality rate

Brief history of the comparison on infant mortality rate between the US and those 19 nations	In the 1960s the US infant mortality rate lower than the average of the 19 nations; in the following decade the US rate higher than the average in the 19 nations, and between 2001 and 2010 76% higher
Factors promoting the relatively high US infant mortality rate	The nation's extensive percentage of poor people, a fragmented health-care system, and an inadequate safety net for economically vulnerable families
The role of the racial factor	African American infants dying at 2.2 times the rate of non-Hispanic whites and, in particular, 3.2 times more likely to die from complications associated with low birth weight; women of color displaying higher rates of medical complications during delivery
The combined impact of poverty and race accelerating in specific locations	Data indicating that children born in Washington, DC's poorest district 10 times more likely to be victims of infant mortality than those born in its wealthiest section; children of color facing the prospect of a high infant mortality rate in certain states. Wisconsin, for instance, possessing a rate for Black infants that is nearly twice as high as Massachusetts and is higher than the rate in such poor countries as Columbia, Jamaica, Tunisia, and Venezuela

Causes for the high infant mortality rate

Sources: Admon et al. 2018; Eskow 2018; Kaplan 2018; National Institutes of Health 2012; Taylor et al. 2019; Thakrar et al. 2018.

Besides their vulnerability to infant mortality, poor children are likely to suffer from a variety of health-related problems. It appears that poverty is like an invading army, which can sweep across a locale bringing a host of painful conditions that at the very least adversely affect youthful residents and sometimes can overwhelm them.

At the moment the focus is on young children—infants, preschoolers, and primary schoolers, covering children up to about the age of 10, and leaving some child-related issues such as poverty's impact on schooling for later chapters.

Poor Youth

While historically poor people have been especially vulnerable to various risk factors, endangerment has been particularly striking for young children. In the late eighteenth and early nineteenth centuries, the youthful poor died much more frequently than their more affluent age peers from intestinal disorders and parasites produced by spoiled food, polluted water, and unhygienic care. Because older family members needed to be earning money, poor children often received minimal care from slightly older siblings or no care at all, making them more susceptible than their counterparts in other social classes to being burned, scalded, or dropped (Klepp 2004, 72–73).

In modern times such vulnerability persists. From the onset of life, being poor besieges people with both physical and mental problems. Poor children disproportionately suffer what the medical community calls a variety of "physical health insults" featuring high-risk exposure to accidents caused by physical abuse or neglect; deficient health care; severe chronic conditions such as diabetes, asthma, and difficulties with hearing or vision; an elevated rate of chronic illnesses; food that is often neither nutritious nor fresh; low immunization to various diseases; and vulnerability to obesity and its associated complications. In addition, among poor children mental-health problems are also prevalent (American Academy of Pediatrics 2016; McCarty 2016, 628–29).

Sometimes physical health affects mental health. For instance, musculoskeletal difficulties, which include a variety of conditions damaging the muscles, joints, and bones, are more common among poor children than in other income groups, leading to higher rates of depression, anxiety, and behavioral/conduct outcomes than their peers without those conditions (Williams and Burnfield 2019).

Many more studies have focused on poor children's physical health than on their mental health (Yoshikawa et al. 2012, 274). A number of factors involving poverty serve as what sociologist Alyn T. McCarty has called "mechanisms of influence," which are pathways connecting poverty to negative outcomes (McCarty 2016, 629). The following three types often affect poor children:

- **Material and social resources:** Poor families tend to have insufficient income to meet their children's food, clothing, and housing needs. Such deprived conditions discourage extensive, emotionally supportive interaction in the family and also undermine close, mutually beneficial relations with outside individuals and groups (McCarty 2016, 630).

When children suffer such material disadvantages, the impact of the family can make a formidable difference in their coping capacity. At the Center for Poverty Research at the University of California, Davis, a pair of investigators found that three factors—mothers' educational level, the family income, and mothers' level of depressive symptoms—affected their children's state of mind and social competence in the opening years. In addition, when those three conditions tended to be positive, the mother/child interaction was generally productive over time, encouraging children to understand emotions more fully and to avoid rebellious behavior as they grew older. The investigators found one particularly interesting, even surprising finding: "Rather than household income, a mother's educational attainment was the strongest, most direct predictor of a child's understanding of emotions at age four" (Winer and Thompson 2013).

A study examining several programs focused on improving outcomes for young children living in poverty found that a distinct contributor involved offering parents social support—for instance, incorporating them into parenting programs where among other issues they could "share parenting challenges and successes within a supportive, safe community of their peers … and discuss strategies for reducing stress and promoting parental health" (Morris et al. 2017, 390). This strategy seems consistent with a straight-forward conclusion that psychologist Suniya Luthar, a long-time researcher of poor families' vulnerability and resilience, asserted—that "[i]f you want a child to be functioning well, tend to the person who's tending the child" (Weir 2017).

Material and social forces tend to interplay, often to the detriment of the poor. To escape the ravages of poverty-stricken areas, those who can manage often move, further eroding the neighborhood quality and leaving those who remain even less involved with and supported by the local community (McCarty 2016, 630).

- **The culture of child poverty**: Historically this perspective favored a blaming-the-victim strategy, labeling poor and/or minority groups as responsible for their own problems and deficiencies. While still examining the culture poor people experience, the current outlook focuses on their values, beliefs, outlooks, and strategies in response to the poverty they encounter in their daily lives as well as their reaction to anti-poverty policies and activities. While this approach downplays victim blaming, it does assess the influence of poor parents on their young children.

Compared to their middle-class counterparts, poor parents are more likely to see their children's development as "an accomplishment of natural growth," permitting them to engage in unstructured free time with family and friends and emphasizing politeness and restraint in dealing with others (McCarty 2016, 630).

According to a team of researchers who studied over 500 families, poor parents, who are more likely than other income groups to suffer such high-risk conditions as low income, teen pregnancy, and depression, tend to have children displaying limited capacity to understand their own and others' mental state, few problem-solving skills, and deficient language ability. With such limitations involving conscious mental activity in place, social reproduction readily comes into play, meaning the children's own children are likely to be adversely affected in similar ways (Wade et al. 2018).

Children's language use is a case in point. Another study also comprised about 500 families, whose members came from diverse social-class backgrounds and in each case possessed a four-year-old child, addressed the issue of parents' dialogue with their children. The findings indicated that poor parents were less likely than their more affluent peers to engage in extended dialogue with their children about various topics. It seems probable that a contributing factor is the previously cited issue of mothers' level of education—that those who are well educated can communicate better with their children than their less educated peers, engaging them more effectively in the lengthy task of preparing them to function well in the modern world. In particular, dialogue is an important element if a parent and child are engaged in a task. Recognizing the role that dialogue plays, parents often carefully explain a task and perhaps provide the child a plan or strategy for completing it.

The absence or near absence of parent–child dialogue in many poor families means that parents offer little or no direction. Dialogue provides not only substantive information about the activity in question but also helps to sustain or build children's self-confidence. The successful child can benefit from such comments as "You're really good at this" or "You got another one right," but equally if not more important, the parent can provide the unsuccessful striver encouragement and suggestions about the attainment of success. The impact on children is likely to be positive and, in contrast, potentially negative if parents do not engage in instructive dialogue during task completion (Barbarin and Jean-Baptiste 2013, 211).

Such parent–child interactions suggest how much easier and more fruitful positive realities of social reproduction can make people's lives. In this case it is more productive for the individual who eventually will be a parent to grow up supported by experience gradually and often unconsciously learned in valuable childhood dialogue with one's own parents than to find oneself as a young mother or father facing such challenges with little or no high-quality childhood exposure to such experiences.

- **The impact of stress:** When people live in disorganized, unstable, high-risk settings, they encounter "toxic stress," which can have destructive impacts on bodily systems, including brain functioning (McCarty 2016, 631). Some specific sources of toxic stress include crowded conditions, little or no money, an inadequate diet, deficient child care, noise including such background noise as a constantly blaring television, household disorder, and family conflict (Blair and Raver 2016; National Institutes of Health 2012).

The connection between toxic stress and its destructive impact on poverty-stricken children is a fairly new subject for investigation. One set of experts observed, "There is mounting evidence that children who grow up poor are more likely to be subjected to stresses like neglect and hunger that act like toxins and hijack the developing brain" (Columbia University 2016). Table 2.2 lists major factors contributing to poor children's mental-health condition, which toxic stress can powerfully affect.

TABLE 2.2 Mechanisms of Influence Affecting Poor Children's Mental-Health Development

Material and social resources	Poverty limiting food and clothing and hindering the development of emotionally supportive relations with family members and others
Culture of child poverty	Poor parents' tendency to emphasize their children's development as "an accomplishment of natural growth" and to engage in less informative dialogue with their offspring than their middle-class counterparts
Impact of stress	Toxic stress such as little or no money or crowded conditions producing bodily impacts, including adverse effects on brain functioning

Sources: Barbarin and Jean-Baptiste 2013, 211; Blair and Raver 2016; McCarty 2016, 629, 630, 631; Wade et al. 2018; Winer and Thompson 2013.

Currently little reason exists to be optimistic about the reduction of poor children's toxic stress since the relative child poverty rate, meaning the percentage of children deprived of minimum income to maintain an average standard of living, is higher in the US than in all the other countries in a study of 35 industrialized nations, with the exception of Romania, which has an economy that is 99 percent smaller than its American counterpart (Children's Defense Fund 2018, 3).

For many children belonging to racial minorities, poverty is often a contributing factor to a disadvantaged childhood.

Young Children of Color

Until their emancipation in 1865, Blacks were born into slavery, with a 1705 Virginia law declaring that with its passage

> all negro, mulatto and Indian slaves … within this dominion shall be held, taken, and adjudged to be real estate … and shall descend unto the heirs and widows of persons departing this life according to the manner and custom of lands of inheritance held in fee simple.
>
> *(Lonang Institute 2018)*

The state of Virginia had legally established that slaves were simply property, which could be passed on to one's heirs.

Frederick Douglass was born in the neighboring state of Maryland, where the standard perception of slaves was similar. Slave owners readily broke up families—in Douglass's case his mother was hired out as a field hand to a man 12 miles away. Occasionally after a long day of work in the fields she would walk the vast distance to see him, often arriving at night and needing to return to start work before sunrise or risk a flogging.

One evening, however, he vividly recalled her visit. His mother brought him a present—"a 'sweet cake' ... in the shape of a heart, with a rich, dark ring glazed upon the edge of it. I was well off for the moment; prouder, on my mother's knee, than a king upon a throne" (Douglass 1994, 155).

It was the last visit from his mother Douglass remembered. Several years later his mother suffered a long illness and eventually died. He was not allowed to visit her as death approached. Douglass wrote, "It has been a life-long, standing grief to me, that I knew so little of my mother; and that I was so early separated from her." He was eight or nine when she died (Douglass 1994, 155).

While seldom enslaved, American Indian children have also suffered the effects of powerful people's inhumane treatment. Until the late 1970s for alleged child-welfare, moral, or religious reasons, state officials, adoption personnel, or members of religious organizations often removed Indian children from their families and placed them for adoption.

In response to this frequent practice, which had been occurring since early in the nation's history, Congress in 1978 passed the Indian Child Welfare Act. The law declared that tribal courts became the authority for deciding whether or not a child should face adoption, sharply reducing both the number of children adopted by outsiders and the trauma they experienced.

In 2018, however, a judge in a US district court in Texas ruled that the Indian Child Welfare Act is discriminatory, violating the Equal Protection Clause (in this case for children of all races) in the 14th Amendment but ignoring the fact that American Indians are the only racial group with a long-established traditional, protective structure (tribal in their case) that precedes US authority. With that background in mind, plaintiffs in possible upcoming cases involving forced adoption are likely to challenge the Texas judge's decision (Akee 2018).

At present many children of color continue to face unusually threatening conditions. A primary care physician at Boston Children's Hospital, who is also a member of the faculty at Harvard Medical School, indicated that children growing up in African American, Hispanic, and American Indian families "are more likely to live in homes with higher unemployment and lower incomes than white children. This means that they are less likely to have good housing, good nutrition, good access to health care, and access to good education" (McCarthy 2019). In short, the combined intersectional impact of both children's race and social class, particularly family income, raise the risk of several major disadvantages (McCarthy 2019).

Not only do young children of color suffer lives where basic resources are often considerably inferior to those most whites enjoy, but they can also be the victims of racist treatment. While it has long been established that children belonging to racial minorities who are 10 and older recognize racial discrimination, no definitive research existed on their younger peers—until 2018 when a pair or researchers published a study that provided insights about younger children. Psychologists Ana Marcelo and Tuppett Yates interviewed 172 seven-year-olds who were Black,

PHOTO 2.1 Like most poor children, these Navaho boys on an arid reservation in Arizona are not living in areas likely to make a healthy, comfortable childhood possible.

Source: Shutterstock/ Meunierd

Latino, and various combinations of Black, Latino, and white and then a year later re-interviewed over 90 percent of the original sample.

At the beginning of the first session, the investigators explained the meaning of racial discrimination and prominent reasons why people engaged in it. The interview featured eight questions about the children's personal experience involving racial discrimination—for instance, whether they had ever had a teacher who treated them as less intelligent because of their racial membership. The results of the study indicated that children in the sample who had perceived racial microaggressions in those different settings were statistically more likely to experience anxiety and depression as well as behavioral problems dealing with teachers and other authority figures (Marcelo and Yates 2018, 255–58).

When interviewed about the study, Tuppett Yates, one of the authors, indicated that it provided important new information about the impact of racial discrimination on young children, reaching an age group once widely believed to be impervious to it. Yates declared, "We must recognize that ethnicity-race is an important part of a person's identify and development even at an early age, rather than profess to operate as a colorblind society" (Warren 2018).

Parents of color often recognize the importance of instructing their young children about the meaning and impact of racism. **Racial socialization** is the process during which parents or others teach children the values, norms, beliefs, and behavior considered appropriate for their racial or ethnic group. For many African Americans racial socialization has included information supporting pride in being Black, warnings about the continuing existence of racial inequalities, and mistrust of or at least caution toward other racial/ethnic groups. On the other hand, some Black parents' racial socialization of their children focuses on deemphasizing the importance of race or encouraging silence about racial matters (Gaskin 2015). While research on this topic continues, mounting evidence suggests that even in kindergarten, children begin to exclude members of other races from play and other activities (Cole and Verwayne 2018).

With such evidence in mind, Howard Stevenson, a psychologist who specializes in racial socialization, questioned the wisdom of parents avoiding discussion about racial issues. He said, [Not giving messages about race] "is fine until it's not." In short, children receiving few messages about race do fairly well until they encounter racial injustice, a condition for which they are often drastically unprepared (Gaskin 2015).

Compared to Black parents, whites are much less inclined to engage in racial socialization with their children, tending, as Tuppett Yates suggested in the earlier quote, to support a sense of a "colorblind society." A related concept is **colorblind racism**, which is whites' assertion that they are living in a world where racial privilege no longer exists while their behavior supports structures and practices perpetuating racial advantage (Bonilla-Silva 2010, 105–15).

Colorblind racism was apparent when three investigators studied 84 European American (white) mothers reading two, racially themed books to their four- to five-year-old children. One book entitled *What If the Zebras Lost Their Stripes?* raised the issue of what would happen if instead of being striped, zebras became either all-black or all-white. The researchers learned that more than 90 percent of the participants made no race-related comments while reading the books, describing them overall as "colormute" or "colorblind." In addition, when tested separately, parents and children were generally unable to assess each others' views about race. A notable finding was that the higher the percentage of mothers' friends who were people of color, the more likely their children rated African Americans as having positive traits (Pahlke et al. 2012, 1167–70, 1174).

Sometimes children in the study made critical comments about racial diversity, and often mothers simply kept on reading. Occasionally at such moments a mother and her child started to discuss the topic. Referring to the zebras, one mother asked whether the black and white zebras would continue to hang out together. "No," the daughter replied. The mother then questioned, "You don't think they'd still hang out together? (pause) "Would different colors be the end of living life as loving friends?" In those relatively few instances where mother and child began to engage in a discussion of race, exchanges like this one ended quickly, without any parental effort to introduce the positive contributions that racial diversity offers (Pahlke et al. 2012, 1171).

Like poverty and race, children's gender can affect them at any early age.

Youthful Girls

Research can often contribute previously unknown information about social change. For instance, in 1972 a team of investigators found that the books winning the celebrated Caldecott Award for the "most distinguished" picture books used by preschool children from 1967 to 1971 displayed 92 percent male and just 8 percent female characters. In addition, the females "were generally inconspicuous and passive in their activities; their roles were usually watching, helping, and waiting. In contrast, boys were often shown as involved in adventures, exciting activities, and camaraderie." The adults "were similarly differentiated" (Oskamp et al. 1996, 28).

About two decades later, a significant change was apparent in the Caldecott winners. Now the number of female characters had markedly increased, and they were much less likely to be locked into traditional female roles and behavioral patterns. While the numerical representation of females was "still a bit shy of full equality with males" (Oskamp et al. 1996 1996, 36) the change was noteworthy.

For preschool children picture books are an early and potentially powerful influence providing gender models for them as both girls and boys and even as women and men. Indicating what the picture books of their era offered females, the 1970s research team concluded that "the little girl reading these books might be deprived of her ego and her sense of self" (Weitzman et al. 1972, 1130). It seems likely that in more recent years young girls reading the modern equivalents will no longer experience a similar sense of diminishment.

As the previous study suggests, some conditions influencing young children's outlook on gender roles can alter in a fairly brief time span. What persists over time, however, is the universal centrality of this topic, starting in the preschool years. Sociologist Jean Stockard wrote, "Long before children understand the nature of religious groups, occupation, or schooling, they recognize that there are two sex groups and that they belong to one of those groups" (Stockard 1999, 215). It is a recognition that extends from early childhood to the end of life.

In the United States, specialists on the topic traditionally accepted that "doing gender" has meant that once a child is assigned to a sex category, everyone, including the children themselves, act in ways considered suitable for that particular assignment (West and Zimmerman 1987). For preschool children the traditional impact of doing gender has been decisive, with three-year-olds generally aware of being female or male and by five "girls prefer dolls, doll accessories, soft toys, drawing, cutting, and pasting—while boys prefer blocks, small vehicles, tools, and rough-house play" (Hesse-Biber and Carter 2005, 115).

Increasingly in modern times, however, many Americans have been challenging such traditional gender-typed standards, and so it seems reasonable to define **doing gender** as a process influenced by the prevailing norms involving the construction and performance of gender while also possessing the potential to resist or ignore those norms (Hirst and Schwabenland 2018; Lindemann 2018).

PHOTO 2.2 While traditionally doing gender often featured separate, different activities for girls and boys, recent standards have become more flexible, sometimes allowing members of both sexes to play on the same soccer team.
Source: MBI / Alamy Stock Photo

Compared to the earlier sense of doing gender, this definition is more fluid, indicating that a traditional, male-favoring designation is now under siege. Recent research provides indications of how doing gender occurs among young children.

In a midwestern city, a study of 99 youthful respondents ranging from three to six-and-a-half years old indicated that in interviews involving activities, occupations, aggressive behavior, and prosocial conduct (which is friendly and meant to encourage acceptance), girls tended to express more traditional outlooks than boys, who generally displayed few if any conventional views (Baker et al. 2016).

As far as the current treatment of their preschool children is concerned, parents in the United States and other western countries do not make stark distinctions between girls and boys. One way they do tend to differentiate involves the types of toys they provide and the activities they encourage, starting from infancy. Campbell Leaper, a psychologist specializing in child development, wrote, "For example, parents are more likely to provide toy vehicles, action figures, and sports equipment for their sons; and they are more likely to give dolls, kitchen sets, and dress-up toys to their daughters" (Leaper 2014).

Besides parents, preschool children's peers serve as a significant influence. From age two or three, children prefer to play with same-sex others, and that tendency increases until they are about 11. Research on preschool children indicated that both girls and boys were about twice as likely to interact with same-sex peers than either other-sex or mixed-sex children.

Young children often turn to same-sex peers to learn rules about gender, and both girls and boys are more likely to experiment with a gender-neutral or cross-gender toy if a same-sex peer does it first. Generally, however, same-sex peers disapprove of cross-gendered-type behavior, with children usually internalizing traditional standards and displaying behavior that becomes increasingly more conventionally gendered the longer they play with same-sex peers (Leaper and Friedman 2007, 569; Lindsay 2016, 239).

A respondent in a study in which college students recalled youthful peers' influence on their gender identity illustrated how preschool peers had pressured her to accept gender conventionality. Sometimes she and her friends acted out the characters in the platform game *Mario Brothers*. The young woman explained that while she protested continuously "I always had to be Princess. I would even cry on some days and demand to be Luigi, or even Bowser. But the kids always said that because I was a girl, I had to play Princess." She indicated that she was "kind of a tomboy and loved to climb trees and the monkey bars," but her peers were unmoved, explaining "that princess just gets chased and waits for Mario or Luigi to save her and … so even my playing style was criticized as it apparently was not very feminine. When I started kindergarten, I faced the same dilemma" (Golshirazian et al. 2015, 15).

For many young girls, however, no such dilemma currently exists. A study of 31 preschool girls aged three to five and 30 of their parents, the majority of whom were Hispanic or white, focused on the impact of the 11 Disney princesses, including Snow White, Cinderella, Sleeping Beauty, Ariel, and seven others, who, the authors noted, "have become cultural icons of childhood and tokens of an idealized girlhood" (Golden and Jacoby 2018, 299). Their research revealed little to dispute that conclusion.

The investigators found that in their encounters with the girls, it was clear that many wanted to be like the princesses, and several themes stood out. Beauty was one of them. A child said, "I want to be this one, this one, this one [pointing at the images of the Disney Princesses]. I want to mix them. Because I can look very cute." Another theme involved costumes and accessories. One youthful interviewee explained, "And mommy put some shiny lipstick on my lips and then she put a little flower right there [points to her hair] and then she put some gloves and necklace. And then I looked like a princess" (Golden and Jacoby 2018, 305). Clearly the princesses entranced many of these preschoolers, perhaps causing readers of this study to wonder to what extent the influence would persist in the years ahead.

An important hurdle young children must face is the challenge of entering school. As they head to kindergarten, an issue that arises is whether or not they are effectively prepared for this new experience.

Preschoolers' School Readiness

During their opening years of life, children develop their "school readiness," which includes "language and literacy, thinking skills, self-control, and self-confidence." These abilities provide a foundation not only for successful performance in kindergarten but also for later academic achievement. Parents and other early caretakers can contribute significantly to children's school readiness (The Urban Child Institute 2011). Because of the deficient social and material resources to which they have access, poor youths and children of color can find effective preschool programs particularly beneficial (Ladd 2017, 31).

A pair of researchers used data from the Early Childhood Longitudinal Study of the Kindergarten Classes of 1998–99 and 2010–11 to measure school-readiness skills, finding that gaps between high- and low-income kindergarten students in both reading and math scores had remained almost the same over more than a decade, in spite of an expansion of anti-poverty programs. However, some exceptions occurred, particularly among the poorest children.

Sharp increases among students deficient in school readiness occurred for those who were Hispanic, lived in homes where the first language was not English, were immigrants, and did not reside with both parents (García and Weiss 2017; Mader 2017).

Other negative factors have also affected school readiness. Research using data from the Fragile Families and Child Wellbeing Study involving over 2,000 respondents found that if poor children's family relocated three or more times before the age of five, it affected their ability to be attentive in school along with their levels of anxiety, depression, aggressiveness, and hyperactivity. Notably these negative responses to multiple family moves occurred only with poor families and not with their more affluent counterparts. The researchers concluded that unlike their wealthier peers, poor families faced relocations that were much more likely to be driven by forced conditions, namely evictions or foreclosures, which could readily produce stress for the preschool children involved (Ziol-Guest and McKenna 2014). Such useful information is largely unknown even by the personnel developing anti-poverty initiatives.

Earlier in this discussion, I noted that in spite of the expansion of anti-poverty programs during a recent 12-year period, the school-readiness gap between poor and affluent children did not reduce. One factor that probably contributed became apparent when an academically diverse research team interviewed poor, primarily African American parents who suggested that the personnel implementing Head Start and other programs concerned with school readiness needed to address not only children's cognitive skills but also their social and emotional growth.

Several parents' thoughtful comments follow. One mother explained, "[F]or me, school-readiness for [my daughter] would be that she's emotionally ready to go to school … [and] [t]hat she is at the stage now where she can sit and pay attention and follow directions." Another mother said,

I think socially is a very important part, to be socially ready for school. Because a lot of children are not used to it, and it's hard to get them away from their mothers. Where I don't think [my daughter] will have that problem because of Early Head Start.

Another parent assessed the bigger picture, making a critical observation about politicians' largely detached efforts to fight poverty and the need for their developing a better understanding of the kinds of problems these children faced. "I wish that a lot of these folks that were making these laws would come and take a walk. Not just take a walk, but really get in and see it" (McAllister et al. 2011). The research team found such observations useful, realizing that programs implementing school readiness needed to take such child-centered insights into account.

Key Terms in the Glossary

colorblind racism
doing gender
mortality rate
racial socialization

Discussion Topics

1. Is it reasonable to conclude that the United States has been successful at lowering its infant mortality rate? How does the US compare with other affluent nations?
2. From the section on the poverty conditions some young children face, choose two factors and explain why they are particularly destructive.
3. Discuss whether or not nonpoor parents have advantages in engaging in dialogue with their preschool offspring.
4. What are sources of toxic stress and why are they damaging to young children?
5. Describe effective way that parents belonging to racial minorities can effectively prepare their young children to enter a world where racism still exists.
6. Based on your observations, do you see evidence that children aged 10 and under continue to be exposed to gender discrimination?
7. For a class project, do research for a paper addressing the major objectives that you believe need to be emphasized in a preschool program for at-risk children. Examine significant difficulties that such activities could encounter.

Bibliography

Admon, Lindsay K., Tyler N.A. Winkelman, Kara Zivin, Mishka Terplan, Jill M. Mhyre, and Vanessa K. Dalton. 2018. "Racial and Ethnic Disparities in the Incidence of Severe Maternal Morbidity in the United States, 2012–2015." *Obstetrics and Gynecology* 132 (October): 1158–1166.

Akee, Randall. 2018. "Forty Years Ago We Stopped the Practice of Separating American Indian Families. Let's Not Reverse the Course." Brookings. (October 11). https://www.brookings.edu/blog/up-front/2018/10/11/40-years-ago-we-stopped-the-practice-of-separating-american-indian-families-lets-not-reverse-course/.

American Academy of Pediatrics. 2016. "Poverty and Child Health in the United States." *Pediatrics* 137 (April). https://pediatrics.aappublications.org/content/137/4/e20160339.

Baker, Erin R., Marie S. Tisak, and John Tisak. 2016. "What Can Boys and Girls Do? Preschoolers' Perspectives Regarding Gender Roles across Domains of Behavior." *Social Psychology of Education* 19: 23–39.

Barbarin, Oscar, and Ester Jean-Baptiste. 2013. "The Relation of Dialogic, Control, and Racial Socialization Practices to Early Academic and Social Competence: Effects of Gender, Ethnicity, and Family Socioeconomic Status." *American Journal of Orthopsychiatry* 83: 207–217.

Blair, Clancy, and C. Cybele Raver. 2016. "Poverty, Stress, and Brain Development: New Directions for Prevention and Intervention." National Center for Biotechnology Information. https://www.ncbi.nlm.nih.gov/pmc/articles/PMC5765853/.

Bonilla-Silva, Eduardo. 2010. *Racism without Racists: Color-Blind Racism & Racial Inequality in Contemporary America*, 3rd ed. Lanham, MD: Rowman & Littlefield.

Carroll, Linda. 2018. "Life-Threatening Birth Complications More Common in Minorities, Study Finds." NBC News. (October 10). https://www.nbcnews.com/health/womens-health/life-threatening-birth-complications-more-common-minorities-study-finds-n918781.

Children's Defense Fund. 2018. "Ending Child Poverty Now." (June). https://www.childrensdefense.org/wp-content/uploads/2018/06/Ending-Child-Poverty-Now.pdf.

Cole, Kirsten, and Diandra Verwayne. 2018. "Becoming Upended: Teaching and Learning about Race and Racism from Young Children and Their Families." National Association for the Education of Young Children. https://www.naeyc.org/resources/pubs/yc/may2018/teaching-learning-race-and-racism.

Columbia University. 2016. "Unequal Stress: How Poverty Is Toxic for Children's Brains." (May 10). Mailman School of Public Health. https://www.mailman.columbia.edu/public-health-now/news/unequal-stress-how-poverty-toxic-children%E2%80%99s-brains.

Douglass, Frederick. 1994. *Narrative of the Life of Frederick Douglass, an American Slave*. New York: The Library of America. First published in 1845.

Eskow, Richard. 2018. "Death by Inequality: Poverty and Racism Are Killing America's Children." *OurFuture*. (January 22). https://ourfuture.org/20180122/death-by-inequality-poverty-and-racism-are-killing-americas-children.

García, Emma, and Elaine Weiss. 2017. "Education Inequalities at the School Starting Gate." *Economic Policy Institute*. (September 27). https://www.epi.org/publication/education-inequalities-at-the-school-starting-gate/.

Gaskin, Ashly. 2015. "Racial Socialization: Ways Parents Can Teach Their Children about Race." American Psychological Association. (August). https://www.apa.org/pi/families/resources/newsletter/2015/08/racial-socialization.

Golden, Julia C., and Jennifer Wallace Jacoby. 2018. "Playing Princess: Preschool Girls' Interpretations of Gender Stereotypes in Disney Princess Media." *Sex Roles* 79 (September): 299–313.

Golshirazian, Sharlene, Manpreet Dhillon, Saskia Maltz, Keisha E. Payne, and Jerome Rabow. 2015. "The Effect of Peer Groups on Gender Identity and Expression."

International Journal of Research in Humanities and Social Studies 2 (October): 9–17. https://www.ijrhss.org/pdf/v2-i10/2.pdf.

Hesse-Biber, Sharlene, and Gregg Lee Carter. 2005. *Working Women in America: Split Dreams.* New York: Oxford University Press.

Hirst, Alison, and Christina Schwabenland. 2018. "Doing Gender in the 'New Office.'" *Gender, Work, & Organization* 25 (March): 159–176.

Johnson, David. 2018. "American Babies Are Less Likely to Survive than Babies in Other Rich Countries." *Time.* (January 9). https://time.com/5090112/infant-mortality-rate-usa/.

Kaplan, Karen. 2018. "Why the United States Is 'the Most Dangerous of Wealthy Nations for a Child to Be Born Into.'" *Los Angeles Times.* (January 8). https://www.latimes.com/science/sciencenow/la-sci-sn-childhood-mortality-usa-20180108-story.html.

Klepp, Susan E. 2004. "Malthusian Miseries and the Working Poor in Philadelphia, 1780–1830," pp. 63–92 in Billy G. Smith (ed.), *Down and Out in Early America.* University Park, PA: Pennsylvania State University Press.

Ladd, Helen F. 2017. "Do Some Groups of Children Benefit More than Others from Prekindergarten Programs?" Pp. 31–36 in Deborah A. Phillips *et al., Consensus Statement from the Pre-Kindergarten Task Force.* https://www.brookings.edu/wp-content/uploads/2017/04/duke_prekstudy_final_4-4-17_hires.pdf.

Leaper, Campbell. 2014. "Parents' Socialization of Gender in Children." *Encyclopedia on Early Child Development.* (August). http://www.child-encyclopedia.com/gender-early-socialization/according-experts/parents-socialization-gender-children.

Leaper, Campbell, and Carly Kay Friedman. 2007. "The Socialization of Gender," pp. 561–587 in Joan E. Grusec and Paul D. Hastings (eds.), *Handbook of Socialization: Theory and Research.* New York: Guilford Press.

Lindemann, Danielle J. 2018. "Doing and Undoing Gender in Commuter Marriage." *Sex Roles* 79 (July): 36–49.

Lindsay, Eric W. 2016. "Same-Gender Peer Interaction and Preschoolers' Gender-Typed Emotional Expressiveness." *Sex Roles* 75: 231–242.

Lonang Institute. 2018. "Of Slaves, Considered as Property, in Virginia." https://lonang.com/library/reference/tucker-blackstone-notes-reference/tuck-3e/.

Mader, Jackie. 2017. "New Research Finds It Hasn't Gotten Any Easier for Poor Kids to Catch Up." Hechinger Report. (October 31). https://hechingerreport.org/new-research-finds-hasnt-gotten-easier-poor-kids-catch/.

Marcelo, Ana K., and Tuppett M. Yates. 2018. "Young Children's Ethnic–Racial Identity Moderates the Impact of Early Discrimination Experiences on Child Behavior Problems." *Cultural Diversity and Ethnic Minority Psychology* 25 (April): 253–265.

McAllister, Carol L., Patrick C. Wilson, Beth L. Green, and Beth L. Baldwin. 2011. "Come and Take a Walk: Listening to Early Head Start Parents on School-Readiness as a Matter of Child, Family, and Community Health." *American Journal of Public Health.* (October 10). https://ajph.aphapublications.org/doi/full/10.2105/AJPH.2004.041616.

McCarthy, Claire. 2019. "How Racism Harms Children." Harvard Medical School. (September 14). https://www.health.harvard.edu/blog/how-racism-harms-children-2019091417788.

McCarty, Alyn T. 2016. "Child Poverty in the United States: A Tale of Devastation and the Promise of Hope." *Sociology Compass* 10 (July): 623–639.

Miller, Cindy Faith, Hanns Martin Trautner, and Diane N. Ruble. 2006. "The Role of Gender Stereotypes in Children's Preferences and Behavior," pp. 293–323 in Lawrence

Balter and Catherine S. Tamis-LeMonda (eds.), *Child Psychology: A Handbook of Contemporary Issues*, 2nd ed. New York: Psychology Press.

Morris, Amanda Sheffield, Jennifer Hays-Grudo, Lara R. Robinson, Angelika H. Claussen, Sophie A. Hartwig, and Amy E. Treat. 2017. "Targeting Parenting in Early Childhood: A Public Health Approach to Improve Outcomes for Children Living in Poverty." *Child Development* 88 (March/April): 388–397.

National Institutes of Health. 2012. "Stresses of Poverty May Impair Learning in Young Children." (August 28). https://www.nih.gov/news-events/news-releases/stresses-poverty-may-impair-learning-ability-young-children.

Oskamp, Stuart, Karen Kaufman, and Lianna Atchison Wolterbeek. 1996. "Gender Role Portrayals in Preschool Picture Books." *Journal of Social Behavior & Personality* 11: 27–39.

Pahlke, Erin, Rebecca S. Bigler, and Marie-Anne Suizzo. 2012. "Relations between Color-blind Socialization and Children's Racial Bias: Evidence from European American Mothers and Their Preschool Children." *Child Development* 83 (July/August): 1164–1179.

Science News. 2013. "Poverty Threatens Health of US Children." (May 4). https://www.sciencedaily.com/releases/2013/05/130504163257.htm.

Stockard, Jean. 1999. "Gender Socialization," pp. 215–227 in Janet Saltzman Chafetz (ed.), *Handbook of the Sociology of Gender*. New York: Kluwer Academic/Plenum Publishers.

Taylor, Jamila, Cristina Novoa, Katie Hamm, and Shilpa Phadke. 2019. "Eliminating Racial Disparities in Maternal and Infant Mortality." Center for American Progress. (May 2). https://www.americanprogress.org /issues/women/reports/2019/05/02/469186/eliminating-racial-disparities-maternal-infant-mortality/.

Thakrar, Ashish P., Alexandra D. Forrest, Mitchell G. Maltenfort, and Christopher B. Forrest. 2018. "Child Mortality in the US and 19 OECD Comparator Nations: A 50-Year Time-Trend Analysis." *Health Affairs* 37 (January): 140–149.

The Urban Child Institute. 2011. "What Do We Mean by School Readiness." (September 16). http://www.urbanchildinstitute.org/articles/research-to-policy/research/what-do-we-mean-by-school-readiness.

Wade, Mark, Sheri Madigan, André Plamondon, Michele Rodrigues, Dillon Browne, and Jennifer M. Jenkins. 2018. "Cumulative Psychosocial Risk, Parental Socialization, and Child Cognitive Functioning: A Longitudinal Cascade Model." *Developmental Psychology* 54 (June): 1038–1050.

Warren, J.D. 2018. "Children as Young as Seven Suffer Effects of Discrimination, Study Shows." Science Daily. (October 22). https://www.sciencedaily.com/releases/2018/10/181022162138.htm.

Weir, Kirsten. 2017. "Maximizing Children's Resilience." American Psychological Association. https://www.apa.org/monitor/2017/09/cover-resilience.

Weitzman, Lenore J., Deborah Eifel, Elizabeth Hokada, and Catherine Ross. 1972. "Sex-Role Socialization for Children in Picture Books for Preschool Children." *American Journal of Sociology* 77 (May): 1125–1150.

West, Candace, and Don Zimmerman. 1987. "Doing Gender." *Gender & Society* 2 (June): 121–151.

Williams, Natalie A., and Judith M. Burnfield. 2019. "Psychological Difficulties and Parental Well-Being in Children with Musculoskeletal Problems in the 2011/2012 National Survey of Children's Health." *Rehabilitation Psychology* 64: 87–97.

Winer, Abby C., and Ross A. Thompson. 2013. "How Poverty and Depression Impact a Child's Social and Emotional Competence." Center for Poverty Research, University of

California, Davis. (July 24). https://poverty.ucdavis.edu/policy-brief/how-poverty-and-depression-impact-childs-social-and-emotional-competence.

Yoshikawa, Hirokazu, J. Lawrence Aber, and William R. Beardslee. 2012. "The Effects of Poverty on the Mental, Emotional, and Behavioral Health of Children and Youth." *American Psychologist.* (May/June): 272–284.

Ziol-Guest, Kathleen M., and Claire C. McKenna. 2014. "Early Childhood Housing Instability and School Readiness." *Child Development* 85 (January/February): 103–113.

3

ADOLESCENCE

A Precarious Life

Adolescence, often considered to range from age 10 to 19 years old, is a time of life posing risks and challenges for members of all social classes. Sharon Levy, a member of the Harvard medical faculty, noted that psychological and social problems, particularly those involving behavior and school activities, are more prevalent during these years than at any other time during childhood. A contributing factor is that teens are much more mobile and removed from parental control than when they were younger. Levy warned that if their misbehavior becomes troublesome, it is sensible to consult a mental-health professional. She noted, "In particular, depression, anxiety, and eating disorders are common during adolescence. Adolescents who have anxiety or mood disorders may have physical symptoms such as fatigue or chronic fatigue, dizziness, headache, and abdominal or chest pain" (Levy 2019). Teens overall are likely to find living stressful, and as Figure 3.1 indicates, the national news provides clear evidence supporting that trend, suggesting that they are more stressed than adults about five issues in the national news.

We begin with some basic statistics about adolescence. In 2016 teens ranging between 10 and 19 represented almost 42 million individuals, about 12.9 percent of the population. By 2050 their numbers will rise to almost 44 million, representing 11.3 percent of the total. Over time the proportion of adolescents belonging to racial minorities is likely to rise—with 53 percent of teens white in 2016 dropping to about 40 percent in 2050. Among the three largest racial minorities, the 2016 to 2050 percentages show Blacks stable at nearly 14 percent of the adolescent population, Hispanics rising from about 24 to 30 percent, and Asians increasing from about 5 to 7 percent.

Generally people of color are less affluent than the overall population, with disproportionately high numbers of families living in poverty. In 2017 about 16 percent of adolescents belonged to poor families, meaning those with income of less than $24,600 a year for a family of four. Among poor families the most vulnerable economically were single-parent units (U.S. Department of Health and Human Services. Office of Population Affairs 2019).

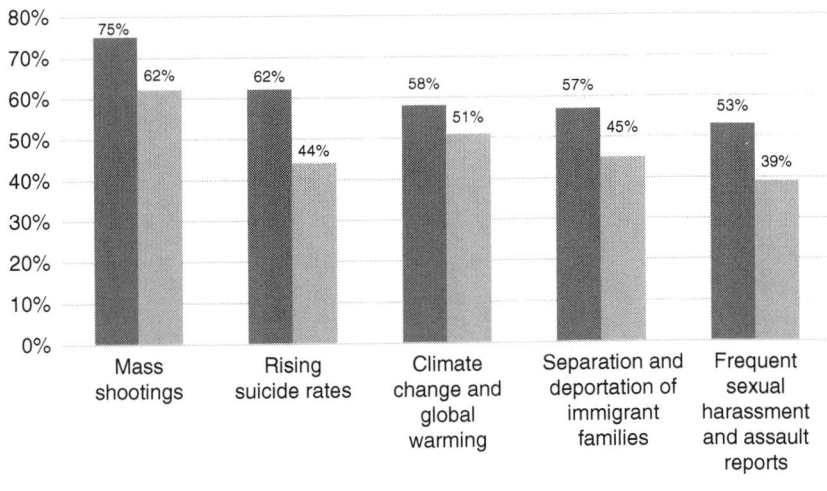

FIGURE 3.1 Adolescents' and Adults' Stressful Reaction to Issues in the National News[1]
Source: American Psychological Association 2018.
Note: As the data demonstrate, teens consistently find national news issues more stressful than adults.
[1] The Harris Poll conducted an online survey for the American Psychological Association containing nearly 3,500 adults 18 and older as well as 300 teens aged 15 to 17.

Like poor people generally, impoverished adolescents commonly face unrelenting, painful challenges.

Teens in Poverty

chaotic environment

Research has shown that the poor often live in a chaotic environment containing toxic stress and featuring "crowding, noise, family instability, and geographic mobility along with fewer structured activities and routines." In such settings it can be difficult or even impossible for young people to believe that they can develop a well-organized life (Fuller-Rowell et al. 2015, 607).

Living in such high-risk communities often produces anxiety and depression for adolescents, making them vulnerable to mental illness and substance abuse. In addition, when chaos and disorder prevail, others, including parents and additional adults, can be adversely affected, producing such outcomes for teens as physical, emotional, or sexual abuse or serious neglect (Lin and Seo 2017; New York Center for Living 2019; Pan American Health Organization 2013).

For poor adolescents the family, especially the parents, can be a critical influence.

The Family in Play

To assess the impact of poor adolescents' parents, analysts have needed to examine the settings in which the families were located. For example, a study of more

189.

than 2,400 low-income children, including a sizable segment of adolescents, found that when the respondents lived in inferior housing, their emotional and behavioral activity was less effective and their cognitive capacities less well developed. Across the different age groups, the investigators found that the children's impeded development was not primarily the result of their own reaction to the housing. Instead a major influence was their reaction to their parents' negative response to the situation (Coley et al. 2013, 1783–85). The researchers indicated that the family processes involving stress and stability affected children in the following manner: "[L]ow-quality housing may induce stress in parents, increase mental health problems, and limit their ability to regulate family activities, in turn affecting children's socioemotional functioning" (Coley et al. 2013, 1785). So, the research team concluded, inferior housing affected the children, generally not directly but indirectly when their parents were negatively impacted by it.

A similar process involving poor parents occurs with the issue of depression. An investigation of non-Hispanic white respondents indicated that among those who were poor, the actual presence of poverty did not cause teens to develop depressive symptoms. Rather they became depressed when their mothers were prone to depression and also when a parent was absent from the household during the respondent's first year of life (Butler 2014, 82, 90–91).

Once revealed, such deep-seated family problems are difficult to resolve. Nonetheless the investigator emphasized that these findings underline "the need for appropriate treatment of childhood depression so as to reduce the adverse consequences in adulthood and for the next generation" (Butler 2014, 82). It is, in short, a situation where the destructive impact of social reproduction can readily extend from one generation to the next.

A review of studies on poor parents' relations with their children indicated that they worried about meeting their offsprings' material needs and were aware of both the benefits and disadvantages of public assistance, realizing that the stresses accompanying poverty limited the youngsters' effective performance. Parents used different approaches in discussing economic circumstances with their children, being more forthright with adolescents than with preteens, and sometimes such major challenges as homelessness or divorce prompted detailed discussion, including extensive exchanges about family finances (Quint et al. 2018, 40–41).

Neighborhood

Poor adolescents grow up in neighborhoods possessing a variety of disadvantaged conditions involving such issues as the amount of violence or quality of housing, with parents' reactions often differing in their assessment of the effect. In a poor Denver neighborhood, about two thirds of parents interviewed felt the locale had a negative impact on their children. One mother explained,

There are drug users knocking at my door at odd hours of the night. I've had to call the police. Someone was almost killed several doors down. I don't let my children play outside. We go from the house to the car. That's it.

(Quint et al. 2018, 28)

Regardless of the neighborhood quality, research has shown that poor teens who received social support from parents or other adult sources were better equipped to develop such coping strategies as effective self-expression, the ability to seek help, and the capacity to reach safety. Without such supports these young people were often unable to resolve the destructive or even dangerous issue at hand (Reife et al. 2019, 209–10).

In addition, with staunch backing from parents and peers, adolescents' capacity to articulate and better comprehend the realities of living in poverty are likely to improve. When asked to write about an issue that was important to them, a sample of low-income, largely African American and Latino teens living in the greater Chicago area thoughtfully examined various problems, which included references to the three at-risk groups in this book. Several examples follow.

One respondent found that the most disturbing issue the residents of poor urban neighborhoods have is fewer chances for success than those in more affluent areas. The youth added, "This upsets me because people in poverty are judged based on the way that they have to survive … [hampered by] limited opportunities." Another emphasized the brutal killing of Black males. "These problems bother me because I feel it's unfair that we constantly fight for justice but we get nowhere" (Roy et al. 2019, 554). Finally a third teen referenced gender discrimination and wrote,

> I don't like the fact that men are displayed more superior than women. They get paid more, they aren't put down like women are and people make it seem like women have to do everything for the man when it shouldn't be that way.
>
> *(Roy et al. 2019, 555)*

Many teens must face the intersectional challenge of dealing with both racism and poverty.

Adolescent Challenges That Racial Minorities Face

As a result of both historical and current discrimination, teens of color can suffer serious effects on their mental health. Over two decades researchers interviewed nearly 2,000 teens and young adults as well as more than 1,000 parents and caretakers living in New York's South Bronx and San Juan, Puerto Rico. They learned that even though the Puerto Rican respondents were poorer, the Americans displayed higher levels of anxiety and depression. Several key influences came into play. The parents in the South Bronx described more neighborhood discrimination and both lower levels of family support and greater amounts of family conflict. The youthful Americans, in turn, also cited less family support as well as weaker ethnic identity. The results of the study prompted the researchers to conclude that such neighborhood-level interventions as youth-civic clubs in after-school programs could prove more effective in reducing anxiety and depression than assistance to individuals (Alegria et al. 2019).

In response to these findings, Margarita Alegria, the lead researcher, offered this generalization. "How others interact with you as a minority can affect your mental health and how you see yourself. The mere experience of growing up as a minority can elevate your psychiatric risks" (ScienceDaily 2019).

Nothing in the pages ahead disputes this conclusion. The material, however, indicates that teens of color encounter a wide variety of conditions—risk factors involving the intersectional combination of race and social class but also a number of positive influences. The discussion begins with the general topic of racial discrimination and then examines parents' efforts engaging in racial socialization to offset it.

Racial Discrimination

The early twenty-first century is hardly the post-Civil War era when whites treated teens belonging to racial minorities as blatantly inferior and considered it normal, even sensible, to keep them in dire poverty. Nonetheless when out in public today, minority adolescents are likely to recognize that in toned-down ways they can be viewed and treated as inferiors.

In Rhonda F. Levine's study of African American youth, she quoted a pair of teenage brothers' reaction to whites observing them. Fifteen-year-old Izzy explained that he would be walking down the street and "I feel they're looking behind their shoulder, you know, and stuff like that, I mean nervous and all." Seeing him, they are inclined to pick up a dog or baby, "just thinking that I'm going to hurt them or something" (Levine 2019, 31).

Curtis, Izzy's 18-year-old brother, expressed similar complaints, indicating that when he and a friend,

> two big dudes, dressed the way we dress, ... [like Black gang members] we look like something that we're not to people who don't truly understand who we are, you know what I mean? White people? .... [W]alk by a car and you hear them lock their doors, you know what I mean? There's been times when I said "Hi" to a little baby because they smiled, and their mother snatched them, like, "No they're dangerous."

(Levine 2019, 31)

While hardly life-threatening, this type of consistently alienating treatment can readily affect teens, possibly supporting a diminished sense of self and impacting negatively on both physical and mental health. In an examination of 214 peer-reviewed articles, theses, and dissertations regarding racial/ethnic discrimination, a team of researchers reached the following significant conclusion: that youth experiences of racism:

[t]he psychological, behavioral, and academic burdens posed by racial/ethnic discrimination during adolescence, coupled with evidence that experiences of discrimination persist across the life course for persons of color, point to discrimination as a clear contributor to the racial/ethnic health disparities observed for African American, Latino, and Native American populations compared with their [w]hite counterparts.

(Benner et al. 2018, 872)

As the following references illustrate, numerous studies suggest the impact of racial influences on teens. In New York City, nearly 600 Dominican, Chinese, and African American early adolescents were surveyed three successive years, generally indicating that while adults' levels of discrimination remained quite stable at low to moderate, the peer amounts tended to drop. The investigators concluded that among adults it was largely those outside of school who contributed significantly to sustaining the level of discrimination (Niwa et al. 2014, 2348–49).

While peers' racial discrimination might generally decline over time, that does not preclude teasing adolescent companions about their racial or ethnic membership. For instance, in a study of 23 racially diverse teens in New York City, a 16-year-old male who described himself as Hispanic and Dominican would tease some of his fellow band members about their ethnicity, admitting that, "Yeah I play around with them, like 'Stop being a lazy Mexican and get on the drums'" (Douglass et al. 2016, 73). **bantering + teasing**

Often such bantering produced no ill effects, but sometimes it could make people angry. An interviewer learned that a Black female had a white friend who made fun of her because she was Black. The interviewer asked what the friend said. "She always says like 'what['s] up, N****r,' like she talks about the slaves too." The interviewer wanted to know how such references made her feel.

> Um[,] one time I got really mad at her, I got offended and I wanted to punch her in the face. But I just let it go …. It's just because … that's a touchy subject to me, like slaves. Because like what happened to them. …. [M]aybe I was having a bad day that day but I remember I just got so mad.
>
> *(Douglass et al. 2016, 73)*

Another factor affecting minority teens' experience with racial discrimination is their personal history. Those who are immigrants are a case in point, with differences developing among the newly arrived teens in their responses to race-related treatment. An investigation of 77 immigrant adolescents of diverse racial or ethnic backgrounds found that those with a greater commitment to their racial or ethnic group felt a stronger belief in social justice and the necessity of stopping racism and ethnic discrimination than their fellows with a weaker commitment to their group (Chan and Latzman 2015, 529).

A study of Asian American ninth graders living in an immigrant community also showed a distinction among research subjects based on the level of involvement with their racial group—that adolescents engaged in the exploration of their own racial origin generally had higher self-esteem than those unengaged in that pursuit. However, one distinct twist appeared in the findings. The teens who were most heavily involved in ethnic exploration ended up with lowered self-esteem, probably because that pursuit could turn out to be costly and worrisome, requiring traveling or spending time with peers engaged in such expensive, demanding tasks as taking language classes or learning to play an ethnic instrument (Stein et al. 2014, 206, 212).

Some adolescents possess traits making them particularly vulnerable to discrimination. A distinct case in point are teens of color belonging to sexual minorities, who experience the effects of a second status that locates them as LGBT outside the perceived mainstream tradition. A study of more than 250 African American or African American mixed teens who were LGBT found that the intersectional combination of being both a member of a racial minority and a sexual minority had a compounded impact in producing depressive symptoms—in short, a double whammy (Thoma and Huebner 2013, 409).

PHOTO 3.1 This lesbian Black couple enjoying each other's company might bring to mind the study indicating that LGBT teens of color are more likely to be happy and satisfied with life if they learn about their sexual minority's contributions and explore the meaning of their minority identities.

Source: Shutterstock/ Kosim Shukurov

While teens belonging to both racial and sexual minorities sometimes encounter emotional problems, research has suggested that they can benefit from exploring both types of membership. A study featuring more than 200 Latino, Asian American, and Black adolescents found that the process of exploring the contributions one's racial and sexual groups have made and examining the meaning of their minority identities encourages positive feelings toward the groups and a stronger sense of attachment, thereby prompting higher levels of self esteem and life satisfaction and reduced levels of depression and anxiety (Ghavami et al. 2011, 81–82, 86).

Since adolescents of color face the distinct prospect of racial discrimination, various adults, notably parents, other relatives, teachers, community workers, and social activists, can provide useful racial socialization. Parents, however, are overall best located and best committed to perform the task.

Parents' Racial Socialization of Their Teenage Children

[handwritten: ethnic + gender norm socialization]

The information and support parents can provide include:

- A sense of racial or ethnic pride in one's group
- Cautions about racial inequalities and injustices
- A forewarning about the physical and psychological dangers the teens might face
- An alternative strategy emphasizing a color-blind approach, downplaying the impact of racism and perhaps also suggesting hard work can overcome any barriers
- The option not to discuss race and racism (Gaskin 2015; Tang et al. 2016; Threlfall 2018).

The previous list makes it clear that parents can make different decisions about how to approach racial socialization. Overall mothers are more involved in children's socialization, including racial socialization, than fathers. Evidence indicates that sometimes the racial group to which parents belong affects how racial socialization develops.

An investigation of 100 dyads involving African American, Latino, and Chinese American mothers and their early adolescent children revealed that when the mothers encountered racial discrimination at work, the teens reported more extensive messages at home advising them about how to respond to discriminatory treatment, with distinct group differences emerging in their content.

In their past African Americans encountered both slavery and a lengthy tradition of racism including extensive discrimination on the job, and since the mothers in this study tended to be well informed about such repressive treatment, they often felt mobilized to confront the challenges of racial socialization. Like Blacks, Latinos are heavily represented in low-skill, low-paying positions where discriminatory treatment has been common, and so these mothers also frequently felt it necessary to provide their children racial socialization that would protect them from the ravages of discrimination.

The Chinese American mothers came from a distinctly different tradition. While they too sometimes felt the effect of discrimination on the job, their response to it tended to differ. They generally believed that the mistreatment was the result of critical perceptions of Asians as foreigners with inadequate capacities to express themselves in English. Unlike the mothers from the other two groups, they did not emphasize the importance of their own tradition but told their teens to learn the language well, work hard at school and on the job, and assimilate into mainstream life (Hagelskamp and Hughes 2014, 550–52, 57).

In addition, within a single racial group, children's responses to racial socialization can vary depending on certain conditions in the family. A study of more than 500 African American parents and their adolescent children from the eighth and eleventh grades provided information on the topic. The data indicated that Black teens were more likely to commit to parents' beliefs and messages about racial issues when there was extensive communication between parents and children. In contrast, when interaction between the generations was limited, the prospect of parents' influence involving racial socialization distinctly diminished (Tang et al. 2016, 1141, 1151).

Many Black parents take an uncompromising view toward racial socialization, believing that their teenage children are best prepared for the world in which they live if they are fully aware of the virulent racism permeating it. In his celebrated book *Between the World and Me,* writer Ta-Nehisi Coates sent a lengthy letter to his adolescent son, laying out his perception of the American racial landscape. Whites, Coates told the boy, had not developed a sense of racial superiority by engaging in such elegant activities as

> wine tastings and ice cream socials, but rather through the flaying of backs; the chaining of limbs; … the destruction of families; the rape of mothers; the sale of children; and the various other acts … to deny you and me the right to secure and govern our own bodies.
>
> *(Coates 2015, 8)*

Continuing the letter, Coates told his son that whites tended to be oblivious to the horrors they had inflicted on Blacks—that they, whom he called the Dreamers, remained immersed in a vision that their country is "exceptional, the greatest and noblest nation ever to exist, a lone nation standing between the white city of democracy and the terrorists, despots, barbarians, and other enemies of civilization" (Coates 2015, 8). His parents, Coates explained, never accepted the Dreamers' view, "not stand[ing] for their anthem…[,] … not kneel [ing] before their God" (Coates 2015, 28). As a child he found that "[f]ear ruled everything around me," and that a connection existed between his fear and the dream shown nightly on TV of whites immersed in their comfortable, affluent lives (Coates 2015, 29).

Meanwhile Blacks, some of them children, face the everyday perils of dealing with whites, particularly the police, who have the authority "to destroy your body," even if the activity is innocent, and rarely do they face the prospect of accountability (Coates 2015, 9).

Toward the end of the letter, Coates told his son that he offered no easy answers—that he saw no way to stop the Dreamers from continuing on their destructive path and that what the boy should do was to recognize and honor critical realities of the world in which he was living. Coates wrote, "I urge you to struggle. Struggle for the memories of your ancestors. Struggle for wisdom. …. Struggle for your grandmother and grandfather, for your name" (Coates 2015, 151).

Inevitably the lion's share of parents engaged in racial socialization are people of color, but sometimes whites participate. In interviews eight middle-class white fathers of early adolescents indicated how they engaged in racial socialization in order to raise their children to be "nonracist." For instance, Tom, a social scientist, explained that the reason he and his wife chose the neighborhood and school their daughter Charlotte attended was that they wanted her to be exposed to "human difference" and to have a chance to meet and get to know children belonging to other racial groups. Tom indicated that he and his wife were happy that

> Charlotte would go to a school that wouldn't be a bunch of rich white kids. … I don't know that I want her to have that super white-bread, sit around with a bunch of, you know, over-achieving … wealthy white Americans, having them as her entire base of everyone she knows. That made us nervous.… Coming to a school that had more racial and economic mixes was appealing.
>
> *(Hagerman 2017, 65)*

In seeking to pinpoint the importance of racial socialization, Tom added, "As her father … what are the good seeds in Charlotte that I'm trying to water?" He went on to explain that unless she contacted people of diverse backgrounds, she would seriously lose out.

> There is a lot of deepening of your human understanding of other people that gets—you miss it.… It makes you … be more thoughtful … and I don't know how that can't make you a better person. It should help you be a kinder human being.
>
> *(Hagerman 2017, 66)*

While her father made no mention of the issue, Charlotte might also have discovered that besides the teen years posing challenges of race, they also raised issues involving gender.

Adolescent Girls' Prospects for Gender Equality

Girls on the brink of adulthood can find that stresses are a common reality involving several sources:

- Plan International conducted a national survey involving more than 1,000 10- to 19-year-olds, showing that at least two thirds of the adolescent respondents indicated that they had found that getting into college or deciding what to do after high school are distinctly stressful prospects. Teens greatly value their future work, and certainly that contributes to their sense of stress. Girls are about as inclined as boys to emphasize that having a career is very important—more important than marrying and having children (Plan International 2018, 6; Smith 2019; Stanford Children's Health 2019).

- Teens have been as likely as adults to believe that sexism remains widespread and a source of stress. In the Plan International study, adolescent boys were considerably more optimistic than girls (44 vs. 21 percent) in believing that gender equality currently exists. In declaring that sexism persists as a major problem, girls often indicated that they felt less respected because they were female, observing that at times they had been treated as a sex object, sometimes felt unsafe because of being a girl, and had heard boys making derogatory sexual statements or jokes about females. One sobering finding was that nearly half of teen boys compared to about a third of girls had heard their fathers or another male relative making disparaging sexual comments or jokes about women, meaning that this potentially powerful impetus to sexism persists (Plan International 2018, 2–5).

- Other prominent sources of adolescent girls' stresses include pressure to experiment with drugs, alcohol, or sex, the challenges of puberty, exposure to sexual harassment or violence, family and peer conflicts, and overloaded schedules that are likely to include the following activities: school work, sports, afterschool programs, social life, part-time employment, and family commitments (Lifespan 2019).

For many adolescents of both sexes, stress is an unrelenting reality. Survey data has indicated that in any previous month about one third or more of teens reported feeling irritable or even angry, being nervous or anxious, sensing fatigue, lying awake at night, or sometimes concluding they were overwhelmed (Smith 2019).

Not surprisingly the specific conditions that girls experience as they grow up can significantly affect their gender-related outlooks and behavior. We consider conditions linked to straight teens and then influences associated with specific racial groups, the members of sexual minorities, and selected female athletes:

- According to the previously cited Plan International survey involving about 1,000 adolescents, a set of findings indicated that girls who primarily played with traditional girls' toys such as dolls and doll houses were more inclined than those who occupied themselves with a combination of girls' and boys' toys to have families where mothers performed most of the child-care duties, to have male friends who asked them for photos showing them sexy or naked, to place less importance on achieving the goal of building a successful career, to feel pressure to be hot or sexy and to dominate or control others, to reject the idea of being a feminist, and to have a father whose sexual comments about women were degrading (Plan International 2018, 8).

The fact that some girls only played with traditional girls' toys did not mean that they were locked into the outcomes listed above. More likely, the girls who only played with girls' toys were generally traditional in experience and outlook, with the distinctly traditional results listed above likely to develop as a result.

- Racial membership can produce a distinct impact, with research showing that this factor is likely to affect female teens' outlooks and behavior. For instance, a study of about 30 low-income, early-adolescent Mexican American and African American females indicated the powerful influence that group affiliation produced.

The Mexican American informants said that parents tended to discourage their dating, fearing that it would lead to sexual activity and pregnancy. Dawn, an informant, declared how dissimilar parental standards were for young women and men. She said,

> That's what I don't get because mostly every boy is allowed to date girls, but almost every girl is not allowed to date. My dad is like, he tells my brother, 'You go ahead and date, just don't get her pregnant.' Now me on the other hand, I can't even mention a boy's name; they say if they ever catch me with a boy, they are going to be thinking that I am pregnant, and I don't know why.
> (Sanchez et al. 2017, 462)

In contrast, African American mothers and fathers were more relaxed, displaying a more open attitude toward dating and sexuality but warning their daughters about the dangers of sexuality and advising them to wait until they were older to engage in it. Many of these Black teens felt they were receiving a mixed parental message, featuring both the distinct advice that they abstain from sex but simultaneously offering assistance in procuring contraceptives (Sanchez et al. 2017, 453, 464–65).

Whether the topic at hand was sexuality or something else, the young African American women in the study reported that their parents generally told them that gender equality prevailed, with no significant power differentials between women and men. For instance, Alicia, reflecting her parents' beliefs, said, "[A husband and wife] should be equal in control. My mama told me, like she always tell me,

'I want you independent.' She don't want me to depend on other people. That's all she's telling me, be independent. Be independent." In contrast, the Mexican American parents tended to instruct their daughters to accept a traditional patriarchal system (Sanchez et al. 2017, 461).

- As previous material involving racial minorities suggested, the adolescent years for gays and lesbians are influential, with a survey indicating that 12 was the median age at which they first felt they might be something other than heterosexual and 17 the median age when they were convinced that they were either lesbian, gay, bisexual, or transgender (Pew Research Center 2013).

Since research has indicated that parents' influence on their children's lives is considerable, it is troubling to learn that a review of the literature indicates that LGBT children in their late teens or early twenties often receive no support from their parents about their sexual status—specifically, a third obtain acceptance, another third rejection, and the remainder have parents who are unaware of their children's sexual orientation because the teens decide not to reveal it. One positive note is that according to the studies, no matter their initial reaction, parents over time generally become more accepting of their children's LGBT status (Katz-Wise et al. 2016, 7).

Parental support can be very beneficial for LGBT teens because as members of a sexual minority they can encounter discrimination in that role, often resulting in a fragile sense of self. Investigation into the parents of sexual minority teens revealed that when mothers and fathers are supportive, adolescents, even if they are vulnerable to mistreatment from peers or others, are more likely to retain a positive sense of themselves, accepting, even embracing their own identity (Bregman et al. 2013, 427–28; Katz-Wise et al. 2016, 4–7).

In short, it is apparent that parents can develop supportive relations with their LGBT children, even if early on they failed to understand them. Shondra's mother explained that when the girl was very young, she was willing to wear dresses, but by the time she was nine, she hated them. In addition, she was often depressed and spent a lot of time alone in her room. Her mother was perplexed, thinking her daughter "willful and disobedient." Then when the child was 12, a counselor contacted the family, requesting a meeting with the mother and explaining that at school Shondra dressed like a boy and asked the students to call her Darnell. It was a learning experience for the mother.

She explained,

> The school counselor told us about transgender. We never heard of such a thing. She thought that Shondra was transgender and she gave us the name of another counselor, … [who] told us what Shondra, I mean, Darnell was feeling when we tried to dress her up and be a certain way. They said that for our child, the way we were acting felt like we were rejecting her … [and] that children like this get very depressed … and [that] they are at very high risk for suicide when their family tries to make them act like a girl.

The information was invaluable. The mother concluded, "We were shocked. We had no idea. So we got our child help and he's much happier now" (Ryan 2009, 3).

- Another category of adolescent girls have been particularly vulnerable to sexist treatment—namely, selected female athletes. While preteens are sometimes sexually mistreated by coaches, doctors, teachers, and other primarily male personnel, a significant portion of the victims are teens. Abuse ranges from verbal badgering to physical assaults, including rape.

Sexual abuse of female athletes has increased over time. In the second half of the twentieth century after the Soviet Union in its first Olympics soundly thrashed the US in women's events, leading politicians and athletic officials began to take women's sports more seriously. Whereas women had previously run almost all female sports programs, men now took the upper hand, becoming the dominant force in such feminine sports as figure skating, swimming, and gymnastics. At present only about 40 percent of women coach female athletes, and about 22 percent of women are athletic directors. Even though increasing numbers of women are becoming medical doctors, men still dominate sports medicine, including the most prestigious power roles.

Title 1x?

A highly publicized case involved Lawrence Nassar, a former USA Gymnastics national team doctor and an osteopathic physician at Michigan State University. In 2018 Nassar was convicted of sexually abusing more than 150 young female athletes

PHOTO 3.2 While Dr. Lawrence Nassar's abuse of more than 150 young female athletes over three decades was a horrifying series of acts, many observers felt that the most troubling issue was the fact that he was able to go largely unchallenged for such a lengthy period of time.

Source: Richard Levine / Alamy Stock Photo

and received a prison sentence of 40 to 175 years. The Nassar case represents a clear illustration of the challenge facing officials trying to eliminate such destructive treatment. Female gymnasts began reporting his abuses in the 1990s. Had coaches and other athletic personnel followed up the complaints and passed them on to law-enforcement authorities, it would have been possible to avoid massive suffering and damage to the victims (Blaschke 2018).

In gymnastics and in other women's sports such as swimming and figure skating, there has been a widespread failure to protect female athletes, starting with preteens and extending to women in their twenties and thirties. The girls and women themselves are often reluctant to report, fearing, as their coaching sometimes warn them, that if they do they will lose their opportunity to become stars. A sociological report on the sexual abuse of young elite athletes suggested that they might be most vulnerable to coaches' sexual overtures when they have attained a high level of performance but are slightly below an elite standard. At that point they recognize the importance of coaches' instruction and support and in many cases are willing to do anything necessary to retain it (Brackenridge and Kirby 1997; Marthe 2016). In an interview with a pair of journalists, one teenage victim explained,

> Gymnastics was my whole world... He threatened to take all that away. That my teammates would lose everything, too. Everything would be my fault. He threatened his own life if I wouldn't, in his words, be his girl-friend... At that point I didn't really resist anymore.
>
> *(Kwiatkowski and Evans 2016)*

To prevent such abuses, all female sports need to establish and maintain norms asserting that regardless of age or consent, no sexual or romantic relationships should exist between coaches and other team officials and their female athletes. It is hardly a breathtakingly innovative idea, causing observers to wonder why such actions have not occurred throughout the female sports world. It turns out that the answer is fairly simple: Olympic administrators backed by their legal councils made the decision that in spite of the dangers involved, it was not their responsibility to address the issue of sexual abuse in sports. Then the U.S. Olympic Committee and the National Sports Governing Bodies also followed suit, fearing the civil cases from coaches that could materialize (Hogshead 2018). Now, however, with the revelation of how widespread and destructive these abuses have become and with athletes less willing to accept them, it seems likely that norms protecting female athletes will become increasingly common.

As teens approach their adult years, many find themselves significantly challenged.

The Uncertain Future for Disconnected Youth

Disconnected youth are teens and young adults between the ages of 16 and 24 who are neither in school nor working. As a result they are often living in a high-risk, stressful limbo. In 2019 the nation contained about 4.9 million in this category, about one in eight members of that age group.

According to the Social Science Research Council, these young Americans "are cut off from the people, institutions, and experiences that would otherwise help them develop the knowledge, skills, maturity, and sense of purpose required to live rewarding lives as adults."

Disconnected youth often belong to two of the three at-risk groups featured in this book. The greater a family's poverty, the higher the likelihood of disconnect. In addition, as Figure 3.2 indicates, race has an impact on the process. Asian Americans have a lower disconnection rate for youths than whites while Latinos, Blacks, and Native American produce a higher frequency, with the Native American rate substantially higher than the others (Measures of America of the Social Science Research Council 2019).

In San Diego Carla was one of the nation's disconnected youths. At 16 she was on her own, either living on the streets or sometimes sleeping on friends' couches. Often she had no idea where to get her next meal. While still in school, she struggled, falling a year behind.

It was a critical time. If Carla failed in school, her ability to establish herself independently would be threatened, seriously undermining her potential for long-term earnings. She was fortunate. Her personal crisis coincided with the development of a program called "Flip the Switch," the brainchild of the San Diego Workforce Partnership (SDWP), a youth summit comprised of more than 500 people representing diverse interests and outlooks but all dedicated to turning "disconnect" into "opportunity." Three staff members from the program described its essence. They wrote,

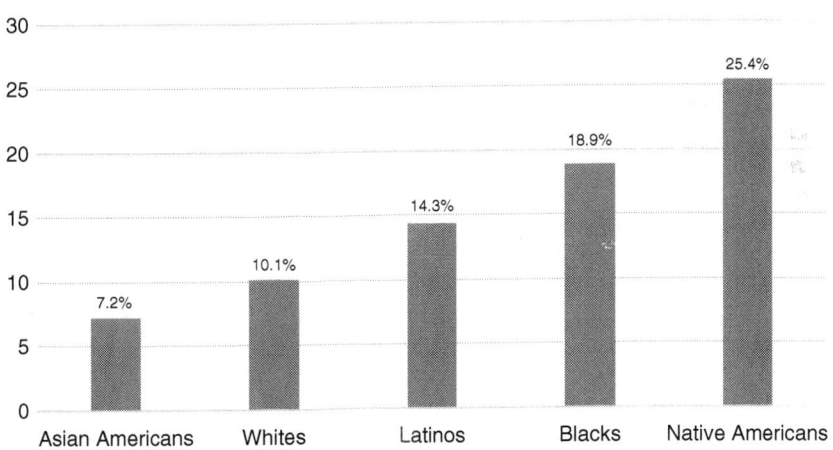

FIGURE 3.2 Major Racial Groups' Youth Disconnection Rates[1]

Source: Measures of America of the Social Science Research Council 2019.

Note: As the graph indicates, the major racial and ethnic groups vary widely in their percentages of disconnected youth.

[1] The data for measuring disconnected youth come from the American Community Survey of the U.S. Census Bureau. These data are obtained annually and are wide-ranging in their coverage, including young people in juvenile or adult correctional facilities and supervised medical programs.

An action plan was begun to achieve …. [a distinct] vision. To be successful, the SDWP implores that we must all work harder to engage more, to listen more and to partner more with our young adults to shape a positive future.

(Marten et al. 2017)

In Carla's case the program did an effective job of helping her surmount the barriers she faced. She graduated high school with good grades and entered SDWP's young adult-employment program. Eventually she obtained a job tutoring students and also earned a nursing-assistant certificate. As a result of these achievements, Carla was obtaining a steady wage, paying rent, saving money, and looking forward to a career in nursing. At age 24 instead of the lonely struggles of her past, she was brimming with optimism about both herself and others. "I think everyone is meant to do something in their life that they love," she said.

A SDWP staff member added that "[a]ll young people can achieve like Carla if pathways and supports are available and barriers are removed" (Marten et al. 2017). While parents are well-located to help teens advance themselves, programs like SDWP make it clear that others sometimes are effectively positioned to transmit the necessary skills and supports for the task.

Key Term in the Glossary

disconnected youth

Discussion Topics

1. Examine the chaotic environment in which poor adolescents often live, suggesting how it must feel to its victims and some of the serious effects it can have on them.

2. Indicate how poor teens' parents can help their children make productive adjustments to living in poverty.

3. How does adolescents' racial background affect their racial socialization? Bring in personal experience when it seems a useful addition to the discussion.

4. Suggest the impact that a racial-minority member in an authoritative position has had on teens of color. For example, you might focus on a prominent politician, a high-school teacher or administrator, or an official in a community organization.

5. Provide detailed information about how a parent or parents with whom you are acquainted engaged in racial socialization.

6. Do you think it's true that girls who play with traditional girls' toys are less likely to develop successful careers or to support feminism than those involved with a combination of girls' and boys' toys? Give illustrations that support your position.

7. Consider how the parents of LGBT children can assist their children in adjusting to their sexual status.
8. What information do you have about coaches' abuse of teen athletes? What seems to be the most effective approach for curtailing such behavior?
9. Gather information and then write about an on-going program helping disconnected youth. Include some references to sources that support the program's activities and goals. It might be a local program or one that is discussed in online sources or journal articles. What appear to be both the most surprising and most important findings you encountered?

Bibliography

Alegria, Margarita, Patrick E. Shrout, Glorisa Canino, Kiara Alvarez, Ye Wang et al.2019. "The Effect of Minority Status and Social Context on the Development of Depression and Anxiety: A Longitudinal Study of Puerto Rican Descent Youth." *World Psychiatry* 18 (October): 298–307.

American Psychological Association. 2018. "Stress in America: Generation Z." (October). https://www.apa.org/news/press/releases/stress/2018/stress-gen-z.pdf.

Benner, Aprile D., Yijie Wang, Yishan Shen, Alaina E. Boyle, Richelle Polk, and Yen-Pi Cheng. 2018. "Racial/Ethnic Discrimination and Well-Being during Adolescence: A Meta-Analytic Review." *American Psychologist* 73: 855–883.

Blaschke, Anne. 2018. The Larry Nassar Case Revealed Nightmarish Abuse against Female Athletes—and the Problem Isn't Going Anywhere." *Insider.* (January 30). https://www.insider.com/larry-nassar-case-abuse-against-female-athletes-2018-1.

Brackenridge, Celia, and Sandra Kirby. 1997. "Playing Safe: Assessing the Risk to Elite Child Athletes." *International Review for the Sociology of Sport* 32 (December): 407–418.

Bregman, Hallie, Neena Malik, Matthew Page, and Kristin Lindahl. 2013. "Identity Profiles in Gay, Lesbian, and Bisexual Youth: The Role of Family Influences." *Journal of Youth & Adolescence* 42: 417–430.

Butler, Amy. 2014. "Poverty and Adolescent Depressive Symptoms." *American Journal of Orthopsychiatry* 84: 82–94.

Chan, Wing Yi, and Robert D.Latzman. 2015. "Racial Discrimination, Multiple Group Identities, and Civic Beliefs among Immigrant Adolescents." *Cultural Diversity and Ethnic Minority Psychology* 21: 521–532.

Coates, Ta-Nehisi. 2015. *Between the World and Me.* New York: Spiegel & Grau.

Coley, Rebekah Levine, Tama Leventhal, Alicia Doyle Lynch, and Melissa Kull. 2013. "Relations between Housing Characteristics and the Well-Being of Low-Income Children and Adolescents." *Developmental Psychology* 49: 1775–1789.

Douglass, Sara, Shina Mirpuri, Devlin English, and Tiffany Yip. 2016. "'They Were Just Making Jokes:' Ethnic/Racial Teasing and Discrimination among Adolescents." *Cultural Diversity and Ethnic Minority Psychology* 22 (January): 69–82.

Fuller-Rowell, Thomas E., Gary W. Evans, Elise Paul, and David S. Curtis. 2015. "The Role of Poverty and Chaos in the Development of Task Persistence among Adolescents." *Journal of Research on Adolescence* 25: 606–613.

Gaskin, Ashly. 2015. "Racial Socialization: Ways Parents Can Teach Their Children about Race." *CYF News.* (August). American Psychological Association. https://www.apa.org/pi/families/resources/newsletter/2015/08/racial-socialization.

Ghavami, Negin, Adam Fingerhut, Letitia A. Peplau, Sheila K. Grant, and Michele A. Wittig. 2011. "Testing a Model of Minority Identity Achievement, Identity Affirmation, and Psychological Well-Being among Ethnic Minority and Sexual Minority Individuals." *Cultural Diversity and Ethnic Minority Psychology* 17: 79–88.

Hagelskamp, Carolin, and Diane L. Hughes. 2014. "Workplace Discrimination Predicting Racial/Ethnic Socialization across African American, Latino, and Chinese Families." *Cultural Diversity and Ethnic Minority Psychology* 20: 550–560.

Hagerman, Margaret Ann. 2017. "White Racial Socialization: Progressive Fathers on Raising 'Antiracist' Children." *Journal of Marriage and the Family* 79 (February): 60–74.

Hogshead, Maker. 2018. "How to Stop Sexual Abuse in Sports." *Athletic Business*. (January). https://www.athleticbusiness.com/athlete-safety/how-to-stop-sexual-abuse-in-sports.html.

Katz-Wise, Sabra L., Margaret Rosario, and Michael Tsappis. 2016. "LGBT Youth and Family Acceptance." *Pediatric Clinics of North America* 63 (December): 1–17. https://www.ncbi.nlm.nih.gov/pmc/articles/PMC5127283/pdf/nihms823230.pdf.

Kwiatkowski, Marisa, and Tim Evans. 2016. "Ex-Gymnast Speaks Out about Her Sexual Abuse." *Indianapolis Star*. (August 27). https://www.indystar.com/story/news/investigations/2016/08/26/kid-they-said-wasnt-worth/89339532/.

Levine, Rhonda F. 2019. *When Race Meets Class: Coming of Age in a Small City*. New York: Taylor & Francis.

Levy, Sharon. 2019. "Overview of Psychosocial Problems in Adolescence." *Merck Manual*. (February). https://www.merckmanuals.com/home/children-s-health-issues/problems-in-adolescents/overview-of-psychosocial-problems-in-adolescents.

Lifespan. 2019. "Managing Stress in Teens and Parents: A Guide for Parents." https://www.bradleyhospital.org/managing-stress-teens-and-adolescents-guide-parents.

Lin, Yi-Ching and Dong-Chul Seo. 2017. "Cumulative Family Risks across Income Levels Predict Deterioration of Children's General Health during Childhood and Adolescence." *PLOS*. (May 16) https://journals.plos.org/plosone/article?id=10.1371/journal.pone.0177531.

Marten, Cindy, Carlos O. Turner Cortez, and Pater Callstrom. 2017. "San Diego Must Do More for Disconnected Youth." *The San Diego Union Tribune*. (April 27). https://www.sandiegouniontribune.com/opinion/commentary/sd-disconnected-youth-20170427-story.html.

Marthe, Emalie. 2016. "'He Threatened to Take All That Away': When Coaches Sexually Assault Athletes." (September 25). *Vice*. https://www.vice.com/en_us/article/qvdpm5/he-threatened-to-take-all-that-away-when-coaches-sexually-assault-athletes.

Measures of America of the Social Science Research Council. 2019. "Disconnected Youth." https://measureofamerica.org/disconnected-youth-2/.

New York Center for Living. 2019. "Adolescent Mental Health Treatment and Risk Factors." https://www.centerforliving.org/blog/adolescent-mental-health-treatment-risk-factors/.

Niwa, Erika Y., Niobe Way, and Diane L. Hughes. 2014. "Trajectories of Ethnic-Racial Discrimination among Ethnically Diverse Early Adolescents: Associations with Psychological and Social Adjustment." *Child Development* 85 (November/December): 2339–2354.

Pan American Health Organization. 2013. "Reaching Poor Adolescents in Situations of Vulnerability with Sexual and Reproductive Health." https://www.paho.org/hq/index.php?option=com_docman&view=download&category_slug=paho-who-scientific-technical-material-6279&alias=25319-reaching-poor-adolescents-situations-vulnerability-with-sexual-reproductive-health-2013-319&Itemid=270&lang=en.

Pew Research Center. 2013. "A Survey of LGBT Americans." (June 13). https://www. pewsocialtrends.org/2013/06/13/a-survey-of-lgbt-americans/.

Plan International. 2018. "The State of Gender Equality for U.S. Adolescents." https:// www.planusa.org/docs/state-of-gender-equality-summary-2018.pdf.

Quint, Janet, Katherine M. Griffin, Jennie Kaufman, Patrick Landers, and Annie Utterback. 2018. *Experiences of Parents and Children Living in Poverty: A Review of the Qualitative Literature. OPRE Report 2018–2030.* (July). https://www.acf.hhs.gov/sites/default/files/ opre/understanding_poverty_cfe_lit_review_final_508.pdf.

Reife, Ilana, Sophia Duffy, and Kathryn E. Grant. 2019. "The Impact of Social Support on Adolescent Coping in the Context of Urban Poverty." *Cultural Diversity and Ethnic Minority Psychology.* (July 22): 1–15.

Roy, Amanda L., C. Cybele Raver, Michael D. Masucci, and Meriah DeJoseph. 2019. "'If They Focus on Giving Us a Chance in Life We Can Actually Do Something in This World:' Poverty, Inequality, and Youths' Critical Consciousness." *Developmental Psychology* 55: 550–561.

Ryan, Caitlin. 2009. "Helping Families Support Their Lesbian, Gay, Bisexual, and Transgender Children." Washington, DC: National Center for Cultural Competence, Georgetown University Center for Child and Human Development. Pp. 1–12. https:// nccc.georgetown.edu/documents/LGBT_Brief.pdf.

Sanchez, Delida, Alaina Flannigan, Crystal Guevara, Sarah Arango, and Emma Hamilton. 2017. "Links among Familial Gender Ideology, Media Portrayal of Women, Dating, and Sexual Behaviors in African American and Mexican American Adolescent Young Women: A Qualitative Study." *Sex Roles* 77: 453–470.

ScienceDaily. 2019. "Experience of Being a Minority Puts US Teens at Higher Risk of Anxiety, Depression." (September 9). https://www.sciencedaily.com/releases/2019/09/ 190909170758.htm.

Smith, Kathleen. 2019. "6 Common Triggers of Teen Stress." Psycom. https://www. psycom.net/common-triggers-teen-stress/.

Stanford Children's Health. 2019. "Puberty: Teen Girl." https://www.stanfordchildrens. org/en/topic/default?id=puberty-adolescent-female-90-P01635.

Stein, Gabriela L., Lisa Kiang, Andrew J. Supple, and Laura M. Gonzalez. 2014. "Ethnic Identity as a Protective Factor in the Lives of Asian American Adolescents." *Asian American Journal of Psychology* 5: 206–213.

Tang, Sandra, Vonnie C. McLoyd, and Samantha K. Hallman. 2016. "Racial Socialization, Racial Identity, and Academic Attitudes among African American Adolescents: Examining the Moderating Influence of Parent–Adolescent Communication." *Journal of Youth & Adolescence* 45: 1141–1155.

Thoma, Brian C., and David M. Huebner. 2013. "Health Consequences of Racist and Antigay Discrimination for Multiple Minority Adolescents." *Cultural Diversity and Ethnic Minority Psychology* 19: 404–413.

Threlfall, Jennifer M. 2018. "Parenting in the Shadow of Ferguson: Racial Socialization Practices in Context." *Youth & Society* 50 (March): 255–273.

U.S. Department of Health and Human Services. Office of Population Affairs. 2019. "The Changing Face of America's Adolescents." (October 3). https://www.hhs.gov/ash/oah/ facts-and-stats/changing-face-of-americas-adolescents/index.html.

4

INEQUALITIES OF THE AMERICAN EDUCATION SYSTEM

The past and the present intertwine to diminish the quality of education for many students who are poor, people of color, female, or some combination of the three. Contributing factors include persistent high rates of poverty, centuries-long housing segregation, economic polarization in many cities dividing districts into those for the affluent and those for the poor, declining efforts to promote racial and economic integration in many schools (Boschma and Brownstein 2016), and persistent denigration of and discrimination toward girls and women.

The impact of such factors can be formidable. Sociologist Sean Reardon indicated that the issue isn't "that sitting next to a poor kid makes you do less well in school." Rather, he said, "it's that school poverty turns out to be a good proxy for the quality of a school." The schools are poorer; the parents are less well educated and thus less capable of advising their children; single-parent families are numerous, meaning mothers have no time to volunteer in the classrooms; and with diminished funding, hiring expert teachers is unlikely (Boschma and Brownstein 2016).

The broad, education-related conditions just described have an intersectional impact, which adversely affects millions of poor students of color. In almost all large American cities, many Black and Hispanic students attend schools where most of their fellow students are poor or low-income, and Figure 4.1 displays this trend at a national level.

The quality of education in these schools reduces students' chances to achieve academic performances preparing them effectively for the working world. Inevitably many suffer the life-diminishing effects of a painfully destructive social-reproduction process. Now we focus on those schools.

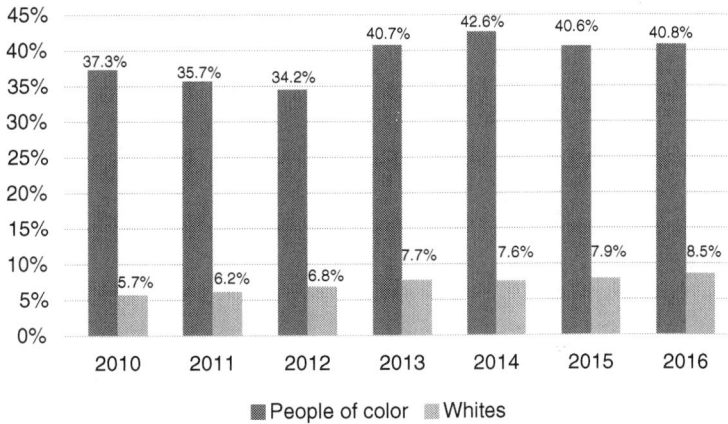

FIGURE 4.1 Students in High-Poverty Schools[1]
Source: National Equity Atlas 2018.
Note: During the seven years represented in this figure, students who were people of color were between about four to six times more likely than whites to attend high-poverty schools.
[1] The National Equity Atlas provides data for the 100 largest cities, 150 largest regions, and all 50 states.

Poor Students in High-Poverty Schools

In a previous chapter, I discussed the idea of the survival of the fittest, an outlook that rationalizes well-off and powerful groups' preferential access to highly valued resources. Funding for public-schools is a prominent illustration.

Unlike most of its affluent European peers, the United States has deemphasized the federal government's contribution to public-school education, with its share just 8 percent of total funding in 2017. At the national level, European countries have tended to develop spending programs that ensured equal school expenditure in poor areas or even above-average spending to compensate for local disadvantages. In contrast, the American decentralized system with its emphasis on local school funding has allowed affluent, powerful groups at the state and local level to establish massive funding differences between high-income and poor districts (Organisation for Economic Co-operation and Development 2014; Roser and Ortiz-Ospina 2019; U.S. Department of Education 2017).

The American system is well entrenched. Over two decades ago when addressing the key question of whether poor American students have the same chance of obtaining a quality education as their wealthier counterparts, educator David Fulton declared, "For most industrialized countries, the answer is yes. For us it's an embarrassing no" (Fulton 2000).

A team of researchers created a concept to convey a sense of the areas in which deprived schools exist. An **urban war zone** is a poor, crime-, and gang-ridden district numerically dominated by people of color in which deteriorated, violent, even war-like conditions and underfunded, largely ineffective schools promote inferior academic performance, including irregular attendance and disruptive or noncompliant classroom behavior (Easley 2016; Garbarino, Dubrow, Kostelny, and Pardo 1992; Good 2012). "A sense of … control is almost totally absent," a writer noted, "just as it would be for any noncombatant in a war zone" (Ogintz 1989). The residents of urban war zones are likely to suffer the effects of "toxic stress" discussed in Chapter 2.

Frequently both politicians and the media manage to publicize urban war zones' most lurid qualities and activities, using hard-hitting racist language to escalate the public's sense of alienation. In this regard Chicago appears to receive extensive attention, sometimes from prominent people. A journalist noted,

> Whenever President Trump or one of his boosters invokes Chicago as a shorthand for urban violence, we hear the racialized subtext loud and clear: Black and brown people here are out of control. You can almost hear the collective exasperated sigh ripple through our neighborhoods as they say Chicago is worse than Afghanistan, or hell, or whatever their default for the worst place in the world might be.
>
> *(Moore 2017)*

In such settings racialized fears and hostilities can readily revitalize.

Whether a school district is in Chicago or elsewhere, it is apparent that because the American system of educational funding is highly dependent on local property tax, public-school quality reflects the level of affluence communities possess. As Luis Santiago, a high-school teacher of history and Spanish in Florida, declared, "What a difference a ZIP code makes." Santiago indicated that he lives in 32259 and teaches in 32065. The school district in which he lives has been top-ranked. He noted,

> Parents are involved in the academic and sports lives of their kids. They have the money for tutoring and special camps. The ZIP code where I work is much different. It's like Dickens' "A Tale of Two Cities." What divides these two … [districts] is a river.
>
> *(Kelley 2020)*

The following topics examine major problems involving poverty-ridden schools:

- Educator Martin Haberman developed the concept pedagogy of poverty which focuses on a set of ineffective even destructive teaching practices in poor schools often imposed on their students. It features:

  1. **Teacher-centered discussions and activity:** Studies have indicated that among young children effective learning requires assignments that include hands-on activities. Such practices encourage students to be actively involved. On the other hand, a distinctly passive learning experience prevails if the teacher directs all or most of the coursework, telling a largely

noninteractive group what to do. Students are unlikely to learn to think independently and creatively.

2. **Low-quality schooling accompanied by limited expectations:** Teachers in high-poverty schools, who are often inexperienced, are likely to doubt that their students can perform well. In many poor primary schools, children spend considerable time making collages and posters and coloring pictures as alleged demonstrations of "hands-on learning." Meanwhile basic reading and math skills receive little attention. Within a few years, many of those students end up tracked into general-education courses and away from the more advanced, stimulating academic offerings (Barr and Parrett 2007, 30–31).

Amy Jenkins, the head of an organization that works with school districts to make their programs better attuned to students' needs, applauded references to the pedagogy of poverty because they alert people to deficiencies that thrive in poor schools and the distinctly healthier conditions that should supplant them. Jenkins explained, "I often find myself in schools within districts where ... all of the students qualify for free and reduced lunch. And sometimes walking those halls, I see the teacher in the front of the classroom giving information, asking right answer questions, and giving low level tasks." She added,

> Sometimes the students are listening, sometimes they are working, but just because they are quiet, doesn't mean that they are engaged. In other schools, I see the opposite. The environments are literacy rich, the students are actively problem-solving, there is collaboration, meaning-making and there are authentic tasks. Those are the classrooms I wish I saw everywhere.
>
> *(Jenkins 2019)*

A probable advantage of such classrooms is that students are likely to find that when they have questions or are confused, their teachers are approachable, helping them with the task at hand and in the course of the interaction implicitly conveying a sense of the wealth that schooling can offer. In poor areas such educational benefits are rare.

- In poverty-ridden schools where low expectations for students often prevail tracking is a common reality. **Tracking** is a process where educators evaluate students and then place them in programs with a curriculum that allegedly is appropriate for their abilities (Chiu et al. 2017, 915–16; Kohli and Quartz 2014; LeTendre et al. 2003, 43–44). A distinction exists between tracking, which involves the assignment of students to different classrooms with different teachers and curricula, and ability grouping, which occurs within a single classroom where students are separated into groups allegedly based on their abilities. Tracking can occur in high school and middle school while ability grouping takes place in elementary school (Brookings 2013).

Criticism of tracking has been extensive, but nonetheless students continue to be placed in tracks according to their short-term performance, and courses continue to be labeled, designating students' eligibility to enter them. The most tracked course is math, with three quarters of eighth-grade students subjected to it, and many school systems use math performance as a basis for allocating students' placement in other courses. No research findings support this approach, but it is likely, particularly given badly funded schools' frequent scarcity of effective math teachers, to prove particularly disadvantageous for poor children (Berwick 2019; Grusky 2001, 575; Moore 2001, 539).

Overall whether they are by themselves in large inner-city schools or in a multi-class setting, poor students plagued by educational deficiency are likely to end up in courses with watered-down offerings like "opportunity math" (designed for students who cannot learn algebra) or vocational preparation, which provides students tracked into low-level courses information about what are generally projected to be decidedly modest job prospects. Usually the slow-learning tracks receive the most inexperienced teachers, who are likely to use the most unchallenging instructional techniques such as worksheets and drills (Barr and Parrett 2007, 144).

Such students have little reason to feel positive about their academic potential. Studies about tracking emphasize that within such a system, participants tend to be decidedly passive, simply accepting their placement and believing that it is correct. Writing about the impact of tracking on students generally, sociologist Kristian Bernt Karlson concluded that they "view track placement as a signal about their academic abilities and respond to it in terms of modifying their educational expectations" (Karlson 2015, 115).

When low-income children fail to master basic skills, they remain in lower tracks and are sometimes forced to repeat the grade. Trapped in a debilitating educational cycle, these students almost never catch up with their age peers and often do not advance from the slow-learning track. In many states under-achieving students, who are disproportionately poor, male, and minority-group members, must leave regular schools and enter alternative low-performing programs where the goal is behavior modification, not educational achievement. Research has found that academic placement of students tracked in lower-level courses tends to produce lower achievement levels and increased performance gaps over time compared to peers located in higher-level courses (Francis et al. 2020; Potter 2019).

It is apparent that tracking represents a prime illustration of the **self-fulfilling prophecy**, namely an incorrect definition of a situation that comes to pass because people accept the incorrect definition and act on it to make it become true (Doob 2019, 286). With this reality in mind, Karlson used the National Educational Longitudinal Study to examine data about eighth- and tenth-grade students in math (6,013) and English (7,217), with 3,169 overlapping in the two samples. Overall she found, students accepted tracking information as a self-fulfilling prophecy, relying heavily on it as a means to increase the likelihood of future educational success. In some instances students lowered their expectations when their high-school evaluations had declined from their middle-school results. Karlson noted, "As expected, these revisions are particularly pronounced when placement is consistent across subjects, and they exist primarily when [low] placements in high school contradict tracking experiences in middle school" (Karlson 2015, 135).

Mike, a poor Black student in a school where tracking was prevalent, experienced such a shift and explained it this way. He said, "I used to do good. I got all A's in grammar school. Now I'm doing shitty. I guess I started out smart and got stupider" (MacLeod 2009, 102). Mike's response was quite typical of low-tracked students, downplaying or even ignoring the impact of tracking and other structural vulnerabilities, taking the responsibility on himself, and fully accepting a self-fulfilling prophecy. Standardized testing is heavily used in tracking systems and has often victimized low-income children.

- The primary motivation for standardized testing is convenience—the development of a test that can easily help educators evaluate students' abilities. In the early 1900s, the French government hired psychologist Alfred Binet to figure out a means of measuring the children who would need specialized educational assistance in a nation that had recently required compulsory education. Binet developed the first intelligence-quotient (IQ) test (Cherry 2019).

In the 1940s Henry Chauncey, the founder of the Educational Testing Service, suggested that multiple-choice questions on intelligence tests could be used to sort individuals into categories based on their abilities. Willingness to use standardized tests was not widespread, but Chauncey believed in the system—that these tests provided the most effective means of determining students' academic potential. An important step Chauncey took to increase their use was to approach James Conant, Harvard's president, with an early version of the SAT, convincing him "that the test was an accurate measure of intelligence, not just of the quality of a test taker's education. Harvard began using the test for scholarship students in 1934 and, starting in 1941, required it for all applicants" (cptv Frontline 2014). Chauncey's faith in SATs was so strong that he believed that individuals who scored highest on these tests should be at the top of the economic and political structures (Afflerbach 2002, 349–50). While it seems unlikely that such a plan will ever materialize, his influence has persisted over time in educational circles.

In particular, Chauncey's emphasis on the efficacy of standardized tests has supported the development of **high-stakes testing**, the use of standardized tests

NCLB

as the basis for accountability, with decisions about students' admission, grade promotion, and graduation as well as teachers' and administrators' salaries and promotion based on students' test scores (Dworkin 2005, 170; Jones and Ennes 2018). In 2002 the No Child Left Behind Act required states to administer standardized reading and math tests to students in the third to eighth grades, imposing increasingly harsh punishments on schools that failed to show "adequate yearly progress" in their results. Poor students, in particular, often must spent considerable time on standardized-test preparation, limiting what many educators believe is effort better focused on more creative topics like hands-on projects and group interactive activities (Mulholland 2015).

A number of studies including a nine-year investigation commissioned by the National Academy of Sciences concluded that the emphasis on high-stakes testing and other standardized tests has produced little improvement in learning while the pressure-laden context in which such activity often occurs has promoted a narrowed curriculum, a decline in individual instruction, and considerable stress for students and teachers (Association of Texas Professional Educators 2015; Hout and Elliott 2011, 30–31, 84–86).

Not surprisingly teachers have expressed limited support for this testing. A survey of 1,500 teachers for grades 3–8 and 10–12 found that 70 percent of the respondents believed that their states' version of high-stakes testing was developmentally inappropriate for their students—that children's capacity to learn something new often varies in age, building on both their past experiences and skills and the concept or idea at hand, and that these tests simply fail to consider those realities. In contrast, standardized tests use a simplistic approach, often rigidly focusing on specific learning objectives for certain grades that tend not to be an appropriate means for judging either students' or teachers' level of success (Walker 2016).

Findings suggest that parents tend to agree with teachers about high-stakes testing. An opinion poll of a 1,000 parents with children of primary- and secondary-school age found that 57 percent believed there was too much emphasis on standardized testing and just 19 percent felt there was not enough (Rasmussen Report 2018).

As we have already seen, a disproportionate number of poor students are people of color.

Racial Minorities' Struggle for Educational Quality

Members of racial minorities and other disadvantaged groups often find that when interacting with them, outsiders are likely to display a **stereotype**, a set of distinctly negative traits that prejudiced people apply to the members of a group against whom they are prejudiced. Stereotypes create images, images that are likely to obscure the possessors' perception, making it difficult or impossible for those observers to evaluate the individuals in question carefully and dispassionately. In addition, stereotypes can trigger such powerful emotions as fear, anger, resentment, or contempt toward a group or an individual.

Once slavery was underway, stereotypes about slaves abounded, claiming Blacks were primitive, simpleminded, lazy, violent, and oversexed. Following the Civil War with whites' economic and political control secured, stereotypes thrived, promoting harsh, discriminatory treatment of Blacks and other people of color.

In the South it was the **Jim Crow era**—fully a century extending from Reconstruction to the 1960s during which laws and customs mandated a castelike separation of Blacks and whites, featuring Blacks' subordination and oppression. The prevailing rule was a separate-but-equal standard—a legal doctrine establishing segregated services and facilities for Blacks and whites. The separate-but-equal standard received considerable support when in 1896 seven of the eight members of the Supreme Court in the famous case *Plessy vs. Ferguson* ruled that the state of Louisiana had the right to designate separate railroad cars for Blacks and to restrict them to remaining there. Three years later the doctrine was applied to public-schools (Elliott 2006; Fireside 1997).

Throughout the southern states, Black schools suffered funding discrimination. For example, in 1930 in Georgia, local school boards allocated over four times the expenditure for a white child that they provided for a Black youth; in Alabama and Mississippi the funding amounts favoring whites were more than five times larger while in South Carolina the disparities were the greatest, with a white youth allotted over ten times what a Black child received (Irons 2004). All in all, the Black and white schools were distinctly separate but light years away from being equal.

The separate-but-equal standard prevailed in the South until 1952 when the Supreme Court dismissed it. For decades, however, local white leadership continued to support the basic principle. In the 1980s a reporter visited a town in South Carolina that had two, racially segregated high schools and a local property tax that could barely support one. "It was like entering a time warp," he wrote.

> The white high school had social studies books that actually had current events in them. Their science books reflected some of the findings of modern science. The white students studied "new" math. Their athletic fields were somewhat new, and maintained.

In line with the state tradition of drastically unequal racial funding previously mentioned, the Black school was vastly inferior. It

> had windows that were broken, but rarely fixed outright. A [B]lack student at Howard would be hard-pressed to recognize the America he or she studied in class, because the textbooks hadn't been replaced since the 1960s. When mechanical things stopped working, they sometimes stayed that way for weeks or even months.
>
> *(Nesbit 2016)*

During the late nineteenth and well into the twentieth century, racial discrimination involving education, though widespread, was often less obvious in the North, where racially segregated schools were not the standard. However, Blacks and other students of color often found themselves in inferior schooling. One contributing factor was that since many families of color tended to possess below-average income, the children were likely to find themselves in low-quality programming, adversely affected by the American public-school system, which places a heavy emphasis on local funding of school districts.

Furthermore the northern states initiated a pair of practices, namely racially restrictive covenants and redlining, that not only prevented people of color from advancing themselves but, in particular, significantly impeded their educational opportunities.

Starting in the late nineteenth century, racial minorities hoping to move into nonpoor areas were likely to encounter a **racially restrictive covenant**, which was a contract among property owners prohibiting specified minorities from buying, leasing, or occupying property in their locale (Massey and Denton 1993, 29–31; Schaefer 1993, 196). For racist whites this arrangement was praiseworthy. One enthusiastic judge, who was a member of the Chicago Real Estate Board, declared that these covenants were "like a marvelous delicately woven chain armor ... [excluding] any members of a race not Caucasian" (Jones-Correa 2001, 559). On the other hand, these covenants offered Blacks nothing positive. In many cities they could only buy property in poor, inner-city districts where the houses had little economic value, "plundering," as a marketing specialist pointed out, "what little bit of wealth [B]lack people were able to cobble together" (Davis 2018). In particular, these covenants significantly limited racial minorities access to quality education, keeping them confined to poor districts and the inferior schooling that occurred within them.

In addition, in the 1930s the federal government started contributing to housing discrimination by creating maps of the cities which designated the alleged riskiness of real-estate investment in different neighborhoods. The areas Blacks inhabited were marked in red, meaning "hazardous" (Meisenhelter 2018). **Redlining** was the discriminatory practice of refusing to provide mortgage loans or property insurance or only providing them at accelerated rates for reasons not associated with any conventional assessment of risk (Doob 2005, 95; Massey and Denton 1993, 51–52). The destructive impact of redlining has persisted, with hundreds of American cities still suffering economic disadvantage because of Blacks' subjection to the discriminatory process (Plumer and Popovich 2020; Wilson 2020). That reality, in turn, has accelerated another destructive trend in those cities—the persistent underfunding of schools in neighborhoods where poor families of color continue to live.

Students of color face additional challenges in their schools. In a study of a multiracial high school in northern California, Rocio, a Salvadoran teen, commented on how racial stereotypes affect perceptions about students' involvement in school programs. Rocio was convinced that each of the four major racial groups has a distinct image shaping the overall perception of members' performance. She noted that "society says that [you] are Latino and lazy, that you are Asian, you are smart, if you are white, Oh God, the best, and if you are [B]lack, you are bad, horrific" (Conchas 2006, 64). It is a stark summary, leaving one wondering how widespread is such stereotypic ugliness in the public-schools and how significant is its influence. Table 4.1 also addresses the significance of race, suggesting it plays an important role in determining students' educational opportunities.

Asian Americans and whites are more likely than Blacks and Latinos to have access to advantageous conditions that improve their likelihood of obtaining extensive schooling. More advanced schooling, in turn, is likely to lead to higher-quality and better-paying employment.

While teachers' stereotypes appear to influence racial minorities' disproportionate appearance in low tracks, social-class background also contributes. Using the Programme of International School Assessment study of school children in 36 developed nations including the United States, researchers found that tracking results corresponded significantly with parents' socioeconomic status, often promoting disadvantaged social reproduction along with racial inequality (Bol et al. 2014).

A team of researchers concluded that

> [o]ne of the most consistent—and frustrating—findings in quantitative educational studies is the persistent score differences among racial and ethnic groups. On many academic achievement and aptitude tests, Asian American students score higher than [w]hite students, who then in turn score higher than Hispanics and African American students.
>
> *(Warne et al. 2014, 571)*

TABLE 4.1 Amount of Schooling Obtained by the Four Major Racial Groups 25 Years of Age and Older[1]

	Asians	Blacks	Hispanics or Latinos	Whites
Less than a high-school diploma	5%	6%	24%	7%
High-school graduates, no college	16%	31%	31%	25%
Some college	8%	20%	15%	15%
Associate's degree	7%	12%	9%	11%
Bachelor's degree and higher	63%	31%	21%	41%

Source: Bureau of Labor Statistics 2018
Note: Asian Americans and whites are more likely than Blacks and Latinos to have access to advantageous conditions that improve their likelihood of obtaining extensive schooling. More advanced schooling, in turn, is likely to lead to higher-quality and better-paying employment.
[1]The data come from the Current Population Survey, a monthly national assessment of about 60 thousand households.

A likely contributor to educational success is family income, which among the four racial groups follows the same pattern as the test scores—namely, for Asians a median income of $101,218, whites $81,976, Hispanics $55,093, and Blacks $53,804 (U.S. Census Bureau 2019). These income differences are particularly significant in the US, where district funding of schools contributes more than in most other countries to the quality of public education. Inevitably the amount of education these groups receive contributes to occupational achievement.

Clearly education is important, prompting interested parties to wonder what are the specific factors determining the level of achievement students belonging to different racial groups achieve. Psychologist Clark McKown has referred to "direct influences" on achievement that children of all racial and ethnic groups encounter in the course of school attendance. McKown cited four direct influences, namely families, the actual schooling, peers, and neighborhoods (McKown 2013, 1122).

- **The families:** Among racial minorities three types of parental activity affect academic achievement (McKown and Strambler 2008, 372–76). First, the quality of family relationships influences children's educational advancement. In poor families of color, financial instability is prevalent, often creating a high-stress atmosphere that can adversely affect the relationship between parents and children and readily influence youths' daily lives, including their school performance.

The quality of parent–child relations appears to be a very important influence in these settings. In a study of nearly 300 poor, Black children in kindergarten, a psychologist came up with a notable finding. She wrote, "In families for whom parent–child conflict was relatively low, children were rated as more academically, psychologically, and socioemotionally prepared for school, even if the parents reported relatively greater financial stress" (Anderson 2018, 65). Clearly, regardless of the family income, parents' impact on their children's school performance can be considerable. She concluded that while the influence of poverty on poor families should not be overlooked, "it is important to also understand the strengths that families living in poverty have and the strategies that they have developed to counteract environmentally adverse circumstances" (Anderson 2018, 66).

A second major way that minority parents can influence their children's educational advancement involves the issue of racial socialization, making them better adjusted to deal with the race-related realities of schooling. A study of 630 African American adolescents found that parental input on the issue of racial socialization reduced the negative impact of teachers' racial discrimination on both students' grade point average (GPA) and their educational ambitions and also decreased the effect of peers' racism on their GPA (Wang and Huguley 2012).

The content of parents' racial socialization is influential but, as previously noted, so is the quality of the relationship between parents and children. Research has revealed that whether it involves schooling or some other endeavor, successful parental racial socialization primarily occurs when the relationship is warm and supportive (Elmore and Gaylord-Harden 2013).

Third, parents' engagement with teachers and administrators affects minority children's educational advancement. More affluent, better educated parents have the knowledge and sense of entitlement along with the contacts to intervene more effectively on behalf of their children's schooling interests than lower-status counterparts. While all four major racial groups are diversified in income and education, the overall pattern is that Asian Americans and whites are more affluent and better equipped educationally for this important task than Hispanics and Blacks.

Maria Teresa Unger Palmer, a writer and advocate for immigrants, commented on this advantage higher-income parents possess. She attended a high-school orientation for rising ninth graders, where an administrator told the largely white students and parents that if a problem developed, they needed to seek help. Palmer wrote, "The parents in attendance were upper-middle class and established members of the community. No ... public housing parents, no Spanish translation." Furthermore unlike many of their less affluent counterparts, the parents at the orientation were hard-nosed, relentless protectors of their children's interests (Palmer 2007, 143–44). That parental influence extends well beyond the issue of dealing with school officials.

Compared to Black parents, whites are more likely to engage in such practices as the involvement of their children in decision-making, the use of parental monitoring, assignment of household chores, and displays of maternal warmth. The differences in racial practices, which are likely to produce a direct effect on students' school performance, reflect the reality that white parents' social-class levels tend to be distinctly higher than Blacks', providing more opportunities to learn about the importance of engaging children in these practices (McKown 2013, 1122–23). Once again, it is apparent that social reproduction frequently comes into play.

- **Quality of schooling:** Sean Reardon, previously quoted about poverty-ridden schools, stated, "The difference in the rate at which [B]lack, Hispanic, and white students go to school with poor classmates is the best predictor of the racial-achievement gap." Poor, disproportionately minority schools tend to be educationally inferior because of such destructive factors as location in chronically poor neighborhoods where child poverty has increased since the onset of the Great Recession, the persistence of housing segregation in many cities, and a widespread retreat from programs to curtail racial or economic integration in public-schools (Boschma and Brownstein 2016). Figure 4.2 indicates that members of the poorer racial groups—African Americans, Latinos, and Native Americans—are distinctly more likely than whites and Asian Americans to conclude that their children's schooling is inferior to that which more affluent groups receive.

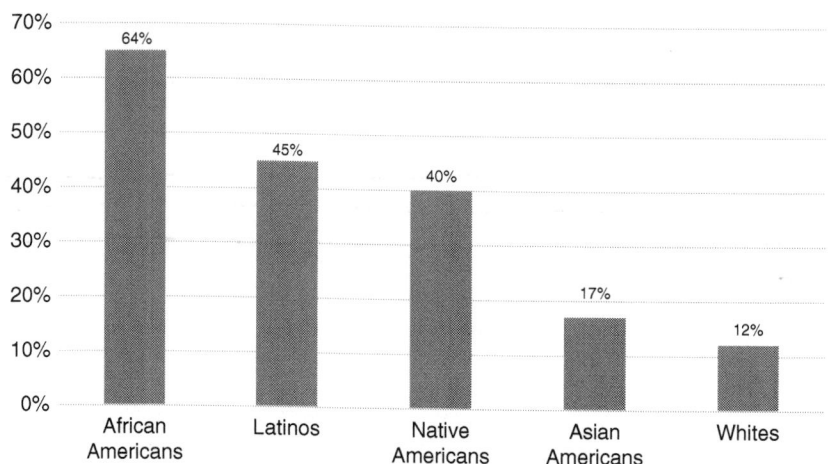

FIGURE 4.2 Percentage of Racial Groups Saying Their Children Denied as Much Chance for a Quality Education as Members of Other Groups[1]
Source: Casey and Levesque 2018.
Note: This sizable sample of adults representing five major racial groups shows stark variations in the subjects' perception of how equitable their group's access is to a quality education.
[1] The survey providing the data used in this figure contained representative samples of the five groups included in it and involved over 1,700 adult respondents.

Largely because of either the schools they attend or more extensive tracking within schools, Hispanic and Black students are more likely than their Asian American or white counterparts to suffer several intersectionality-linked disadvantages— fewer experienced teachers, greater conflict with teachers, especially when they do not belong to students' racial group, larger classes, fewer challenging courses for college preparation, less parental outreach, and placement in lower-track classrooms (Carnoy and García 2017; Cook 2015; Mahatmya et al. 2016; McGrady and Reynolds 2013; Oakes 2005; U.S. Department of Education 2014).

All in all, students of color can find their schooling difficult and nonproductive, with their white teachers, at times perhaps unwittingly, treating them less positively than they act toward their white students. At Parlington High School, a facility containing all four major racial groups and a student body with 80 percent either poor or low-income, Black students observed their teachers, sometimes concluding that their behavior was discriminatory. For instance, Marques indicated that "the teachers … they socialize a lot with the white students … And while they're doing that, they're also isolating the [B]lack students who are just sitting there twirling their thumbs" (Levine 2019, 56). His sister Serena described a situation involving a friend who was "the only [B]lack student in a class … And the teacher would make references to how [B]lack students aren't able to learn as quick as most white students, and all that stuff" (Levine 2019, 57). These quotes clearly show that on occasion the teachers in question would behave in ways that were hurtful and harmful for their Black students, hardly promoting their educational advancement.

A report published by the U.S. Department of Education suggested an additional deficiency in minority-dominated schools. Drawing data from roughly 97,000 public-schools, it provided information about discipline, beginning in preschool where Black students represented just 18 percent of the total but 42 percent of those suspended and 48 percent of those suspended more than once. Alerted by these figures, the writers indicated $Suspension!$

> particular concern… for our nation's young men and boys of color, who are disproportionately affected by suspensions and zero-tolerance policies in schools. Suspended students are less likely to graduate on time and more likely to be suspended again.
>
> *(U.S. Department of Education 2014)*

- **Peers:** Compared to research on families and schools, there has been considerably less investigation of peers' impact on academic achievement for students of color. While several studies suggest that Black students have same-race peers who are more inclined than their white counterparts to discourage academic achievement, other research indicates limited or no impact of peers' race regarding their educational efforts (McKown 2013, 1124).

At previously mentioned Parlington High School, evidence suggested that many Black students needed supportive same-race peers to do well in school. A case in point involved Brandy's friend. Brandy was an honor student in the ninth grade, who had developed largely white friends, and as a result her previous Black friends stopped talking to her. Brandy missed some of her former Black friends, particularly one. She explained, "Like I really miss hanging out with [my middle-school friend], because we were like really close friends. …. And now that we stopped hanging out, she's always in trouble. She never goes to school or anything" (Levine 2019, 66).

Like Brandy young people of color who are successful students can find it difficult to sustain peer support. In certain challenging academic areas, notably the STEM (science, technology, engineering, and mathematics) fields, students of color can feel isolated and keenly aware of the absence of same-race peers' support. A researcher noted that Black men in STEM fields were more likely to change majors or drop out of college than their white counterparts. Erik, a Black student who was taking computer science and math courses, indicated that it might sound silly to say it, but invariably entering a classroom featuring one of those two subjects, he would feel "surprised." He explained,

> I say surprised because I'm often surprised when I walk in the [computer science] or [math] classroom and all of a sudden I'm like a nobody. In my fraternity, everybody knows me. In [my residence hall], they all know me. I'm kind of popular but when I walk in my major … [classrooms], it's back to being a nobody it feels like. Usually I don't care what people think of me but it really bothers me.

Erik added,

> And then when I'm in there and nobody knows me or cares to know me, I'm like … damn, here comes some racist sh*t, like always. They be like [sic] … your hair is so big, or you're such … [a] good dresser, or like don't worry, we'll do the homework and share our answers with you … like 1 can't do it myself. Sometimes I feel like screaming and running away to hang with my boys in the frat.
>
> *(Strayhorn 2015, 59)*

It seems apparent that in such situations where same-race peers are often absent, the resulting racially frigid atmosphere can make life much more difficult and potentially affect racial minorities' academic performance.

- **The neighborhood:** Investigation on this topic has been limited, but preliminary research has suggested that in cohesive neighborhoods, where people work together to accomplish shared goals, improved academic outcomes for students of color can be one of the results (McKown 2013, 1124). A study of 88 Black elementary-school children produced findings consistent with this conclusion, indicating that those students who internalized a worldview

PHOTO 4.1 Since Asian Americans often have the benefit of high-quality schooling, they are likely to be less isolated from their racial group in STEM courses than other students of color.

Source: Tom Wang / Alamy Stock Photo

drawing on African cultural traditions and emphasizing a spiritual, communal identity with a greater collective involving family, community, and race were more likely to receive support encouraging them to be confident and effective in their academic endeavors (Shin 2011, 222).

Like racial minorities girls and women have faced discriminatory treatment in schooling.

The Advancement of Education for Girls and Women

Sometimes historical outcomes occur for unexpected reasons. In 1642 the Puritan leadership of the Massachusetts Bay Colony passed a law requiring local authorities to make certain that all children could read and write. The chief motivation for the law seems to have been the Puritans' belief that achieving literacy would prepare people to read the Bible, giving them access to the one source that they believed could protect them from Satan. Clearly the law promoted literacy. By best estimates two thirds of males and one third of females in the founding generations were literate. By the mid-nineteenth century the figures rose to 90 percent for males and 80 percent for females (Daniels 2012, 111–12), unusually high figures for that era.

However, the advancement of girls' and women's educational rights have usually occurred because of conscious efforts to promote them. In 1972 Congress passed Title IX, a law declaring that females of all ages in educational organizations receiving federal funds for any programs would not encounter discriminatory treatment (Albrecht and Strand 2010, 18). Since the law's passage, girls' and women's sports programs have enlarged and improved significantly. While many people believe Title IX primarily applies to sports, it has also influenced major reforms involving protection for pregnant students allowing them to remain in school, challenges to gender stereotypes in classrooms and textbooks, documentation of and mobilization against sexual abuse and assaults in educational programs, and greater access for women to teaching jobs in colleges and universities (Chadband 2012; U.S. Department of Education 2015).

Following Title IX's passage, statistics indicate that women have sharply increased their involvement in higher education. In 1972, 57 percent of college students were men and only 43 percent were women. By 2010 the numbers had reversed, with 57 percent of college students female and 43 percent male. A similar trend has occurred with doctorates; while in 1970 men obtained eight times as many as women, currently women earn more doctorates than men. In addition, before Title IX, law, medical, and dental schools came close to barring women from entering them while nowadays the numbers in those fields are equal.

Title IX has also sparked controversy. For instance, as the Obama administration applied the law to sexual harassment, some individuals and groups of varied political persuasions were critical, asserting that the newly developed guidelines threaten both freedom of speech and due process (Melnick 2020).

While girls and women have benefited from the support that Title IX has provided, it is clear that legislation alone cannot produce gender equality in the education system. A concept relating to that conclusion is the **hidden curriculum**—the important but unofficial messages about values, beliefs, and behavior that teachers and administrators can implicitly communicate to students (Edwards and Carmichael 2012; Glossary of Education Reform 2015). Most of the time school officials, parents, and children are unaware of the hidden curriculum because it is just that—hidden. However, studies have indicated that various vulnerable groups, notably children who are poor, belong to racial minorities, or are female, can fall victim to it.

A team of specialists on international education has raised the question of whether nowadays "education institutions allow girls effective participation, and whether the existing situations of girls and women are enhanced or diminished by the schooling they receive" (Aikman et al. 2005, 45). The following evidence examines the educational impact that the hidden curriculum has on females.

- **Girls and women less valued:** Some recent research has focused on the perceptions supporting the hidden curriculum that persist in American society. For instance, two experiments involving a total of more than 1,100 subjects, over half of whom were women, revealed that these individuals were about 25 percent less inclined to refer a woman to a position where the job description emphasized the importance of intellectual ability than if it did not. Furthermore the data showed that when intellectual ability was stressed, women were more likely to support the female candidates than men and also people of color were more inclined to back these female candidates than whites. Children too have shared the perception that females are not as smart as men. In a third experiment when choosing teammates for a game requiring smart players, nearly 200 children aged five to seven equally divided between girls and boys were less likely to take girls than boys (Bian et al. 2018, 1143–49). Clearly the hidden curriculum remains a persistent presence for both adults and children.

Having found similar support for the hidden curriculum among teens, Richard Weissbourd, the head of a research team at the Harvard Graduate School of Education, indicated that findings about the hidden curriculum were likely to surprise many adolescents. He said, "Some of them may question whether gender biases even exist." He added, "And the idea that biases can be implicit or unconscious is something many teenagers may never have thought of before" (Walsh 2015).

The research team supplied teachers a number of suggestions they could use to help their students begin to understand the hidden curriculum existing in their high schools. For instance, the instructors could have their teens engage in reflective exercises where the girls would write about the experience of being a girl and boys would describe what they believed it would feel like to be a girl. In addition, they could reverse the situation, with the boys detailing what they experienced and the girls trying to imagine being a boy. If the students seemed comfortable with the idea of sharing papers with each other, the teachers might encourage them to do it.

Another exercise involved the teens interviewing a woman from an older generation, seeking to learn how she was treated growing up, her perception of the changes in the expectations for women over time, and what principal challenges the interviewee felt remained for women (Walsh 2015). Hopefully exercises like the two just summarized would encourage adolescent students to bring gender issues out of the closet, allowing them to become more aware of them and better equipped to confront the persistent inequalities.

For women one means of confronting the hidden curriculum is to major in a STEM field. Women, however, are only 30 percent of the graduates in STEM majors, and they are less likely than men to find a job in a STEM field. Those who do, however, average about 35 percent more earnings than their counterparts in non-STEM positions (Economics and Statistics Administration 2017; Gu 2018).

A team of investigators interested in the hidden curriculum obtained data from 330 female and male undergraduates, including an assessment of six traits that different majors might possess and that could influence the choices they made—namely, the extent to which there is an emphasis on math, a central role for science, helpfulness provided by the profession, gender bias against women, high salaries, and creativity.

Seeking to add information from a much larger sample, the researchers turned to an earlier survey of nearly 5,000 students for whom they had majors but not the data about the traits influencing choice of majors. As a proxy for those data, the researchers matched the two sets of informants on their characteristics, predicting that shared traits for respondents in the two studies made it likely that students' views in the earlier study would coincide with those the later interviewees held.

Making that assumption, the researchers found that the findings from the two investigations indicated that among the STEM majors, one factor stood out for female college students as negative, namely gender bias against women (Ganley et al. 2018). Joseph Cimpian, a participant in the study, emphasized that the research showed that female students assessing STEM majors did not find their math or science content intimidating, but they "don't like to be discriminated against" (EAB 2019). In choosing their majors, these women clearly kept a sense of the hidden curriculum in mind.

It is hardly surprising that female students reached this conclusion. STEM faculty members tend to be the first authoritative people students encounter in these fields, and the preponderance of research evidence indicates that both female and male college STEM teachers tend to spend more time mentoring males, are more likely to answer men's emails, and are more inclined to call on males in class (Grunspan et al. 2016).

PHOTO 4.2 The hidden curriculum can be a subtle process, with male teachers, especially in STEM courses, often failing to recognize that they are more inclined to interact with males and to call on them in the classroom than they do with females, possibly discouraging girls and women from speaking out publicly.

Source: Shutterstock/ Alexander Raths

Discrimination toward females in the classroom, in fact, goes well beyond the STEM fields. Inevitably what happens in the classroom has a major impact on females' educational goals and activities.

- **Gender roles in the high-school and grade-school classroom:** Generally teachers pay more attention to boys than girls—in part, according to a report by the American Association of University Women, because boys are more likely to shout out answers to teachers' questions, even if the teacher did not call on them. In addition, teachers tend to call on boys more often and to ask them more complicated questions. Such favoritism is likely to discourage many girls from speaking out even if they feel certain they have something interesting or useful to contribute.

Another difference involves the issue of distance, with teachers tending to speak to boys from farther away. Contrasting perceptions involving the genders comes into play here, with teachers likely to conclude they should deal with boys in a highly public, business-like manner but be more nurturing and intimate with girls. The upshot is that while the entire class can often hear boys' conversations with teachers, girls tend to have their teacher contacts limited to private conversations, preventing them from receiving the experience and recognition of participation in the more public, male-dominated exchanges.

While teachers often intend to treat girls and boys equally, there are frequently distinct gender-related differences in the praise and criticism offered. Boys, for example, tend to be praised more extensively than girls for providing correct answers in class; their incorrect answers are more likely than girls' to be overlooked or downplayed. As a result students readily reach the conclusion that the information boys provide is more valuable (Johnson 2019; Pronin 2020; Sadker and Sadker 1994).

In addition, some teachers have stereotyped notions about girls' and boys' respective abilities, especially beliefs that females are less capable in mathematics, the sciences, and computer studies than males (Leaper and Friedman 2007, 578; Wang and Degol 2017).

Gender discriminations are often well entrenched, following distinct patterns. For instance, psychologists Eleanor K. Chesnut and Ellen M. Markham suspected that the choice of words could influence the perception of gender inequities. They studied 640 English-speaking adults to determine the effect of language on their evaluation of girls' and boys' potential. They divided the respondents into two sections, presenting them with slightly but significantly different statements about gender-related math ability: "Girls do just as well as boys at math" or "Boys do just as well as girls at math."

While 71 percent of the respondents reading the first sentence opted in favor of boys having more natural ability at math, less than half as many, namely 32 percent, took that position after encountering the second statement. The two conclusions produced significantly different impacts, with the gender category receiving second mention often providing the standard against which the one listed first was measured. People in the experiment, in fact people generally, were unlikely to be aware of the distinction, but nonetheless, as the results show, the specific phrasing affected them (Chesnut and Markham 2018; Shashkevich 2018). Markham concluded, "We thought that swapping 'boys' and 'girls' in the sentence would have an effect, but we didn't expect a … [major] reversal of the stereotype" (Shashkevich 2018).

At this time it seems useful to examine an important educational issue that affects not only females but also the poor and people of color.

American Apprenticeship Programs

Compared to its wealthy European peers, the US has not been successful in apprenticeship training of high-school graduates for decently paying, middle-skill jobs. An **apprenticeship** is a worker's on-the-job training accompanied by classroom instruction for which the individual receives wages and also an industry-recognized credential after one to six years on the job (Amoyah and Brown 2018).

Statistics on the topic indicate that in 2018 the U.S. Department of Labor recorded about 585,000 apprentices in over 23,000 registered apprenticeship programs. The occupations included boilermakers, carpenters, electricians, elevator installers and repairers, insulation workers, ironworkers, pipe fitters, plumbers, and sheet metal workers.

For workers who complete the programs, the payoff is very satisfactory, both for them and their employers. An individual finishing these programs averages about $50,000 a year and earns in a lifetime more than $300,000 in wages and benefits than middle-skill employees without apprenticeships. In addition, the organizations hiring apprentices retain over 90 percent of them once they have completed their programs.

With such positive results, it is informative to find out that the number of apprenticeships completed is currently insufficient in the modern American economy. While the middle-skill jobs involving apprenticeships include about 250 occupations comprising about 53 percent of the nation's workforce, only about 43 percent of the individuals holding those jobs receive apprenticeship training for them.

In fact, in the opening decade of the twenty-first century, the proportion of businesses invested in apprenticeship training declined. Several factors appear to be contributing to this outcome. Some organization leaders seem to believe that the costs outweigh the benefits. For small or medium-sized companies hiring one or two new workers a year, this belief might be valid. Furthermore, while in the past labor unions cooperated with employers in training apprentices, such collaborative ventures have declined as union activity has decreased. In addition, research has revealed that some business officials consider poaching from competitors to be a significant drawback from investing in such programs. Finally, in some firms managers are likely to feel pressure to maximize short-term profits, cutting costs by eliminating or curtailing the expense of apprenticeship training that primarily produces long-term growth (Amoyah and Brown 2018; Hanks 2016; Hennen 2018; Torpey and Farrell 2019).

Businesses in France, Germany, Great Britain, Switzerland, and other European countries tend to take a very different approach. While fewer than 4 percent of Americans engage in apprenticeships, nearly 60 percent of Germans sign up for them, entering occupations that provide few or no apprenticeships in the US, such as advanced manufacturing, banking, hospitality, and information technology.

In Switzerland an even higher 70 percent of all young people become apprentices, with a proportion of young people entering apprentice training that is 20 times greater than what the United States possesses. If the US maintained the Swiss rate, it would mean that instead of starting just 150,000 new apprenticeships a year, the figure would be over 3 million (Amoyah and Brown 2018; Dixon 2017).

Besides producing a large number of apprenticeships, Switzerland's programs represent high-quality opportunities for young people. A prominent Swiss political leader, who completed an apprenticeship himself as a laboratory assistant, wrote a book about the major contribution these programs have made to the economy. After researching the subject, he concluded, "Someone who has completed an apprenticeship is three times less likely to become unemployed or be without work for a long period" (House of Switzerland 2019).

Reducing or overcoming educational disadvantages is likely to be a complex, demanding task. However, this final commentary suggests the importance and the efficacy of keeping in mind the kind of simple truths the following study emphasized.

An Attack on the Hidden Curriculum

A team of investigators conducted two experiments with 269 high-school students involving their likelihood of signing up for a college course on introductory computer science. They chose this course because computer science has the greatest gender disparities of the four broad fields included in STEM, with women earning just 18 percent of the bachelor's degrees (National Girls' Collaborative Project 2018). The researchers suggested that a major contributing factor has been that girls are much less likely to enroll in "pipeline courses" like introductory computer science. Based on a previous study, they surmised that girls were distinctly more likely to feel that they did not belong in the course, with prevailing stereotypes among instructors in the field signaling their inappropriateness.

The research team undertook two experiments, which differed somewhat in their settings but emphasized a similar concern with girls' reaction to facing stereotypes in STEM courses. In one instance the experimental subjects saw a photo of the classroom in an introductory course in computer science showing conventional objects associated with the field such as "Star Wars/Star Trek items, electronics, software, tech magazines, computer parts, video games, computer books, and science fiction books." In the other experiment, students viewed a very different photo of the course's classroom that displayed "nature pictures, art pictures, water bottles, pens, a coffee maker, lamps, general magazines, and plants." Both photos contained a teacher's table and chair, students' desk, a side table, and a storage unit (Master, Cheryan, and Meltzoff 2016, 427).

Whether the classroom appearance was typical or not had little influence on boys' interest in taking a computer science course, but the impact on girls was decisive, with their "self-reported interest in enrolling in an introductory computer science course … significantly increased when the classroom environment was altered so that it did not fit high school students' current … [male-favoring setting for] computer science" (Master et al. 2016, 430).

This research seems provocative, providing clear evidence that when a group feeling at-risk for exclusion from a certain field—in this instance high-school girls' belief that a hidden curriculum discourages them from taking an introductory computer science course—receives subtle but decisive support for taking the course, they are likely to feel encouraged to make the leap.

This is a gender issue, but it seems probable that if comparably fruitful supportive actions become available to poor youths and students of color, they will respond and benefit in a similar way.

Key Terms in the Glossary

apprenticeship
hidden curriculum
high-stakes testing
Jim Crow era
pedagogy of poverty
racially restrictive covenant
redlining
self-fulfilling prophecy
separate-but-equal standard
stereotype
tracking
urban war zone

Discussion Topics

1. Consider how the American system of public-school funding differs from those used in affluent European nations. What, if anything, would you change about the American system?
2. Have you attended a school that used tracking? Discuss the experience, assessing its effectiveness. If you haven't experienced tracking, indicate what impressions you have about it.
3. Is it reasonable to conclude that in the South the separate-but-equal standard has had an historical impact on African Americans' social reproduction? Explain.
4. Material in the chapter analyzes the impact of several factors on racial minorities' school performance. Which one or two factors seem(s) most influential and why?
5. Have you been aware of the hidden curriculum affecting girls and women in school? Can you give an interesting example of how it has affected you or someone you know? Would you expect that the hidden curriculum has been declining over time? On the last issue, include a specific reference to STEM fields.
6. The chapter finishes with an account of two experiments where high-school students saw photos of the classrooms providing two sharply contrasting settings for introductory computer-science courses. Does it surprise you that girls reacted very differently than boys to the two settings? Can you think of other effective ways school officials could promote girls' interest in taking STEM courses and perhaps entering STEM fields?

7. Pick one of the three at-risk groups featured in this book and consider its members' relationship with public education. Write a paper on the topic, detailing the students' challenges and struggles by using a variety of sociological and popular sources, including references to organizations and initiatives that have attempted to address the system's inadequacies.

Bibliography

Afflerbach, Peter. 2002. "The Road to Folly and Redemption: Perspectives on the Legitimacy of High-Stakes Testing." *Reading Research Quarterly* 37: 348–360.

Aikman, Sheila, Elaine Unterhalter, and Chloe Challender. 2005. "The Education MDGs: Achieving Gender Equality through Curriculum and Pedagogy Change." *Gender and Development* 13 (March): 44–55.

Albrecht, Jay, and Bradford Strand. 2010. "A Review of Organized Youth Sport in the United States." *YouthFirst: The Journal of Youth Sports* 5 (Spring): 16–20.

Amoyah, May, and David Brown. 2018. "Apprenticeship America: An Idea to Reinvent Postsecondary Skills for the Digital Age." *Third Way*. (June 11). https://www.thirdway. org/report/apprenticeship-america-an-idea-to-reinvent-postsecondary-skills-for-the-digital-age.

Anderson, Riana Elyse. 2018. "And Still We Rise: Parent–Child Relationships, Resilience, and School Readiness in Low-Income Urban Black Families." *Journal of Family Psychology* 32: 60–70.

Association of Texas Professional Educators. 2015. "Written Testimony to the Senate Committee on Health, Education, Labor and Pensions (HELP) on 'Fixing No Child Left Behind: Testing and Accountability.'" (January 30). https://www.teachthevote.org/blog-content/uploads/2015/01/ATPE-Written-Testimony-to-the-Senate-Committee-on-HELP_Testing-and-Accountability-01-21-15.pdf.

Barr, Robert D., and William H.Parrett. 2007. *The Kids Left Behind: Catching Up the Underachieving Children of Poverty*. Bloomington, IN: Solution Tree.

Berwick, Carly. 2019. "Is It Time to Detrack Math?" George Lucas Educational Foundation. (August 9). https://www.edutopia.org/article/it-time-detrack-math.

Bian, Lin, Sarah-Jane Leslie, and Andrei Cimpian. 2018. "Evidence of Bias against Girls and Women in Contexts That Emphasize Intellectual Ability." *American Psychologist* 73: 1139–1153.

Bol, Thijs, Jacqueline Witschge, Herman G. Van de Werfhorst, and Jaap Dronkers. 2014. "Curricular Tracking and Central Examinations: Counterbalancing the Impact of Social Background on Student Achievement in 36 Countries." *Social Forces* 92 (June): 1545–1572.

Boschma, Janie, and Ronald Brownstein. 2016. "The Concentration of Poverty in American Schools." *The Atlantic*. (February 29). https://www.theatlantic.com/education/archive/2016/02/concentration-poverty-american-schools/471414/.

Brookings. 2013. "The Resurgence of Ability Grouping and the Persistence of Tracking." (March 18). https://www.brookings.edu/research/the-resurgence-of-ability-grouping-and-persistence-of-tracking/.

Bureau of Labor Statistics. 2018. "Educational Attainment of the Labor Force Age 25 and Older by Race and Latino or Hispanic Ethnicity, Hispanic or Latino Annual Averages." https://www.bls.gov/opub/reports/race-and-ethnicity/2018/home.htm.

Carnoy, Martin, and Emma García. 2017. "Five Key Trends in U.S. Student Performance." Economic Policy Institute. (January 12). https://www.epi.org/publication/five-key-trends-in-u-s-student-performance-progress-by-blacks-and-hispanics-the-takeoff-of-asians-the-stall-of-non-english-speakers-the-persistence-of-socioeconomic-gaps-and-the-damaging-effect/.

Casey, Logan, and Elizabeth Mann Levesque. 2018. "New Survey of Minorities Adds Dissenting View to Public Satisfaction with Schools." Brookings. (January 11). https://www.brookings.edu/blog/brown-center-chalkboard/2018/01/11/new-survey-of-minorities-adds-dissenting-view-to-public-satisfaction-with-schools/.

Chadband, Emma. 2012. "Nine Ways Title IX Has Helped Girls and Women in Education." *neaToday*. (June 21). http://neatoday.org/2012/06/21/nine-ways-title-ix-has-helped-girls-and-women-in-education-2/.

Cherry, Kendra. 2019. "Alfred Binet and the History of IQ Testing." *Verywell Mind*. (July 2). https://www.verywellmind.com/history-of-intelligence-testing-2795581.

Chesnut, Eleanor K., and Ellen M. Markham. 2018. "'Girls Are as Good as Boys at Math' Implies That Boys Are Probably Better: A Study of Expressions of Gender Equality." *Cognitive Science* (June 28).

Chiu, Ming Ming, Bonnie Wing-Yin Chow, and Sung Wook Joh. 2017. "Streaming, Tracking and Reading Achievement: A Multilevel Analysis of Students in 40 Countries." *Journal of Educational Psychology* 109: 915–934.

Conchas, Gilberto Q. 2006. *The Color of Success: Race and High-Achieving Youth*. New York: Teachers College Press.

Cook, Lindsey. 2015. "U.S. Education: Still Separate but Equal." *U.S. News & World Report*. (January 28). https://www.usnews.com/news/blogs/data-mine/2015/01/28/us-education-still-separate-and-unequal.

cptv Frontline. 2014. "Americans Instrumental in Establishing Standardized Tests." https://www.pbs.org/wgbh/pages/frontline/shows/sats/where/three.html.

Daniels, Bruce Colin. 2012. *New England Nation: The Country the Puritans Built*. New York: Palgrave Macmillan.

Davis, Angelia. 2018. "Racial Restrictions in Old Property Deeds Have Shaped Today's Neighborhoods in Upstate South Carolina." *Greenville News*. (July 6). https://www.greenvilleonline.com/story/news/2018/07/06/racial-restrictive-covenants-part-greenville-clemson-past/549802002/.

Dixon, Lauren. 2017. "Corporate Education Differences: Germany's Apprenticeships versus U.S. Partnership Model." *Medium*. (August 14). https://medium.com/@AurenDisson/corporate-education-differences-germanys-apprenticeships-versus-u-s-partnership-model-8acca90f33b4.

Doob, Christopher Bates. 2005. *Race, Ethnicity, and the American Urban Mainstream*. Boston, MA: Allyn & Bacon.

Doob, Christopher B. 2019. *Social Inequality and Social Stratification in US Society*, 2nd ed. New York: Routledge.

Dworkin, A. Gary. 2005. "The No Child Left Behind Act: Accountability, High-Stakes Testing, and Roles for Sociologists." *Sociology of Education* 78 (April): 170–174.

EAB (formerly Education Advisory Board). 2019. "Female Students Worry They'll Face Gender Bias in STEM Majors."(May 8). https://eab.com/insights/daily-briefing/workplace/female-students-worry-theyll-face-gender-bias-in-stem-majors/.

Easley, Jonathan. 2016. "Trump Casts Inner Cities as War Zones in Pitch to Minority Voters." *The Hill*. (August 22). http://thehill.com/blogs/ballot-box/presidential-races/292283-trump-casts-inner-cities-as-war-zones-in-pitch-to.

Economics and Statistics Administration. 2017. "Women in STEM: 2017 Update." (November 13). http://www.esa.doc.gov/reports/women-stem-2017-update.

Edwards, Richard, and Patrick Carmichael. 2012. "Secret Codes: The Hidden Curriculum of Semantic Web Technologies." *Discourse: Studies in the Cultural Politics of Education* 33 (October): 575–590.

Elliott, Mark Emory. 2006. *Color-Blind Justice: Albion Tourgée and the Quest for Racial Equality from the Civil War to Plessy V. Ferguson*. Oxford: Oxford University Press.

Elmore, Corinn A., and Noni K. Gaylord-Harden. 2013. "The Influence of Supportive Parenting and Racial Socialization Messages on African American Youth Behavioral Outcomes." *Journal of Child and Family Studies* 22 (January): 63–75.

Fireside, Harvey. 1997. *Plessy v. Ferguson: Separate but Equal?* Springfield, NJ: Enslow Publishers.

Francis, Becky, Nicole Craig, Jeremy Hodgen, Becky Taylor, Antonina Tereshchenko, and Paul Connolly. 2020. "The Impact of Tracking by Attainment on Pupil Self-Confidence over Time: Demonstrating the Accumulative Impact of Self-Fulfilling Prophecy." *British Journal of Sociology of Education* 41 (June): 626–642.

Fulton, David. 2000. "Teach the Children: Who Decides?" *The New York Times* (September 19): A19.

Ganley, Colleen M., Casey E.George, Joseph R.Cimpian, and Martha B. Makowski. 2018. "Gender Equity in College Majors: Looking beyond the STEM/Non-STEM Dichotomy for Answers Regarding Female Participation." *American Educational Research Journal* 55 (June): 453–487.

Garbarino, James, Nancy Dubrow, Kathleen Kostelny, and Carol Pardo. 1992. *Children in Danger: Coping with the Consequences of Community Violence*. San Francisco: Jossey Bass.

Glossary of Education Reform. 2015. "The Hidden Curriculum." (July 13). https://www.edglossary.org/hidden-curriculum/.

Good, Dave. 2012. "'It's a War Zone Down Here." *San Diego Magazine*. (February 17). http://www.sandiegomagazine.com/San-Diego-Magazine/March-2012/Its-a-War-Zone-Down-Here/.

Grunspan, Daniel Z., Sarah L. Eddy, Sara E. Brownell, Benjamin L. Wiggins, Alison J. Crowe, and Steven M. Goodreau. 2016. "Males Under-Estimate Academic Performance of Their Female Peers in Undergraduate Biology Classrooms." *PLOS ONE* 11 (January 14). https://journals.plos.org/plosone/article?id=10.1371/journal.pone.0148405.

Grusky, David B. 2001. "Review." *Contemporary Sociology* 30 (November): 574–576.

Gu, Jackie. 2018. "Women Lose Out to Men Even before They Graduate from College." Bloomberg. https://www.bloomberg.com/graphics/2018-women-professional-inequality-college/.

Hanks, Angela. 2016. "Now Is the Time to Invest in Apprenticeships." Center for American Progress. (November 18). https://www.americanprogress.org/issues/economy/reports/2016/11/18/292558/now-is-the-time-to-invest-in-apprenticeships/.

Hennen, Anthony. 2018. "Why Aren't There More Apprentices in America? The James G. Center for Academic Renewal." (January 12). https://www.jamesgmartin.center/2018/01/arent-apprentices-america/.

House of Switzerland. 2019. "Apprenticeships the Recipe for Swiss Success." (April 26). https://houseofswitzerland.org/swissstories/economics/apprenticeships-recipe-swiss-success.

Hout, Michael, and Stuart W. Elliott. 2011. *Incentives and Test-Based Accountability in Education.* Washington, DC: National Academies Press.

Irons, Peter. 2004. "Jim Crow's Schools." American Federation of Teachers. https://www.aft.org/periodical/american-educator/summer-2004/jim-crows-schools.

Jenkins, Amy. 2019. "Personalized Learning and the Shift from a Pedagogy of Poverty to a Pedagogy of Plenty." *Education Elements.* (March 6). https://www.edelements.com/blog/personalized-learning-and-the-shift-from-pedagogy-of-poverty-to-pedagogy-of-plenty.

Johnson, Jesse. 2019. "6 Ways You Can Promote Gender Equality in Your Classroom." *TeachThought.* (September 19). https://www.teachthought.com/education/6-ways-can-promote-gender-equality-classroom/.

Jones-Correa, Michael. 2001. "The Origins and Diffusion of Racial Restrictive Covenants." *Political Science Quarterly* 115 (Winter): 541–568.

Jones, M. Gail, and Megan Ennes. 2018. "High-Stakes Testing." *Oxford Biographies.* (February 22). https://www.oxfordbibliographies.com/view/document/obo-9780199756810/obo-9780199756810-0200.xml.

Karlson, Kristian Bernt. 2015. "Expectations on Track? High School Tracking and Adolescent Educational Expectations." *Social Forces* 94 (September): 115–141.

Kelley, Lora. 2020. "Without Fixing Equality, the Schools Are Really Going to Struggle." *The New York Times.* (May 14). https://www.nytimes.com/interactive/2020/05/14/opinion/inequality-schools-teachers.html.

Kohli, Sonali, and Quartz. 2014. "Modern-Day Segregation in Public Schools." *The Atlantic.* (November 18).

Leaper, Campbell, and Carly Kay Friedman. 2007. "The Socialization of Gender," pp. 561–587 in Joan E. Grusec and Paul D. Hastings (eds.), *Handbook of Socialization: Theory and Research.* New York: Guilford Press.

Levine, Rhonda F. 2019. *When Race Meets Class: Coming of Age in a Small City.* New York: Taylor & Francis.

McGrady, Patrick B., and John R. Reynolds. 2013. "Racial Mismatch in the Classroom: Beyond Black-White Differences." *Sociology of Education* 86 (January): 3–17.

McKown, Clark. 2013. "Social Equity Theory and Racial-Ethnic Achievement Gaps." *Child Development* 84 (July/August): 1120–1136.

McKown, Clark, and Michael J. Strambler. 2008. "Social Influences on the Ethnic Achievement Gap," pp. 366–396 in Stephen M. Quintana and Clark McKown (eds.), *Handbook of Race, Racism, and the Developing Child.* Hoboken, NJ: John Wiley & Sons.

Massey, Douglas S., and Nancy A. Denton. 1993. *American Apartheid: Segregation and the Making of the Underclass.* Cambridge, MA: Harvard University Press.

Master, Allison, Sapna Cheryan, and Andrew N. Meltzoff. 2016. "Computing Whether She Belongs: Stereotypes Undermine Girls' Interest and Sense of Belonging in Computer Science." *Journal of Educational Psychology* 108: 424–437.

Meisenhelter, Jesse. 2018. "How 1930s Discrimination Shaped Inequality in Today's Cities." National Community Reinvestment Coalition. (March 27). https://ncrc.org/how-1930s-discrimination-shaped-inequality-in-todays-cities/.

Melnick, R. Shep. 2020. "The Strange Evolution of Title IX." *National Affairs.* (Winter). https://www.nationalaffairs.com/publications/detail/the-strange-evolution-of-title-ix.

Moore, Mignon R. 2001. "Review." *American Journal of Sociology* 107 (September): 538–540.

Moore, Natalie Y. 2017. "When They Say Chicago Is a War Zone, We Know What They Really Mean." *BuzzFeedNews.* (November 1). https://www.buzzfeed.com/nataliemoore/if-chicago-is-a-war-zone-who-is-the-enemy?utm_term=.mjQ1QpKR7#.ugaw92Ad4.

Mulholland, Quinn. 2015. "The Case against Standardized Testing." *Harvard Political Review.* (May 14). http://harvardpolitics.com/united-states/case-standardized-testing/.

National Equity Atlas. 2018. "Percent of Students in High-Poverty Schools: United States, All Public Schools 2010–2016." https://nationalequityatlas.org/indicators/School_poverty.

National Girls' Collaborative Project. 2018. "*Statistics.*" https://ngcproject.org/statistics.

Nesbit, Jeff. 2016. "Separate High Schools, Unequal Everything." *U.S. News and World Report.* (March 29). https://www.usnews.com/news/articles/2016-03-29/delayed-desegregation-separate-sc-high-schools-unequal-everything.

Oakes, Jeannie. 2005. *Keeping Track: How Schools Structure Inequality,* 2nd ed. New Haven, CT: Yale University Press.

Ogintz, Eileen. 1989. "Children Are Caught in Urban War Zone." *Chicago Tribune.* (April 30). https://www.chicagotribune.com/news/ct-xpm-1989-04-30-8904080440-story.html.

Organisation for Economic Co-operation and Development. 2014. "Education Policy Outlook: Netherlands." http://www.oecd.org/education/EDUCATION%20POLICY%20OUTLOOK_NETHERLANDS_EN%20.pdf.

Palmer, Maria Teresa Unger. 2007. "'Desperate to Learn:' The Schooling Experience of Latinas in North Carolina," pp. 120–144 in Erica Frankenberg and Gary Orfield (eds.), *Lessons in Integration: Realizing the Promise of Racial Diversity in American Schools.* Charlottesville: University of Virginia Press.

Plumer, Brad, and Nadja Popovich. 2020. "Housing Policy Left Neighborhoods Sweltering." *The New York Times.* (April 24). https://www.nytimes.com/interactive/2020/08/24/climate/racism-redlining-cities-global-warming.html?referringSource=articleShare.

Potter, Halley. 2019. "Integrating Classrooms and Reducing Academic Tracking." The Century Foundation. (January 29). https://tcf.org/content/report/integrating-classrooms-reducing-academic-tracking-strategies-school-leaders-educators/?session=1.

Pronin, Emily. 2020. "Women and Mathematics: Stereotypes, Identity, and Achievement." College Board. https://www.google.com/search?q=teachers%27+stereotypes+of+girls+in+math+and+scienc&oq=teachers%27+stereotypes+of+girls+in+math+and+scienc&aqs=chrome..69i57j69i60.24257j0j7&sourceid=chrome&ie=UTF-8.

Rasmussen Report. 2018. "Americans, Parents See Too Much Focus on Standardized Tests." (April 19). https://www.rasmussenreports.com/public_content/lifestyle/education/americans_parents_see_too_much_focus_on_standardized_tests.

Roser, Max, and Estaban Ortiz-Ospina. 2019. "Financing Education." Our World in Data. https://ourworldindata.org/financing-education.

Sadker, David, and Myka Sadker. 1994. *Failing at Fairness: How America's Schools Cheat Girls.* New York: Macmillan Publishing Company.

Schaefer, Richard. 1993. *Racial & Ethnic Groups,* 5th ed. New York: HarperCollins.

Shashkevich, Alex. 2018. "Some Well-Meaning Statements Can Spread Stereotypes, New Stanford Study Says." *Stanford News Service.* (July 10). https://news.stanford.edu/press-releases/2018/07/10/well-meaning-sta-unintentionally/.

Shin, Richard Q. 2011. "The Influence of Africentric Values and Neighborhood Satisfaction on the Academic Self-Efficacy of African American Elementary School Children." *Journal of Multicultural Counseling and Development* 39 (October): 218–228.

Strayhorn, Terrell L. 2015. "Factors Influencing Black Males' Preparation for College and Success in STEM Majors: A Mixed Methods Study." *Western Journal of Black Studies* 39: 45–63.

Torpey, Elka, and Ryan Farrell. 2019. "Apprenticeships: Outlooks and Wages in Selected Occupations." U.S. Bureau of Labor Statistics. (November). https://www.bls.gov/careeroutlook/2019/article/apprenticeships-outlook-wages-update.htm.

U.S. Census Bureau. 2019. Table 4.7. "Type of Family (All Races) by Median and Mean Income." https://www.census.gov/data/tables/time-series/demo/income-poverty/historical-income-families.html.

U.S. Department of Education. 2014. "Expansive Survey of America's Public Schools Reveals Troubling Racial Disparities." (March 21). https://www.ed.gov/news/press-releases/expansive-survey-americas-public-schools-reveals-troubling-racial-disparities.

U.S. Department of Education. 2015. "Title IX and Sex Discrimination." https://www2.ed.gov/about/offices/list/ocr/docs/tix_dis.html.

U.S. Department of Education. 2017. "The Federal Role in Education." https://www2.ed.gov/about/overview/fed/role.html.

Walker, Tim. 2016. "Survey: 70 Percent of Educators Say State Assessments Not Developmentally Appropriate." *neaToday*. (February 18). http://neatoday.org/2016/02/18/standardized-tests-not-developmentally-appropriate/.

Walsh, Bari. 2015. "Confronting Gender Bias at School." Harvard Graduate School of Education. (September 8). https://www.gse.harvard.edu/news/uk/15/09/confronting-gender-bias-school.

Wang, Ming-Te, and Jessica L. Degol. 2017. "Gender Gap in Science, Technology, Engineering, and Mathematics (STEM): Current Knowledge, Implications for Practice, Policy, and Future Directions." *Educational Psychology Review* 29 (March): 119–140.

Wang, Ming-Te, and James P. Huguley. 2012. "Parental Racial Socialization as a Moderator of the Effects of Racial Discrimination on Educational Success among African American Adolescents." *Child Development* 83 (September/October): 1716–1731.

Warne, Russell T., Myeongsun Yoon, and Chris J. Price. 2014. "Exploring the Various Interpretations of 'Test Bias'." *Cultural Diversity and Ethnic Minority Psychology* 20: 570–582.

Wilson, Ben. 2020. "Urban Heat Management and the Legacy of Redlining." *Journal of the American Planning Association*. (May 22). https://www.tandfonline.com/doi/full/10.1080/01944363.2020.1759127.

5

RISKY BUSINESS

Latina wages

In 2019, November 20th was Latina Equal Pay Day. That was the day when Latinas' earnings from the previous year and up to that time in 2019 would on average equal those of white men's for 2018. Another way to address the comparison is to point out that Hispanic women's pay averaged $0.53 to white men's dollar—a double pay gap based on the intersectional combination of gender and ethnicity. The pay gap narrows slightly to $0.66 to the dollar when the combination of education, years on the job, and location are taken into account.

A major contributing factor to Latinas' modest pay is that a substantial number work in low-wage positions as maids and housecleaners, cashiers, and retail salespeople. A sobering finding is that as Hispanic women move into occupations requiring more schooling, the pay gap with white men actually expands. Economist Elise Gould wrote,

> Even Hispanic women with an advanced degree earn less than white men who only have a bachelor's degree. That statistic bears … [further comment]: white non-Hispanic men with only a college degree are paid, on average, $6.81 *more* [an hour] than Latinas with an advanced degree!
>
> *(Gould 2019)*

In short, more schooling, as desirable as it might be, is not the entire means for attaining Latinas' equal job opportunity.

It is hardly surprising that Gould stressed the necessity for such workforce protections as equal pay for equal work. The last point suggests a troubling issue: Job discrimination continues to be prevalent in modern job settings, and as research later in the chapter reveals, the activities producing it often remain hidden from public view. In the upcoming section, it becomes apparent that overall employment for the working poor is seldom a positive experience.

Struggles of the Working Poor

Throughout the nineteenth century, depressions and mechanization on farms threatened many low-paying jobs for farmers, unskilled laborers, and craftsmen. These workers, who once had steady employment, became a "floating proletariat," often traveling extensively to find jobs (Iceland 2006, 12; Katz 2003, 228; Trattner 1994, 22). In spite of that reality, the myth prevailed that the able-bodied could always find work. Frustrated by such claims as they applied to a group of 700 unemployed job seekers, Josiah Quincy, a future Harvard president, told a roomful of scholars, "These men long for work; they anxiously beg for it; yet it is not to be found" (Katz 2003, 228).

In the mid-nineteenth century, thousands of workers validated Quincy's claim about the scarcity of jobs, traveling hundreds of miles to dig canals for a dollar a day. They were working in swamp conditions which often made them sick. At the end of their employment, many returned to their families with little cash and their health ruined. However, other men needed work so badly that they readily replaced those who left (Katz 2003, 228).

Never in the nation's history has any program significantly alleviated the plight of the working poor. In December 1967 about a century after the canal diggers just described, Martin Luther King, Jr., indicated that he planned a major protest, which he called the "Poor People's Campaign." He envisioned "a trek to the nation's capital by suffering and outraged citizens who will go to stay until some definite and positive active [sic] is taken to provide jobs and income for the poor." In addition, the Poor People's Campaign would demand federal funding to assure full employment and a guaranteed, above-poverty income. King invited others to join him at the National Mall in Washington, DC. (Diamond 2018).

King was assassinated the following year, but a protest did develop, lasting 42 days with 3,000 tents in the Mall's "Resurrection City." While no significant legislation followed the protest, the mobilization was significant for many participants, who decades later continue to feel the influence of the experience. One participant was Dr. Lenneal Henderson, a professor of government, who said, "It was exciting to be part of something that potentially, at least, could make a difference in the lives of so many people who were in poverty around the country" (Diamond 2018).

The Institute for Policy Studies indicated that in the intervening half-century since the Poor People's Campaign, 60 percent more people were living in poverty. Meanwhile the most affluent have been thriving. The top 1 percent now receives nearly twice the share of national income it obtained in 1968 (IPS Staff 2017).

In 2017 39.7 million people, representing 12.3 percent of the US population, lived below the poverty line. That year the working poor represented 2.9 percent of full-time workers, with their part-time job holders employed 27 weeks a year or fewer representing over three times as great a percentage at 10.9 percent of all employees. More women than men tend to be among the working poor, and African Americans and Latinos represent more than twice the percentages of Asians and whites (U.S. Bureau of Labor Statistics 2019a). Table 5.1 provides basic information about the working poor.

TABLE 5.1 Prominent Traits of the Working Poor (2017)[1]

Workforce size	4.5 million, with part-time employment much more common than full-time
Percentages belonging to major racial groups	Individuals who worked 27 weeks or more during the year: 2.9 % of Asians, 3.9 % of whites, and 7.9 % of both Blacks and Hispanics
Gender membership	3.8 million women worked 27 weeks or more compared to 3.1 million men, with women having a higher working-poor rate—5.3 % to 3.8 %
Education	The greater people's education, the less likely they belonged in the working-poor category. Among those who worked 27 weeks or more, 13.7 % of those with less than a high-school diploma while only 1.5 % of those with a bachelor's degree
Occupation	Individuals with jobs involving extensive education and higher earnings the least likely to be included. For example, 1.4 % of those with positions in management, the professions, and related occupations qualified as members of the working poor. In contrast, those with jobs requiring only limited schooling and providing low pay often members of the working poor—for instance, the 2.3 million job holders in service work representing 36 % of the total membership of the working poor
Families with children	Families with at least one member in the labor force distinctly more likely to be living below the poverty line if they had children than if they did not. A working-poor rate for single women with children under 18 of 21.5 %, 10.9 % for single men, and 7.1 % for married couples

Source: U.S. Bureau of Labor Statistics 2019a.
[1] The data in this report come from the Current Population Survey, which is a monthly survey of about 60,000 eligible households.

Individuals hired in service occupations are more likely to belong to the poor than to be members of other social classes (U.S. Bureau of Labor Statistics 2019a). Additional poverty-level jobs involve retail sales, cooking and food preparation, cleaning buildings, food and beverage serving, and personal care and service work such as child care and patient care (Ross and Bateman 2019, 11).

[handwritten margin note: hourly wages]

While the positions the working poor obtain are diverse, certain traits are commonplace. Inevitably these job holders receive low wages. Fifty-three million individuals, 44 percent of all workers between 18 and 64, obtain a median hourly wage of $10.22 or less and a median annual income of no more than $17,950, well below the poverty cutoff for a family of four. About half of these workers are the primary earner in their family or a major contributor, and a quarter are the sole providers (Ross and Bateman 2019, 9; U.S. Department of Health and Human Services 2020).

Many members of the working poor, especially individuals who are female, people of color, and have a high-school diploma or less schooling, find themselves trapped in low-wage positions, sometimes shifting from one job to another but generally unable to obtain higher wages (Escobari et al. 2019; Ross and Bateman 2019, 9). Locked into jobs with little promise of advancement, the working poor have no option but to hold on to their current positions; bosses are fully aware of this situation and take advantage of it, often pressuring employees to increase their output.

A writer who once worked at a McDonald's explained that the vast fast-food industry is

> far from the leisurely time implied by "flipping burgers." One of my co-workers put it best: "Fast food is intense! And it's stressful! You're always feeling rushed, you're on a time crunch for literally eight hours straight, you're never allowed to have one moment just to chill."
>
> (Guendelsberger 2019)

[handwritten note: mental health for working poor #1]

Another drawback of the jobs the working poor have is that the tasks in which they engage are often unpleasant and stressful, sometimes including disturbing surprises. For instance, a journalist lost his job, and the only position he could locate was in retail sales. He discovered that in the sporting-goods store where he worked the management personnel were obsessed with theft, and so frequent searches took place. "If you go outside or leave the store on your break, me or another manager [will] have to look in your backpack and see the bottom," ... [his boss] explained. "And winter's coming—if you're wearing a hoodie or a big jacket, we'll just have to pat you down. It's pretty simple." It was unwelcome news for a Black man who had been stopped and frisked by police, and yet he had no choice but to endure the painful treatment for the low pay he needed to survive (Williams 2014).

One might recall that in Chapter 2 when discussing the poor, the idea of toxic stress was introduced, emphasizing that in their immediate environments stressful conditions could actually do bodily harm. Notably the low-wage positions that the working poor fill can lead to psychologically and physically harmful outcomes. It appears, in fact, that these employees face a double trap.

First, as previously noted, they tend to be stuck in low-level positions, unable to find work in higher-level, better-paying employment. Research involving nearly 700,000 individuals covered in the 2011 to 2017 rounds of the March Supplement of the Current Population Survey indicated that within a 12-month period only about 5 percent of low-wage workers found better jobs (Gabe et al. 2018). A major impediment is that individuals in service jobs or other manual-labor positions often need to develop cognitive and interpersonal skills to perform well in such better-paying occupations as clerks, entry-level administrators, bank tellers, customer-service representatives, or cashiers, but, generally speaking, their modest education has not prepared them for such activities (Waddell 2018).

Second, on the job, the working poor often encounter another type of trap. The former McDonald's worker quoted earlier pointed out that electronic monitoring over time has become more sophisticated, making positions like the one she had "inescapably, chronically stressful." Speaking from experience, she added, "It can be hard to understand the stress of having someone constantly looking over your shoulder if you haven't recently—or have never—had to work a job like this" (Guendelsberger 2019). Covid #10

One of the harsh realities for the working poor is that when they encounter stress and other destructive impacts, they generally have fewer protections than more affluent counterparts. When COVID-19 hit the United States, the working poor disproportionately encountered two major risks—massive layoffs following local or state stay-at-home orders; and increased exposure to the contagious disease for many remaining at such service jobs as home health aides, factory workers, grocery clerks, restaurant workers, and housekeepers—all positions requiring close contact with the public (Joint Economic Committee, the Senate 2020).

A writer noted that while many poor service workers were appreciative of staying on the job when so many were losing theirs, they felt intimidated, working in tightly packed assembly lines and checking in for their shift using fingerprint scanners. One factory worker, who like others spoke anonymously because of possible job retaliation, explained, "There's parts of the line where you're literally rubbing elbows with each other …. I'm washing my hands more, but I'm still worried" (Sanchez 2020).

Along with other disadvantages, the United States has provided poverty-level workers little chance to obtain high-quality vocational schooling and to participate in well-proven apprenticeship programs similar to those in Germany, Switzerland, and other Europeans nations. As a result individuals seeking service and sales jobs are often poorly prepared (Novello 2018).

Not surprisingly, racial minorities, who are disproportionately poor, have often found the American work world a difficult, harsh place.

Embattled Workers of Color

All workplaces have rules, which, among other things, establish the legitimacy of the current employment system. Some workplaces, however, are less equality-oriented than others. In *Black Boy* Richard Wright's autobiography, the renowned writer described a job he held as a 16-year-old living in Jackson, Mississippi, in 1924.

Things started well. Wright met Mr. Crane, the boss of an optical company, who asked him about his schooling and seemed pleased to find out that he had completed two years of algebra. Perhaps he would like to learn the trade the boss said, and Wright replied that he definitely would. Crane introduced Wright to Pease and Reynolds, two white workers, and explained that they should start instructing him in grinding and polishing lenses. Meanwhile his job involved keeping the office clean.

Eventually a week and then a month passed, and Pease and Reynolds told Wright nothing about the optical work. So one afternoon Wright approached Reynolds and asked him to explain how the work was done.

From that moment Wright was exposed to a barrage of microaggressions. "What are you trying to do, get smart, n****r?" Reynolds asked. Wright said no, but he was confused and then thinking that perhaps Reynolds simply didn't want to help, he went to Pease with the same request, reminding him that the boss had said he should be given a chance to learn the work. "N****r, you think you're white, don't you?" "No, sir," Wright replied. Then he added that he was only doing what the boss said he should do. Infuriated, Pease shook his fist at Wright and said, "This is a *white* man's work around here" (Wright 1991, 180).

From that moment the relations between Wright and the two white men deteriorated; they no longer said good morning, and if he was somewhat slow in performing some duty he was called "a lazy black sonofabitch." Then one day the situation reached a climax. Pease called Wright over to his workbench, saying that Reynolds told him that he, Wright, had referred to him as "Pease," failing to call him "Mr. Pease." It was clearly a trap. Wright wrote,

> If I had said: No, sir, Mr. Pease, I never called you *Pease*, I would by infer-ence have been calling Reynolds a liar: And if I said: Yes, sir, Mr. Pease, I called you *Pease*, I would have been pleading guilty to the worst insult that a Negro can offer to a southern white man [calling him by just his last name].

Wright hesitated, and then pressured by Pease he said that he couldn't remember calling him Pease. The reply hardly satisfied Pease, who slapped Wright repeatedly, saying that, indeed, he had called him Pease. Wright begged him to stop the beating and knowing that they were trying to force him to resign said that he would do so. Pease and Reynolds gave him a minute to leave and warned him not to show up again or to tell the boss what had happened (Wright 1991, 182).

TABLE 5.2 Occupational Categories for the Major Racial Groups[1]

	Asians	Blacks	Hispanics	Whites
Management, professional, and related occupations	54%	31%	22%	41%
Natural resources, construction, and maintenance	3%	6%	17%	10%
Production, transportation, and material moving	10%	16%	16%	11%
Sales and office	17%	22%	21%	22%
Service	17%	24%	24%	16%

Source: U.S. Bureau of Labor Statistics 2019b.
Note: It is apparent that Asians and whites, who tend to have more extensive schooling, are more likely to work in management, professional, and related occupations while Blacks and Hispanics produce higher percentages in several categories requiring less formal education.
[1] The data in this report come from the Current Population Survey, which is a monthly survey of about 60,000 eligible households.

Employees of color no longer have to endure the blatantly abusive conditions Wright described, but in numerous job settings they find themselves seriously disadvantaged. Whether because of discrimination, educational differences, or both, Table 5.2 indicates that the members of the major racial groups are distributed differently into job categories.

It is apparent that Asians and whites, who tend to have more extensive schooling, are more likely to work in management, professional, and related occupations while larger proportions of Blacks and Hispanics produce higher percentages in several categories requiring less formal education. *resumes + interv.*

To assess discrimination, researchers have done experimental studies involving job *#9* applications using testers (experimental subjects working for the investigators) from different racial groups. Twenty-four field experiments conducted during the quarter century from 1989 to 2014, involving over 55,000 applications for over 26,000 positions, revealed that when the candidates' qualifications were matched, the whites received 36 percent more callbacks than Blacks and 24 percent more than Latinos (Quillian et al. 2017). *Criminal record* *# 9*

Another tester study featured Black and white men supplied with résumés that alternated between those indicating that the experimental subjects had spent time in prison and others showing that they had not. Highly revealing was the finding that whites with a criminal record received more callbacks than Blacks without a criminal past (Pager and Pedulla 2003).

Some people of color have tried to reduce the job discrimination they encounter. One tactic African Americans have often used involves casting a wider job-seeking net than white applicants (Pager and Pedulla 2003; Pedulla and Pager 2015).

PHOTO 5.1 Job interviews can be both nerve-racking and discriminatory. The hard truth is that two dozen field experiments conducted over a quarter century reveal that after an initial interview, whites have a decided advantage over Blacks and Hispanics for receiving a callback.

Source: Shutterstock/ Fizkes

Another means available to racial minorities is to attempt to manipulate the hiring personnel's perception of them. In a study of minority applicants, many indicated that their racial membership was less important than how they represented themselves when applying for a job. For instance, "résumé whitening" could often prove useful (Kang et al. 2016, 469). These job candidates would often decide how to portray themselves as they assessed the prospective employers who were examining them. When one of the researchers interviewed a Black student about whether or not her résumé would refer to her membership in a Black organization, she explained,

> If the employer is known for like trying to employ more people of color and having like a diversity outreach program then I would include it because in that sense they're trying to broaden their employees, but if they're not actively trying to reach out to other people of other races then, no, I wouldn't include it.
>
> *(Kang et al. 2016, 482)*

For minority job applicants, this approach is likely to produce practical results. A review of six studies suggested that whites tended to react negatively toward minorities who supported improved rights and opportunities for their group members, and the strongest opposition came from whites who were committed to the status quo in the job world (Kaiser and Pratt-Hyatt 2009). Inevitably that type of opposition affects the distribution of racial minorities in various occupations.

People of color are often underrepresented in many highly valued, well-paid careers. Evidence indicates that relatively few Blacks and Hispanics are in STEM jobs. While members of those two groups represent 27 percent of the overall workforce, they fill just 16 percent of STEM positions. Studies have suggested that contributing factors to the underrepresentation have been the scarcity of Black and Hispanic mentors encouraging young people from their groups to seek STEM work, limited access to the requisite science courses, and low-income backgrounds that discourage students' pursuit of STEM-related coursework.

Once on the job, African American STEM employees are particularly likely to have reported discrimination in current or previous jobs—62 percent compared to 44 percent of Asians and 42 percent of Hispanics (Funk and Parker 2018).

The U.S. Equal Employment Opportunity Commission (EEOC) is the agency that is supposed to investigate job complaints where discrimination because of a person's race, color, or sex produces a violation of federal laws involving job applications or employee treatment (U.S. Equal Employment Opportunity Commission 2020). Each year the EEOC and its state and local partner agencies examine about 100,000 cases, with individuals receiving some form of compensation such as money or a change in working conditions about 18 percent of the time. Cases involving race are among the most common and have the lowest success rate, about 15 percent (Jameel and Yerardi 2019).

The proponents of equal opportunity believe that besides discriminated job applicants launching complaints, there is a pressing need to change the culture of the settings in which businesses operate—for instance, altering the norms for hiring and operating in the business world. Almost every Fortune 500 company holds diversity training for staff members, but the reality is that the impact of such exposure generally lasts only a few days.

What appears to be a more effective means of reducing racial discrimination involves companies' commitment to including a fairly high proportion of people of color in their applicant pool, and then once the hiring process begins keeping the process as race-blind as possible (Strauss 2019).

Such a commitment is often missing. Experts estimate that about one third of jobs are obtained through family, friends, or colleagues and that many of them are never listed publicly. Such hiring networks tend to be racially homogenous, with whites receiving most of the better job offerings.

An effective way to limit this bias is for prospective employers to post jobs publicly, particularly using such sites as colleges and universities containing large numbers of students of color and also contacting organizations like Handshake, which can provide students, including applicants of color, with information about available jobs and internships (Abowd et al. 1999; Strauss 2019).

Once on the job, many people of color feel intimidated discussing race, suggesting the need to create a comfortable setting where they can examine such issues without fear of retribution. Drawing from a study of more than 3,700 respondents representing the major racial/ethnic groups, researchers found that 58 percent of Black professionals experienced microaggressions on the job, more than Latinos at 41 percent and Asians at 38 percent. Nearly two fifths of Black professionals felt the largely white leadership considered it inappropriate for them to speak out about the racist comments they had encountered. As a result their sense of isolation and alienation increased (Center for Talent Innovation 2019, 5; Connley 2019).

These are the kinds of oppressive situations that those trying to equalize job opportunities for people of color are trying to change. "People often are scared to say anything because they worry that if they say anything wrong, they might get fired," said Angela Nino, a prominent human-resource specialist. "It is important to create a space where people feel safe to have honest conversations where nobody feels singled out or different" (Hirsch 2018).

While Nino was referring to a psychological sense of safety, people of color on the job can be particularly vulnerable to situations involving physical safety. Prominently represented among the working poor, people of color found that once the coronavirus pandemic started, they often encountered one prominent disadvantage on the job previously discussed as associated with that group. In short, racial minorities found themselves disproportionately in front-line jobs with frequent contact with the public and as a result increased vulnerability to catching the virus (Gould and Wilson 2020).

Blacks are the racial group with the highest disproportionate representation in front-line jobs, filling 18 percent of those positions while comprising just 12 percent of all workers. They are most heavily overrepresented in child care and licensed practical nursing attending to sick, injured, or disabled patients while Hispanics are most likely to be found in farm work and building-cleaning services. Overall workers of color are particularly overrepresented in the following front-line positions—bus driving, trucking and warehousing, building-cleaning services, various health-care occupations, and several child-care and social-service positions (Ryo et al. 2020; U.S. Department of Agriculture 2020).

In addition, as the pandemic descended, both female and male Blacks had higher job-loss rates than their white counterparts (Gould and Wilson 2020) while Latinos' job-loss rates were the highest among the three groups (Palavi 2020).

Historically and currently women in the work world also encounter many risks.

Gender on the Job

In Ohio during the early 1800s, factory work became an option for women. Although they received one half to two thirds a man's pay, these jobs did provide support for their families. Besides low pay, factory jobs also featured poor working conditions—no heating and little ventilation and insufficient light. In the early nineteenth century, organizations like the Female Protective Union formed, with the intention of improving women's working conditions and increasing their pay. Such groups had some success in achieving their goals (Ohio History Central 2020). In fact, in various cities in the late nineteenth and early twentieth centuries, working women associated with the suffrage movement and empowered by it joined labor unions and protested for higher pay and improved working conditions (National Women's History Museum 2020).

In modern times, however, employment results for women have often been discouraging. In its first five years of ongoing research, McKinsey & Company conducted a study featuring more than 250,000 individuals in nearly 600 companies surveyed about their jobs (Huang et al. 2019).

While company personnel often applauded gender diversity, actual progress had stalled. Clearly women have been making the commitment, earning more bachelor's degrees than men and, in spite of a widespread belief to the contrary, staying in the workforce at the same rate as men. If women's representation is going to increase, the onus falls on the companies, where gender diversity needs to become an actual priority.

On the issue of income, women overall in 2019 earned about $0.79 for every dollar that a man earned. Comparing females and males employed in the same jobs and possessing similar qualifications, the differences shrunk considerably to the woman obtaining $0.98 to the man's dollar (PayScale 2019). The last finding suggests a fairly obvious conclusion—that a ferocious attack on the gender gap in hiring at all pay levels would sharply curtail gender inequality in pay. Figure 5.1 provides data on median income for women in the major racial groups.

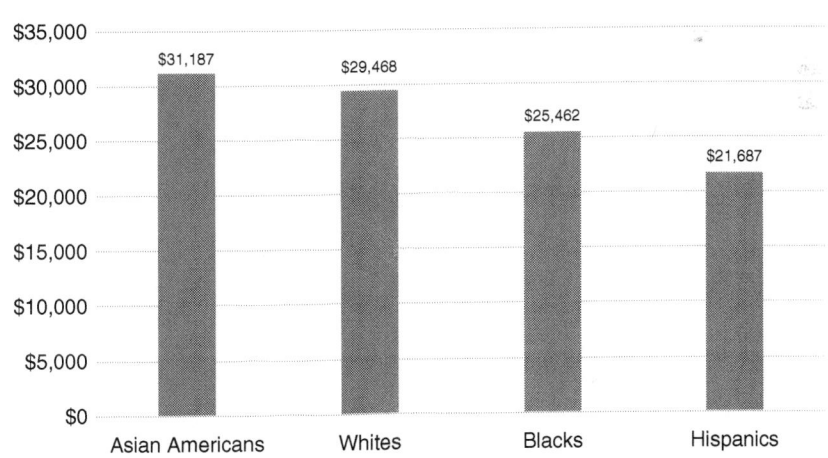

FIGURE 5.1 Median Income for Women in the Major Racial Groups (2018)[1]
Source: U.S. Bureau of the Census 2019.
Note: In 2000, income for the women in the four groups represented here followed a similar pattern to what it was nearly two decades later, with Asians having the highest and Hispanics the lowest.
[1] The data provide income information for Americans aged 15 years and older.

The current reality is that in spite of their good educational credentials, women are underrepresented at all levels in most companies. This deficiency exists at the entry level, and the disparity widens for management positions, with women less likely to be hired for those jobs and much less likely to be promoted into them.

Besides the inequality in job level and pay women often face, another major issue involves the features of the job setting. Workforce interaction occurs most harmoniously when employees enjoy a pleasant, relaxed context where women and men are encouraged to interact in a positive, equality-oriented way. Gender discrimination, sexual harassment, and women alone on the job are three conditions that effectively discourage such a setting (Krivkovich et al. 2018).

- Gender discrimination is rampant in the work world. A McKinsey & Company study has found that female employees often encounter microaggressions, indicating distinct doubts about judgments they make or demanding that they provide more evidence of their competence than male colleagues would be expected to supply.

Black women, in particular, often must face a large number of microaggressions, widely forced to endure extensive questioning about their competence. They can also find that white bosses and coworkers confront them with stereotypes, and whether conscious or not, these are self-serving, asserting the dominant group's superiority and seeking to justify the maintenance of the economic, political, and social status quo. In addition, these stereotypes can savagely erode Black female employees' self-image and performance (Krivkovich et al. 2018).

To avoid microaggressions, women of color are likely to feel compelled to adjust their behavior. In a study in which the author, a Black woman, interviewed 10 women of color operating in the corporate world, one issue raised was the common perception among whites that Black women are aggressive. One of the interviewees explained that her advisors at work talked to her "about dimming my light. I always thought I had to bring that down to make people comfortable." The researcher herself also encountered this advice.

> I've been told to smile in the office and, at the risk of coming across as too aggressive, I tend to wait until everyone else has spoken before choosing to weigh in. …. I've been conditioned by society and its predominantly white institutions to feel that as a [B]lack woman I come across as aggressive, bossy, and selfish when I speak my mind compared to a man or white woman making the same statements.
>
> *(Cheeks 2018)*

During the 2020 vice-presidential debate, Kamala Harris, the Democratic nominee, who is Black and Indian, faced numerous interruptions from Vice President Mike Pence, her opponent. Fully aware of stereotypes about angry Black women, Harris defended herself by smiling, looking directly at Pence, and repeatedly saying in a quiet but forceful voice, "Mr. Vice-president, I'm speaking." Usually he would back off (Gambino 2020).

Another gender-linked set of minorities vulnerable to discrimination on the job are people belonging to sexual minorities, namely LGBT workers. Historically in the US, no federal legislation has protected employees from dismissal based on sexual identity, and 28 states containing about 52 percent of LGBT employees have provided no support if they were harassed on the job, turned down for promotion, or fired (Catalyst 2020; Miller 2019). For LGBT employees, risky work has continued to be a widespread reality.

However, in June 2020 the Supreme Court, which at the time tended to take conservative positions on issues, reached an unexpected, even surprising decision. In a 6-to-3 ruling, Justice Neil M. Gorsuch, writing for the majority, stated,

> An employer who fires an individual for being homosexual or transgender fires that person for traits or actions it would not have questioned in … [someone with a traditional sexual orientation]. Sex plays a necessary and undisguisable role in the decision, exactly what Title VII forbid.

Title VII, a section in the renowned Civil Rights Act of 1964, prohibits discrimination because of personal characteristics, and being homosexual or transgender, or for that matter LGBT of any type, are clear examples of such traits (Supreme Court of the United States 2020, 2).

A journalist suggested that transgender people's rights have become "a political battlefield," with the issue sometimes arising because of President Trump's efforts to eliminate transgender individuals' health protections. The journalist added that with its decision on workplace discrimination against LGBT people, the Supreme Court made clear its position on the issue (Zurcher 2020).

Besides discrimination facing employees, sexual harassment or assault are frequent gender-related problems on the job.

- The estimates of the prevalence of sexual misconduct at work vary from about 25 percent of female employees experiencing it to over three times that figure— about 80 percent. A major factor in determining the estimates is the decision about what constitutes sexual harassment. For instance, should the assessment include such verbal expressions as whistles or catcalls? (Chatterjee 2018; Krivkovich et al. 2018; Stop Street Harassment 2018; U.S. Equal Employment Opportunity Commission 2014). Sexual Harassment

Evidence from one large study suggests that individuals challenging traditional feminine expectations, namely women in senior leadership positions, lesbians, and employees in technical fields, are particularly vulnerable to sexual harassment (Krivkovich et al. 2018).

While such categories of women are widely harassed, a very different set of female workers are also frequent victims of such mistreatment. A report by the Restaurant Opportunities Center indicated that female restaurant workers who depend on tips felt particularly vulnerable, forcing them to tolerate behavior that made them uncomfortable or nervous. Over half of these workers claimed that managers, coworkers, or customers had often sexually harassed them, but the majority never reported it, with two thirds fearing financial loss, public humiliation, or termination if the harasser came from management and nearly half if he were a coworker (U.S. Equal Employment Opportunity Commission 2015).

A study of sexual harassment involving over 500 women at work included quotations about the experience—both details about what happened and also how they felt and reacted to the mistreatment. For instance, a high-level executive described a situation where she was wearing a sweater dress and high boots, and in front of another woman a male colleague said that she looked like "an alluring zorro" [fox]. Later as the man was driving her home and "grinding his choppers" under his breath, he said,

> "I'll bet you're really nasty in the bedroom," and I was like, "Did I just hear that right?" He's like, "Whips and chains and high heeled boots," and I was like, "Did I just hear that correctly?" I'm in this car with him going through Years Square and I want to dive roll out of the car but I'm just going to pretend I did not hear that. I just totally dismissed it and changed the subject.

The woman wanted to tell her boss about the incident, but the harasser was her superior, and so she realized the outcome of making a report could easily be damaging to her career (Keplinger et al. 2019).

PHOTO 5.2 While many women might like to strike back physically or even just verbally when a boss is sexually harassing them, they are likely to restrain themselves, fearing the job-related consequences.
Source: Viacheslav Iakobchuk / Alamy Stock Photo

The team of researchers who did this study indicated that regardless of their work, female employees who suffer sexual harassment are likely to experience one or more of the following types of reactions, including "negative mood, eating disorders, alcohol abuse, job withdrawal, greater stress, greater self-doubt, lower self-esteem, and lower overall mental health" (Keplinger et al. 2019).

While sexual harassment and gender discrimination at work result from men's explicit mistreatment of women, the following issue occurs because of a persistent historical pattern offering women less access than men to the job world.

being the only woman @ work

- Being "the only one" or one of few women in the room at work is a fairly common experience. Data from the massive McKinsey & Company study cited earlier indicated that one in five women face this solitary experience. The research indicated that these women were not just lonely—that over 80 percent experienced microaggressions compared to 64 percent for working women overall. In addition, matched with women workers in settings where they are more prevalent, those who were alone were nearly twice as likely to have faced sexual harassment at some time in their careers (Krivkovich et al. 2018).

Certain categories of women, such as members of racial minorities, are particularly likely to be alone in the office, especially in higher-status jobs. An African American woman, quoted in the report involving 10 women of color cited earlier, was often very discouraged by the way her white colleagues viewed the world. It was a lonely existence. She was on a business trip with colleagues, and one evening she was by herself in a hotel room, receiving the painful news that a police officer had shot a Black man. That same day a prominent Hollywood couple had broken up, and most of the media attention focused on that, saying little about the killing. The woman recalled, "I remember watching [the shooting] and crying in my hotel bed. And then having to go to work. And no one checked in for your wellbeing." The author added, "This is the reality for many [B]lack women at work in America. They care deeply about the issues affecting the [B]lack community but that feeling isn't generally supported or acknowledged in the workplace" (Cheeks 2018).

Another category of women who tend to find themselves the only member of their sex at work are those in traditional men's working-class jobs. Sociologist Jeanie Ahearn Greene interviewed 17 female blue-collar workers and aptly named her book *Blue-Collar Women at Work with Men: Negotiating the Hostile Environment* (2006). The respondents were employed in trucking, construction, loading ships, manufacturing, policing, security, carpentry, printing, commercial painting, and various other positions.

While all the jobs were difficult and demanding, the quality of supervision could determine whether the situation was tolerable or intolerable. Beth, who did electrical contracting, had a supervisor who supported women at work and recruited her into a meter-repair-and-assembly shop, encouraging her to study the subjects to qualify for the position. The supervisor stated, "'Women are my best workers.' .... And that was the way he let us know we were welcome there." Beth suggested that such a supportive outlook eventually can permeate an entire organization (Greene 2006, 118–19).

In contrast, some supervisors could make a hard job intolerable, even forcing women to leave their positions. The punitive supervisors were often more vigilant about overseeing women's work than men's, particularly on the topic of sick and injury time—a sensitive subject because it relates to stereotyping of women being weak or lazy. Sonja indicated that two days after she was hurt in a fall her supervisor asked when she would resume working. She told him that in several days she would have tests, and then she would let him know. The supervisor was unsatisfied, saying that staying home would not get the job done. Sonja told him, "I fell. I hurt myself. I did not do it on purpose ..., and if you're taking this personally, maybe you should talk to somebody because this isn't personal. This is a business" (Greene 2006, 119).

Lastly on the relationship between gender and work, information provided earlier in this chapter has indicated that from the onset of the COVID-19 pandemic, both the working poor and people of color have been overrepresented in front-line jobs. An additional reality is that women are extensively involved in such work, representing about half of all workers but nearly two thirds of those in working-poor or working-class front-line jobs. They have been most prevalent as health-care workers (excluding physicians), child-care and social-service employees, cashiers, retail salespeople, customer-service personnel, pharmacy technicians, and fast-food and counter workers (Ryo et al. 2020).

The chapter closes with an important issue about women's work currently receiving little attention.

The Largely Ignored Issue of Unpaid Work

When the Organisation for Economic Co-operation and Development gathered data from 30 primarily affluent countries about the amount of unpaid work women and men do around the house, namely tasks involving shopping for household goods, cooking, cleaning, child care, and other unpaid domestic activities, women in every country did more. The nations with the closest totals for the sexes were Sweden, Denmark, and Norway, which have extensive safety-net organizations supplying care for both children and elderly people. In the United States, women provide about four hours of unpaid labor per day compared to men's two-and-a-half (Organisation for Economic Co-operation and Development 2020; Wezerek and Ghodsee 2020).

In spite of the fact that women's unpaid labor represents a massive contribution to the society, it generally goes unnoticed by economists since no explicit financial transactions take place: The universal assumption simply exists that family members should perform the tasks for free. However, it would be possible to quantify the related economic issues, moving these normally hidden figures from obscurity into the public arena.

Using 2019 data from the Organisation for Economic Co-operation and Development, a pair of journalists concluded, "If American women earned minimum wage for the unpaid work they do around the house and caring for relatives, they would have made $1.5 trillion last year" (Wezerek and Ghodsee 2020). Is this just an astounding figure that can serve as a conversation piece, or in upcoming years might growing awareness of this reality help generate support for a system providing American women compensation for their unpaid household contribution?

Discussion Topics

1. List and discuss the basic traits of the working poor.
2. Why do people get trapped in low-wage jobs? Have you ever had that type of work?
3. Assess the impact of electronic monitoring on the job. From either personal experience or what you have heard from others, how do people in low-wage jobs react to it and why?
4. The text provides an example of the racist treatment a 16-year-old Richard Wright experienced dealing with his white bosses at an optical company in Mississippi in the 1920s. Do you know of other situations that show how African Americans or other workers of color were treated on the job in the past?
5. Had you previously heard of résumé whitening? Are there other techniques job applicants might use to curtail discrimination?
6. Is gender discrimination on the job likely to remain prevalent or will it decline in the future? Take a position and build a case for it.
7. How do people you know regard sexual harassment in the workplace? If possible, provide contrasting examples.
8. Have you ever thought about or discussed women's unpaid work in the home? In your opinion what, if anything, would be the most productive action countries could take?
9. Choose one of the three groups described in this chapter whose members were at-risk in a front-line job during the COVID-19 pandemic. Using various sources, write a paper describing in detail the employees' job settings, their reactions to it, and also the means of promoting comfortable, safe working conditions.

Bibliography

Abowd, John M., Francis Kramarz, and David N. Margolis. 1999. "High Wage Workers and High Wage Firms." *Econometrica* 67 (March): 251–333.

Catalyst. 2020. "Lesbian, Gay, Bisexual, and Transgender Workplace Issues: Quick Take." (June 15). https://www.catalyst.org/research/lesbian-gay-bisexual-and-transgender-workplace-issues/.

Center for Talent Innovation. 2019. "Being Black in Corporate America: An Intersectional Exploration." https://www.talentinnovation.org/_private/assets/BeingBlack-KeyFindings-CTI.pdf.

Centers for Disease Control and Prevention. 2020. "COVID-19 in Racial and Ethnic Minority Groups." (June 25). https://www.cdc.gov/coronavirus/2019-ncov/need-extra-precautions/racial-ethnic-minorities.html.

Chatterjee, Rhitu. 2018. "A New Survey Finds 81 Percent of Women Have Experienced Sexual Harassment." *npr.* (February 21). https://www.npr.org/sections/thetwo-way/2018/02/21/587671849/a-new-survey-finds-eighty-percent-of-women-have-experienced-sexual-harassment.

Cheeks, Maura. 2018. "How Black Women Describe Navigating Race and Gender in the Workplace." *Harvard Business Review.* (March 26). https://hbr.org/2018/03/how-black-women-describe-navigating-race-and-gender-in-the-workplace.

Connley, Courtney. 2019. "Corporate America's Diversity and Inclusion Efforts Are Still Failing Black Employees, New Report Says." *CNBC.* (December 13). https://www.cnbc.com/2019/12/13/report-corporate-americas-diversity-efforts-fail-black-employees.html.

Diamond, Anna. 2018. "Fifty Years Later Remembering Resurrection City and the Poor People's Campaign of 1968." *Smithsonian Magazine* 49 (May). https://www.smithsonianmag.com/history/remembering-poor-peoples-campaign-180968742/.

Escobari, Marcela, Ian Seyal, and Michael J. Meaney. 2019. "Realism about Reskilling: Upgrading the Prospects of America's Low-Wage Workers." (November 7). https://www.brookings.edu/research/realism-about-reskilling/.

Funk, Cary, and Kim Parker. 2018. "Blacks in STEM Jobs Are Especially Concerned about Diversity and Discrimination in the Workplace." Pew Research Center. (January 9). https://www.pewsocialtrends.org/2018/01/09/blacks-in-stem-jobs-are-especially-concerned-about-diversity-and-discrimination-in-the-workplace/.

Gabe, Todd, Jaison R. Abel, and Richard Florida. 2018. "Can Low-Wage Workers Find Better Jobs?" Federal Reserve Bank of New York. (April). https://www.newyorkfed.org/medialibrary/media/research/staff_reports/sr846.pdf.

Gambino, Lauren. 2020. "Kamala Harris and Mike Pence Clash over Coronavirus Response in Vice-Presidential Debate." *The Guardian.* (October 8). https://www.theguardian.com/us-news/2020/oct/07/debate-kamala-harris-mike-pence-latest-news.

Gould, Elise. 2019. "Latina Workers Have to Work Nearly 11 Months into 2019 to Be Paid the Same as White Non-Hispanic Men in 2018." Economic Policy Institute. (November 19). https://www.epi.org/blog/latina-pay-gap-2019/.

Gould, Elise, and Heidi Shierholz. 2020. "Not Everyone Can Work from Home." Economic Policy Institute. (March 19). https://www.epi.org/blog/black-and-hispanic-workers-are-much-less-likely-to-be-able-to-work-from-home/.

Gould, Elise, and Valerie Wilson. 2020. "Black Workers Face Two of the Most Lethal Preexisting Conditions for Coronavirus—Racism and Economic Inequality." Economic Policy Institute. (June 1). https://www.epi.org/publication/black-workers-covid/.

Greene, Jeanie Ahearn. 2006. *Blue-Collar Women at Work with Men: Negotiating the Hostile Environment.* Westport, CT: Praeger.

Guendelsberger, Emily. 2019. "I Was a Fast-Food Worker. Let Me Tell You about Burnout." *Vox*. (July 15). https://www.vox.com/the-highlight/2019/7/6/20681186/fast-food-worker-burnout.

Hirsch, Arlene. 2018. "Taking Steps to Eliminate Racism in the Workplace." The Society for Human Resource Management. (October 22). https://www.shrm.org/resourcea ndtools/hr-topics/behavioral-competencies/global-and-cultural-effectiveness/pages/taking-steps-to-eliminate-racism-in-the-workplace.aspx.

Huang, Jess, Alexis Krivkovich, Irina Starikova, Lareina Yee, and Delia Zanoschi. 2019. "Women in the Workplace 2019." McKinsey & Company. (October). https://www.mckinsey.com/featured-insights/gender-equality/women-in-the-workplace-2019.

Iceland, John. 2006. *Poverty in America: A Handbook*. Berkeley: University of California Press.

IPS Staff. 2017. "Report: The Poor People's Campaign, 50 Years Later." (December 4). https://ips-dc.org/report-poor-peoples-campaign-50-years-later/.

Jameel, Maryam, and Joe Yerardi. 2019. "Workplace Discrimination Is Illegal. But Our Data Shows It's Still a Huge Problem." *Vox*. (February 28). https://www.vox.com/policy-and-politics/2019/2/28/18241973/workplace-discrimination-cpi-investigation-eeoc.

Joint Economic Committee, the Senate. 2020. "The Impact of the Coronavirus on the Working Poor and People of Color." https://www.jec.senate.gov/public/_cache/files/bbaf9c9f-1a8c-45b3-816c-1415a2c1ffee/coronavirus-race-and-class-jec-final.pdf.

Kaiser, Cheryl R., and Jennifer S. Pratt-Hyatt. 2009. "Distributing Prejudice Unequally: Do Whites Direct Their Prejudice toward Strongly Identified Minorities?" *Journal of Personality and Social Psychology* 96: 432–445.

Kang, Sonia K., Katherine K. DeCelles, András Tilsik, and Sora Jun. 2016. "Whitened Résumés: Race and Self-Presentation in the Labor Market." *Administrative Science Quarterly* 61: 494–498.

Katz, Michael B. 2003. "In the Shades of the Poorhouse: A Social History of Welfare in America," pp. 225–253 in Dalton Conley (ed.), *Wealth and Poverty in America: A Reader*. Malden, MA: Blackwell.

Keplinger, Ksenia, Stefanie K. Johnson, and Liza Y. Barnes. 2019. "Women at Work: Changes in Sexual Harassment between September 2016 and September 2018." *PLOS ONE*. (July 17). https://journals.plos.org/plosone/article?id=10.1371/journal.pone.0218313.

Krivkovich, Alexis, Marie-Claude Nadeau, Kelsey Robinson, Nicole Robinson, Irina Starikova, and Lareina Yee. 2018. "Women in the Workplace 2018." McKinsey & Company. (October). https://www.mckinsey.com/featured-insights/gender-equality/women-in-the-workplace-2018.

Miller, Susan. 2019. "'Shocking Numbers:' Half of LGBTQ Adults Live in States Where No Laws Ban Job Discrimination." *USA Today*. (October 8). https://www.usatoday.com/story/news/nation/2019/10/08/lgbt-employment-discrimination-half-of-states-offer-no-protections/3837244002/.

National Women's History Museum. 2020. "Working Women in the Suffrage Movement." http://www.crusadeforthevote.org/working-women-movement.

Novello, Amanda. 2018. "11 Ways American Workers Are Falling Behind the Rest of the World." The Century Foundation. (September 7). https://tcf.org/content/commentary/11-ways-american-workers-are-falling-behind-the-rest-of-the-world/?session=1.

Ohio History Central. 2020. "Women in the Industrial Workforce." https://ohiohistor ycentral.org/w/Women_in_the_Industrial_Workforce.

Organisation for Economic Co-operation and Development. 2020. "Employment: Time Spent in Paid and Unpaid Work by Sex." (March 5). https://stats.oecd.org/index.aspx?queryid=54757#.

Pager, Devah, and David S. Pedulla. 2003. "The Mark of a Criminal Record." *American Journal of Sociology* 108 (March): 937–975. https://scholar.harvard.edu/pager/publications/mark-criminal-record.

Palavi, Gogoi. 2020. "Why a Historic Wave of Latino Prosperity Is Under Threat Now." *npr*. (May 10). https://www.npr.org/2020/05/10/853049239/historic-wave-of-latino-prosperity-is-threatened-by-devastating-job-losses.

PayScale. 2019. "The State of the Gender Pay Gap 2019." https://www.payscale.com/data/gender-pay-gap.

Pedulla, David S., and Devah Pager. 2015. "Here's How Minority Job Seekers Battle Bias in the Hiring Process." *The Conversation*. (July 21). https://theconversation.com/heres-how-minority-job-seekers-battle-bias-in-the-hiring-process-43897.

Quillian, Lincoln, Devah Pager, Ole Hexel, and Arnfinn H. Midtbøen. 2017. "Meta-analysis of Field Experiments Shows No Change in Racial Discrimination in Hiring over Time." *Proceedings of the National Academy of Sciences of the United States of America.* (September 12). https://www.pnas.org/content/early/2017/09/11/1706255114.

Ross, Martha, and Nicole Bateman. 2019. "Meet the Low-Wage Workforce." Metropolitan Policy Program at Brookings. (November). https://www.brookings.edu/wp-content/uploads/2019/11/201911_Brookings-Metro_low-wage-workforce_Ross-Bateman.pdf.

Ryo, Hie Jin, Hayley Brown, and Shaun Fremstad. 2020. "A Basic Demographic Profile of Workers in Frontline Industries." Center for Economic and Policy Research. (April). https://cepr.net/wp-content/uploads/2020/04/2020-04-Frontline-Workers.pdf.

Sanchez, Melissa. 2020. "'Essential' Factory Workers Are Afraid to Go to Work and Can't Afford to Stay Home." *ProPublica*. (March 24). https://www.propublica.org/article/coronavirus-essential-factory-workers-illinois.

Stop Street Harassment. 2018. "A National Study on Sexual Harassment and Assault." http://www.stopstreetharassment.org/wp-content/uploads/2018/01/Survey-Questions-2018-National-Study-on-Sexual-Harassment-and-Assault.pdf.

Strauss, Becky. 2019. "Battling Racial Discrimination in the Workplace." D.C. Policy Center. (January 24). https://www.dcpolicycenter.org/publications/battling-racial-discrimination-in-the-workplace.

Supreme Court of the United States. 2020. "Bostock v. Clayton County Georgia." (June 15). https://www.supremecourt.gov/opinions/19pdf/17-1618_hfci.pdf.

Trattner, Walter I. 1994. *From Poor Laws to Welfare State*. New York: Free Press.

U.S. Bureau of the Census. 2019. Table P-2. "Race and Hispanic Origin of People by Median Income and Sex: 1947 to 2018." https://www.census.gov/data/tables/time-series/demo/income-poverty/historical-income-people.html.

U.S. Bureau of Labor Statistics. 2019a. "A Profile of the Working Poor, 2017." (April). https://www.bls.gov/opub/reports/working-poor/2017/home.htm.

U.S. Bureau of Labor Statistics. 2019b. "Labor Force Characteristics by Race and Ethnicity, 2018." (October). https://www.bls.gov/opub/reports/race-and-ethnicity/2018/home.htm.

U.S. Department of Agriculture. 2020. "Farm Labor." (April 22). https://www.ers.usda.gov/topics/farm-economy/farm-labor/.

U.S. Department of Health and Human Services. 2020. "Poverty Guidelines." (January 8). https://aspe.hhs.gov/poverty-guidelines.

U.S. Equal Employment Opportunity Commission. 2014. "Women in the American Work-force." https://www.eeoc.gov/eeoc/statistics/reports/american_experiences/women.cfm.

U.S. Equal Employment Opportunity Commission. 2015. "Testimony of Fatima Goss Graves Vice President for Education and Employment National Women's Law Center." (January 14). https://www.eeoc.gov/eeoc/meetings/1-14-15/graves.cfm.

U.S. Equal Employment Opportunity Commission. 2020. "Overview." https://www.eeoc.gov/eeoc/.

Waddell, Kaveh. 2018. "The Quicksand of Low-Wage Work." *Axios*. (July 18). https://www.axios.com/low-wage-work-automation-1531881974-ca596ad4-cea8-4849-a165-c4c9adf2313c.html.

Wezerek, Gus, and Kristen R. Ghodsee. 2020. "Women's Unpaid Labor Is Worth $10,900,000,000,000." *The New York Times*. (March 4). https://www.nytimes.com/interactive/2020/03/04/opinion/women-unpaid-labor.html.

Williams, Joseph. 2014. "My Life as a Retail Worker: Nasty, Brutish, and Poor." *The Atlantic*. (March 11). https://www.theatlantic.com/business/archive/2014/03/my-life-as-a-retail-worker-nasty-brutish-and-poor/284332/.

Wright, Richard. 1991. *Black Boy*. New York: The Library of America. Originally published in 1945.

Zurcher, Anthony. 2020. "Supreme Court LGBT Ruling: Why It Is Such a Big Deal." BBC News. (June 15). https://www.bbc.com/news/world-us-canada-53055937.

6

FACING FORMIDABLE CHALLENGES

✳ #19 throughout. similar to 16

One morning in the fall of 2017, Kiarra Boulware caught a bus to Baltimore's Bon Secours Hospital, where she would struggle to reduce the approximate 200 excess pounds she carried on her 5-foot-2-inch body. Her weight was hardly the only major problem Kiarra faced. She had grown up in a community filled with death, drugs, and violence, and recently had overcome her alcoholism. However, she continued to engage in binge eating, consuming plates of quesadillas or mozzarella sticks in minutes. Kiarra's heaviness produced additional serious conditions for the 27-year-old woman—sleep apnea, diabetes, and menstrual dysregulation, which made her worry that she wouldn't be able to have children.

At the hospital Kiarra told the doctor, "I don't want to be fat …but I don't know how to not be fat." Kiarra had struggled with the feeling that diet is a mystery she might never solve. Still, she would try to counteract binge eating, sometimes developing a meal plan for the week but then succumbing to a massive intake of Popeye's fried chicken by midweek. Like many of the inhabitants of her community where obesity and diabetes are prevalent, Kiarra blamed herself for her poor health, but other factors also came into play.

In Baltimore, neighborhoods differ considerably in healthiness. Sandtown, where Kiarra grew up, is 97 percent Black, with half its inhabitants living in poverty. It was a difficult setting. The author of the article describing Kiarra's struggles spent a year in Baltimore, particularly in her neighborhood, and learned that child molestation and drug addiction were widespread. Kiarra became pregnant at 12 and gave birth at 13. Within a year the baby died unexpectedly, and Kiarra was so traumatized she spent a month in a psychiatric unit. Once home her boyfriend physically and sexually abused her. For solace Kiarra turned to food—binge eating, a common response for victims of abuse (Khazan 2018). Figure 6.1 indicates that Kiarra is a member of the racial group that appears to have the greatest risk of high obesity levels.

13

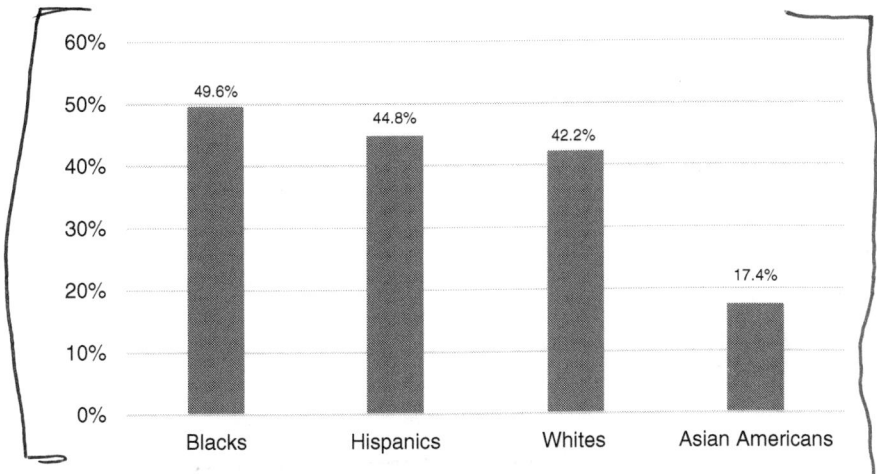

FIGURE 6.1 Racial-Group Members' Self-Reported Obesity Levels[1]
Source: Centers for Disease Control and Prevention 2020a.
Note: Diet is one factor contributing to group members' differences in their obesity. Undoubtedly levels of education, income, and perhaps genetics also play a role.
[1] The data come from the Behavioral Risk Factor Surveillance System of the Centers for Disease Control and Prevention.

A major factor making Kiarra's life difficult was the neighborhood in which she lived, one of the issues about to be examined. Instead of focusing on the three at-risk groups, the upcoming chapter looks at six issues—neighborhoods, food and nutrition, health care, elderly people's longevity and lifestyle, climate change and inequality, and finally blacks' incarceration—indicating how deficiencies and dangers associated with those issues affect the disadvantaged groups.

The Neighborhood Impact

In his research, sociologist William Julius Wilson has emphasized the influence that neighborhoods have had on poor people—an influence, he cautioned, that observers often overlook. For instance, Wilson cited a study in Pittsburgh where Black and white youths were compared without taking into account their neighborhoods, and the results showed that the African Americans were more often delinquent than the whites. However, 41 percent of Black youths and only 2 percent of their white counterparts lived in poverty-stricken neighborhoods featuring extensive unemployment and single-parent families, prominent conditions promoting delinquency. In fact, when researchers compared Black and white youths from nonpoor families, the differences in delinquent behavior simply disappeared (Wilson 1996, 265).

Wilson was impressed by the neighborhood deterioration that Blacks and other minorities often face, indicating it was distinctly different from his experience. Growing up in the 1940s and 1950s, he conceded that Black families like his "were poor ... but we didn't feel trapped in poverty." Even in low-income areas, the schools were different, with deeply committed teachers. "I remember a white teacher calling me in and telling me that I had a very high I.Q. and it was time I started living up to my potential" (American Public Media 1988). Furthermore in Wilson's childhood, whites were both in the neighborhood and at school, and while some racism occurred, he generally felt comfortable with them. Modern inner-city Black children, Wilson indicated, "have practically no contact at all with white people, and when they do encounter white people they are intimidated." Generally young Blacks are without role models emphasizing how life could be different, perhaps better, and "[o]n the contrary ... [t]hey are exposed to an environment that provides a vast opportunity for crime, drugs, hustling, [and] illicit sex" (American Public Media 1988).

Like Wilson current social scientists have considered the influence that neighborhoods, particularly poverty-level neighborhoods, have on their residents. So in the 1990s a government project called Moving to Opportunity (MTO) recruited more than 4,000 families, primarily headed by Black or Hispanic mothers coming from five cities, and sent them to three neighborhoods that varied in residents' income and that will be described in more detail presently (Chang 2018; Kling 2008).

Two decades later economists Raj Chetty and Nathaniel Hendren, eventually joined by Lawrence F. Katz, assessed MTO while also undertaking a much larger study. Gathering data from over 5 million families around the country, the investigators found that the adult earnings for children moving to better neighborhoods, as compared to results for children already living there, would improve depending on how much time they lived in the new locale. While earlier studies focused on adults and older youths, these investigators determined it was important to study young children to predict their later earnings (Chetty and Hendren 2015, 1–7). The researchers emphasized that "our findings imply that much of the variation across neighborhoods documented in observational studies does in fact reflect causal effects of place, but that these effects arise through accumulated childhood exposure rather than impacts on adults" (Chetty and Hendren 2015, 8).

Once they finished the national study, the economists focused on families that had been involved in the MTO project, expecting to find valuable detail from the data. The study involved over 8,000 children, three quarters of whom were born before 1991. The families had been randomly placed in three types of neighborhoods before the children were 13 years old and had remained in them until at least the age of 18. In one district the families had received a subsidized housing voucher requiring them to settle in a neighborhood with a poverty rate under 10 percent; in a second group, the recipients obtained a subsidized housing voucher but were not restricted in their residential location; and finally a set of families received no vouchers but had access to public housing. Some of the families with the voucher prompting them to relocate to a neighborhood with a poverty rate under 10 percent did not make that move when the MTO study took place. As a result neighborhood poverty rates for that segment of families were somewhat higher than would have been expected if all of them obeyed the directive; nonetheless a distinct pattern did emerge.

The economists' findings indicated that the poverty rates for the three types of neighborhoods were 19 percent for those with vouchers directed to the low-poverty locations, 29 percent for families who received a voucher but were unrestricted regarding their residential area, and 41 percent for those in public housing. Notably, by their middle twenties, the children growing up in the fairly low poverty settings earned nearly $3,500 a year more than their counterparts who lived in public housing, and the children whose parents received vouchers not restricting their location ended up in the middle, earning about $1,600 more than their public-housing peers (Chetty et al. 2016, 860–62, 856–58).

Chetty et al. wrote,

> We conclude that the Moving to Opportunity experiment generated substantial gains for children who moved to lower-poverty neighborhoods when they were young. We estimate that moving a child out of public housing to a low-poverty area when young [at age eight on average] ... will increase the child's total lifetime earnings by about $302,000.
>
> *increase in lifetime earnings*   (Chetty et al. 2016, 859–60)

It is a noteworthy conclusion, suggesting a success rate for the MTO project that would be hard to rival with any other approach.

One's neighborhood can have an impact in other ways. A study of nearly 9,000 Chicago residents found that the more affluent women were, the less vulnerable they felt to such potentially dangerous people as public drunks or loitering strangers. The conclusion seems reasonable. As women become more active in the economy, they are more indispensable to the community at large and become more confident that the police and other local organizations will readily mobilize on their behalf. In contrast, women of color and immigrants, who tend to be less affluent and well connected, have considerably less reason to feel supported in their neighborhoods (Jackson et al. 2017, 204–05).

African American women's vulnerability within their communities is often readily apparent. Since the days of slavery and the subsequent Jim Crow era, they have often been completely unprotected from sexual abuse and exploitation and, brutalized as they have been, often feel it is hopeless to report assaults. A study featuring 25 in-depth interviews suggested that in poor communities the prevailing standards "continue to cultivate the perception of Black women as being unvictimizable" (Norwood 2018, 98). In other words within these neighborhoods, violence against African American women has been so common that regardless of the level of brutal treatment inflicted, many Americans are incapable of visualizing them as victims. A reference in Chapter 7 addresses the growing recognition of police killings of Black women following Breonna Taylor's death.

For the women themselves, however, the ever-present dangers have been a constant reality. Lynn, one of the interviewees in the study just cited, spoke matter-of-factly about violence in the neighborhoods in which she had lived. She told the author,

> [One] of my friends, she's dead. She didn't make it to 22, so, you know what I'm saying? I'm 45. It's hard out—you're in here. You're not out there … I'm out there. I see things. I see all kinds of things. I see a girl in the alley one day; I lean back, she's getting raped. At least I took a phone and called 911. In broad daylight. This stuff happens [here], you know what I'm saying? I move to Cypress [another poor, largely black neighborhood]. It doesn't make a difference. It's bad there, too.
>
> *(Norwood 2018, 113)*

Like the impact of neighborhoods, food and nutrition are factors that can also have a significant influence on people's quality of life.

A Struggle Involving Food and Nutrition food insecurity

In the course of a normal year, about 11 percent of American households, including 7 percent of children, are food insecure, possessing insufficient funds and other resources to provide food for active, healthy, hunger-free living (Coleman-Jensen et al. 2019). Upcoming information indicates that during the pandemic the numbers rose appreciably.

Poor caretakers have a number of food-related challenges with which they deal. One is the dire reality of simply lacking the money to pay for food. Research from the San Francisco Bay area on more than 160 families varied in income indicated that unlike middle-class caretakers, who avoid hunger and can afford to emphasize the importance of nutrition, the poor mothers in the study took advantage of a temporary food supply by allowing their children whatever they desired. While they recognized that children's choices might not be nutritionally ideal, many wanted to compensate for painful times when they could not provide their children enough to eat.

Elissa, an Hispanic single mother who lived below the poverty line, was a case in point. She could recall having almost no money for food, and so when she worked overtime or found a supermarket sale, she simply let her children eat their favorite foods. She explained,

> They'll be like, "Can I get some Hot Pockets, Mom?" Or "Can I get some pizza bites?" …. Or "Can you get me a soda?" I think they pretty much have all … they want … to feel comfortable with what they're eating.
>
> *(Fielding-Singh 2017, 435)*

Another local condition affecting poor families facing hunger concerns their access to food supplies. For example, Black and Native American neighborhoods are often distant from chain supermarkets with their fairly high-quality and fresh products—foods that tend to support a healthy lifestyle and reduce or eliminate the prospect of obesity (Odoms-Young et al. 2012).

Additionally research has indicated that through the second decade of the twenty-first century, poor racial minorities tend to have diets that feature suboptimal intake of fruits, vegetables, and whole grains and an excess of fast foods and sweetened beverages. Once settled in the US, immigrant Hispanic children and adults tend to increase their amounts of both fast foods and sweetened drinks. Overall these consumption patterns are unhealthy, supporting higher rates of obesity among some racial minorities than among whites (Haroldson et al. 2015; Odoms-Young et al. 2012; Truesdale et al. 2019).

While people who are food insecure face serious difficulties, the following study makes it clear that families facing this challenge have some proven tactics for dealing with the issue.

Poor Caretakers' Coping Strategies for Obtaining Food   *Coping Strategies*

An investigation of 12 African American caregivers, most of whom were mothers with preschool children, found that they had several methods of maximizing their food intake and avoiding food insecurity.

A standard approach was to shop at discount stores, studiously choosing economical products. Keisha was particularly committed to making her choices after carefully reading and comparing grocery-store flyers. She said, "So if the meat is on sale here, then I'll get that from there. If the pop or the dairy products are on sale at Strack-Van-Til's then I will … stop in" (Jarrett et al. 2014, 199).

Another purchasing tactic involved buying so-called "family packages," thereby saving on the cost of individual items. Like Keisha, Ayana carefully compared stores' offers, particularly on large quantities. She explained,

> [At] the Meat House … a half a slab of pork chops gonna' run me about $12…. I got at least 20 or 21 pork chops…. I go to Fair Play to buy some meat. I buy a pack of pork chops, goin' to cost me about $7. You got about five or six of 'um in there?
>
> *(Jarrett et al. 2014, 201)*

Several caregivers found that undershopping, saving money for what might be a lean month coming up, was a useful food-buying practice. Claudia explained, "Me as a mother … I don't overspend…. If I had more in my budget, I will hold that until the next budget…. I have to feed them [my children] the next month and I might not have enough" (Jarrett et al. 2014, 201).

Another approach, which came into play at crisis times, involved such food-consumption savings as stretching leftovers, eating less, and rationing certain foods. Stretching leftovers could involve some planning. Candice explained that when facing a food shortage, she

> can usually stretch something out. There are always leftovers in the freezer.... If I cook a lot ... I know somethin's goin' to be left over. Put it in zip lock bags, put it in the freezer. Later on ... I just pull it out and heat it up and do the sides, maybe, corn, and potatoes.
>
> *(Jarrett et al. 2014, 202)*

At times Candice gave her children less to eat, with fairly good results. She would tell them,

> You used to eatin' three times a day. Now you're eating twice.... But when you know it's nothin' you can do, you just have to build a bridge and get over it.... So then you've got to get adjusted. But normally it's just for a short period. So everybody seems to work together on it.
>
> *(Jarrett et al. 2014, 203)*

An additional tactic, which some of the caretakers occasionally used, involved seeking help from social networks, most frequently extended kin as well as friends and neighbors. Sometimes families found that governmental sources and community resources could provide food assistance. While government programs could alleviate food insecurity, their eligibility standards were often difficult to navigate. Only three of nine households in the study that qualified for the WIC (Women, Infants, and Children) program sponsored by the Food and Nutrition Service of the U.S. Department of Agriculture participated and spoke positively about it (Jarrett et al. 2014, 204–07).

The COVID-19 pandemic brought unprecedented food insecurity for many American families. In July 2020, Feeding America, a nonprofit organization, which controls the nation's largest network of over 200 food banks and pantries, distributed 715 million pounds of food, a 62 percent increase from the average monthly amount before the pandemic. At that time the Brookings Institution reported that the childhood increase in food insecurity was particularly notable—about 14 million American children, 16.5 percent of households with children, were not getting enough to eat, a rate that was 5.6 times greater than two years earlier (Arango 2020; Bauer 2020). It appears highly regrettable that various government agencies did not make a greater organizational and financial contribution.

When the pandemic struck, many families contained members who had good jobs but either lost them or had their hours sharply reduced. One single mother said that previously "I felt myself finally in the middle class." Another woman explained that after she lost her job and her husband's hours were drastically cut, she awoke each morning to a sense of "impending doom" (Arango 2020).

Like shortages of food, disadvantaged groups often suffer distinct deficiencies in medical treatment.

Health-Care Inequities

Throughout the nation, health-care administration has always faced financial challenge. The dire situation became more evident with the onslaught from the coronavirus when the depleted state and local health departments suddenly found themselves facing a number of expensive tasks produced by the pandemic (Bosman and Fausset 2020). Disadvantaged groups have been particularly vulnerable.

Poor People's Health Risks and Health-Care Programs

Widespread evidence demonstrates that when comparing the poor and the non-poor on issues related to health, one finds significant differences in both exposure to risk factors and in access to health care. Low-income individuals suffer higher rates of such chronic diseases as diabetes, stroke, and heart disease and are more often susceptible to such dangerous conditions as smoking, substance abuse, physical inactivity, and obesity. *residence + health*

Less affluent communities tend to have such structural conditions contributing to chronic diseases and obesity as lowered access to fresh foods, extensive fast-food locations selling items that are often filled with large amounts of sugar, fat, and other unhealthy ingredients, and less open space, e.g. an absence of parks encouraging residents to exercise. In addition, their residential areas often contain such unhealthy conditions as the frequent presence of violence, high levels of environmental pollution, crowding, and the absence or scarcity of effective heating, air conditioning, water, and electricity and for some the actual loss of housing (Khullar and Chokshi 2018).

Besides health-related disadvantages in their communities, the American poor have always faced deficient health-care programming. Poor people are less likely to have medical insurance and access to high-quality medication, technology, and competent medical personnel. *among other countries ↓*

A six-country study in 2006 indicated that compared to residents in Australia, Canada, Germany, New Zealand, and the United Kingdom, low-income Americans suffered a greater disparity between the quality of their health care and that which more affluent individuals received than did their counterparts in the other five nations (Hospitals & Health Networks 2006).

More recently an investigation found a similar pattern with 32 wealthy and middle-income nations—that when the quality of respondents' self-rated health were assessed, Americans revealed a larger gulf in the responses between the most affluent third of the citizens and the least affluent third than did their counterparts in all but two of the other countries (Hero et al. 2017).

#3 on quiz

Joachim O. Hero, the lead author in the study, indicated that a higher per-centage of Americans than respondents in the other countries noted that many of their fellow residents lacked access to the health care they needed. On the other hand, US participants were less likely than other interviewees to assert that it was unfair for the more affluent to receive better health care. Hero concluded, "The combination of those two things raises this question: Is there a lack of political will to address the issue of disparities in the U.S., relative to countries where we know they do a lot better on this issue?" (Johnson 2017). Currently the answer seems clear.

Not surprisingly, people of color, who are disproportionately less affluent than whites, are more likely to suffer deficient medical treatment.

Racial Minorities' Dire Health-Care Outcomes

Compared to whites, racial minorities obtain less access to such important pre-ventative practices as inoculations and screening. An ominous reality is that with such factors as income, residential location, and health-insurance type taken into account, people of color still receive lower-quality care. Given that finding, it is hardly surprising that outcomes for certain serious medical conditions are often less satisfactory for racial minorities—for instance, a comparison between Blacks and whites on mortality rates for heart disease, breast cancer, and stroke. (Hostetter, and Klein 2018).

A significant finding indicates that Black and Native American women are two to three times more likely than white women to die from a pregnancy-related cause. While research has indicated that on average women of color have less effective health care and hospital facilities than whites as well as higher rates of diabetes, hypertension, and obesity, many expert observers are convinced that racist treatment comes into play (Centers for Disease Control and Prevention 2020b; Martin and Montagne 2017). Supportive evidence appears in over 200 stories of African American mothers that ProPublica and National Public Radio collected in which "the feeling of being devalued and disrespected by medical providers was a constant theme" (Martin and Montagne 2017).

In her book *Just Medicine: A Cure for Racial Inequality in American Healthcare*, Dayna Bowen Matthew, a lawyer specializing in public-health issues, suggested that while very few white medical personnel admit to maintaining negative views about racial groups, many unconsciously do. Such discriminatory treatment of patients of color involves **implicit racism**—the unconscious, biased perceptions of and behavior toward members of a racial group. Matthew suggested that such views and the actions that follow from them have a major impact on the quality of health care people of color receive (Matthew 2015, 55–74).

Other sources have provided supportive evidence. For instance, an online survey of 86 pediatricians found that their views of racial groups correlated with the treatment they provided their young patients—for instance, that the more racially biased in favor of whites, the greater the likelihood that these doctors prescribed pain-management medication for white children but not for their black peers (Sabin and Greenwald 2012).

White nurses have also displayed implicit racism. Hakima Tafunzi Payne, an African American mother of nine children and a former labor-and-delivery nurse, has been both a patient and a caregiver. She explained, "The nursing culture is white, middle-class, and female, so is largely built around that identity. Anything that doesn't fit that identity is suspect" (Martin and Montagne 2017).

While white medical personnel often appear to be largely unaware of their racist biases, the victims, people of color subjected to deficient health care, are painfully aware as interviews with 51 adults belonging to all the major racial groups demonstrated. An African American female respondent said angrily, "They [clinic staff] shun you. No compassion. You want to say something, but I don't because I need treatment, and who knows what they'll do" (D'Anna et al. 2018, 14). A Latina patient basically agreed. She explained,

> It feels bad. It feels ugly. You feel, well, discriminated and that you have no worth as a person. And then you think could it be because I am old... that I'm ugly, or what? If you see that other people are being called in and you had an [earlier] appointment. I at least notice and say something.
>
> *(D'Anna et al. 2018, 16)*

In this study men of color fared no better. A Black male stated,

> [You're] made to wait all day because of your color. You have an appointment but have to wait all day. They put everyone before you and you're the last to be seen ... I was the last one in the office.
>
> *(D'Anna et al. 2018, 19)*

Finally, it seems worth mentioning that this situation involving white medical staff members' implicit racism is similar to the pattern involving the hidden curriculum discussed in Chapter 4. In that instance the reference was to covert messages teachers and other school officials communicate to children, particularly on gender-related issues, and, once again, often unconsciously. One other similarity involving the issues: In both cases the victims can find the treatment damaging. Inevitably a similar process can occur with women.

Health Care for Women: A Critical Inequity

Once again, the focus involves a comparison of an American outcome with those in other wealthy countries. A study involving 11 affluent nations found the US behind the others in women's access to quality health care. In the course of treatment, American women were more likely to encounter various negative conditions, including the greatest tendency to skip costly treatments and the highest percentage of maternal mortality because of difficulties from pregnancy or childbirth. The study concluded, in fact, that American women were about three times more likely to die during child delivery than their counterparts in Sweden or Norway, indicating that the US is a dangerous country for giving birth (Gunja et al. 2018; Seervai 2019).

Participating in the US health-care system, Americans are likely to be unaware of its deficiencies compared to other wealthy nations. However, a foreigner experiencing the system for the first time is likely to spot stark differences right away. Before residing in the US, Roosa Tikkanen, a researcher in health policy and practice, had lived in Australia, England, Germany, and Norway. She said,

> Well, living in the U.S. was the first time I experienced being uninsured. Right after I had graduated from Harvard. To me, that was the biggest irony of all—a fresh master's ... [as a] public health graduate, having just spent nine months learning how unfair the American healthcare system can be—experiencing it myself.
>
> *(Seervai 2019)*

It appears that two factors primarily account for women's decided disadvantages:

- One contributor is implicit sexism, much like implicit racism previously examined. **Implicit sexism** is men's unconscious, biased perceptions of and behavior toward women.

Research suggests that male doctors' biases often produce a reduced interest in treating women's illnesses, leading to more inaccurate diagnoses for serious conditions like strokes and heart attacks and particularly for illnesses that primarily or only affect women.

The gender gap in treatment is clearly apparent when the issue is women's pain. A study indicated that in emergency rooms female patients need to wait longer for painkillers and, in fact, are more likely to be denied them. Many male doctors seem inclined to believe that women are overly sensitive, simply neurotic about pain.

Doctors' gender can often lead to different outcomes for female patients. For instance, in research conducted over two decades in Florida hospitals, investigators found that women treated for heart attacks by male doctors died at a higher rate than men, but with female physicians similar survival rates occurred (Cedars-Sinai 2019; Greenwood et al. 2018; Harvard Heart Letter 2009; Harvard Women's Health Watch 2017; Miller 2018).

Like disadvantaged victims discussed in previous chapters, female patients sometimes find ways to reduce or eliminate their discriminatory treatment. At age 19 Katie Ernst began suffering a host of symptoms—rashes, joint pains, hair loss, intense fatigue, and occasionally fainting spells and heart palpitations. When tests for autoimmune and cardiac diseases were negative, doctors told her that she was either depressed or suffering panic attacks. Ernst, now a lawyer, said, "I'm a go-getter … Being told that I was malingering was incredibly frustrating." Later when she married, Ernst decided to bring her husband to her appointments. Eventually she found a physician who discovered that she had lupus, a disease which more often affects women than men. The doctor admitted, "It was a good idea to bring your husband along … I have another patient with similar symptoms, and I've always assumed hers were psychosomatic" (Miller 2018). For that physician was this a lesson learned?

The second factor promoting women's disadvantaged health care is men's domination of major medical activities.

- While at present women are nearly half of all medical students, they comprise only 38 percent of medical-school faculty and only a small percentage of the leadership—21 percent of full professors, 15 percent of department chairs, and 16 percent of deans. Because of both men's control of medical facilities and their frequent sexist outlooks, the male-dominated medical establishment has historically paid less attention to studying women's bodies and the ailments that they encounter.

Maya Dusenbery, a journalist and the author of the well-known *Doing Harm: The Truth About How Bad Medicine and Lazy Science Leave Women Dismissed, Misdiagnosed, and Sick,* explained,

Because medicine has traditionally been a male-dominated field, it has invested relatively little in research to explain women's symptoms scientifically. Then when women have symptoms that health care providers can't explain, those symptoms are dismissed as made up, exaggerated, or psychogenic—all in the patient's head.

(Miller 2018)

It can take considerable perseverance to push forward to obtain a cure for one of the "women's diseases" when the male-dominated medical structure consistently fails to take female patients seriously. Meghan Cleary was a 45-year-old writer who had intense menstrual cramps and pelvic pain for over three decades. She explained, "The first doctor I went to told me I needed to get in touch with my body" (Miller 2018). Other male physicians suggested exercise or laxatives or simply learning to survive with the pain. Cleary kept looking for a solution, and she eventually received a diagnosis of endometriosis, where tissue similar to the lining of the uterus forms outside of it, and a surgeon burned away some endometriosis lesions. Afterwards, though, Cleary found the pain even more intense.

Finally Cleary discovered online a procedure called Laparoscopic Excision, considered by doctors who manage to cure the disease as the gold standard for its treatment. This approach permits the removal of diseased tissues but leaves

PHOTO 6.1 Research has shown that often unknowingly male doctors display implicit sexism, with the possibility of seriously affecting female patients' recovery. To offset that possibility, those doctors who become aware of the danger can consider consulting with female colleagues.

Source: Shutterstock/ Gorgev

surrounding areas and organs undamaged (Center for Endometriosis Care 2020). The surgery was a success, and for the first time since childhood Cleary was free of pain. The experience, she explained, transformed her life, but it angered her that the procedure was not better known and made available to many more women. Cleary concluded, "You've got millions of women who've had multiple instances of these burning surgeries with no relief. Yet ob-gyns [obstetricians-gynecologists] don't learn about the latest techniques for treating this disease in medical school. It's really heartbreaking" (Miller 2018).

Like health care, growing old is hardly a topic favoring the three disadvantaged groups we have been examining.

People Particularly At-Risk Growing Old

When it comes to the three categories of people examined in this book, the disadvantages they suffer are often significant. That is the case with the issue of longevity, where various risk factors are frequently close at hand.

The Poor and Their Prospects for Longevity

Extensive research has concluded that the smaller people's income, the shorter their life expectancy (Isaacs and Choudhury 2017). It is hardly a surprise.

What researchers found instructive was that certain factors played a highly influential role. When economist Raj Chetty and his research team obtained data from 1.4 billion records for Americans' earnings between 1999 and 2014, they focused on three risk factors strongly linked to longevity—obesity, lack of exercise, and smoking, with smoking the most lethal (Chetty et al. 2016; Woolf and Schoomaker 2019). In fact, even before the Chetty study, several investigations concluded that these sorts of "unhealthy behaviors" correlated with social class—that the higher people's membership, the less likely they were to engage in them (Pampel et al. 2010).

Smoking is a major case in point, with certain factors suggesting why poor people engage in it more extensively than their more affluent peers. Research reported by the Centers for Disease Control has indicated that people living below the poverty level smoke cigarettes on average for twice as many years as individuals whose income is three times the poverty rate. That reality suggests that within impoverished families, parents are more likely to be smoking, and that can be a powerful influence on the children.

Furthermore, this source reported, cigarette retailers have targeted poor areas, especially women, offering discount coupons, point-of-sale discounts, and the production of brands these women find particularly attractive (Centers for Disease Control and Prevention 2019).

Consider a case in point where Crystal R., a local resident, was taking photos in her neighborhood as part of a program publicizing the photography of women raising children in poverty. A pair of journalists observed, "Among Crystal's photos of piles of trash, abandoned lots and barbed wire fences is a striking

TABLE 6.1 Major Findings about Smoking and Social Class

Income and smoking	The poor averaging three times as much as individuals with income three times the poverty level
Education and smoking	High-school graduates smoking twice as much as college graduates
Lung-cancer effect	Less affluent classes, particularly the poor, suffering higher rates
Access to health care	Low-income groups having less access to health care, delaying treatment for lung cancer and other smoking-related diseases
The dangers of second-hand smoke	Greater exposure for the poor and other less affluent groups

Source: Centers for Disease Control and Prevention 2019.

picture: large advertisements for 'special prices' of cigarettes promising 'Kool – be true' that greet her on her way to shop for food" (Sandel and Boynton-Jarrett 2014). Table 6.1 summarizes major findings about the relationship between smoking and social class, once again suggesting disadvantaged circumstances poor people often face. A prevailing pattern is that individuals from lower social classes tend to smoke more heavily.

A disproportionate number of people of color are poor or low-income, affecting their life expectancy.

Elderly People of Color: Longevity and Lifestyle

While historical records about life expectancy do not generally meet current standards, the US did conduct a census each decade starting in 1790. The available data for 1850 indicated that whites' lives averaged 25.5 years and while battling lower living standards, more physically demanding work, and inferior medical care, Blacks only attained 21.4 years. A major contributor to both groups' short life expectancy was that about one quarter of infants died in the first year (Stanford School of Medicine 2020).

Modern records show some distinct differences in the racial groups' longevity averages. The overall national figure in 2018 was 78.86 years, and, extending from the highest to the lowest in years, Asian Americans were at 86.67, Hispanics at 82.89, whites at 79.12, African Americans at 75.54, and Native Americans at 75.06 (World Life Expectancy 2018). Between 2018 and 2060, the number of Americans who are 65 or older is expected to almost double from 52 to 95 million, with people of color increasing from 23 to 45 percent of the total (Mather et al. 2019).

In studying racial groups' longevity, researchers have raised some provocative issues, seeking insight into detail about racial-group differences. In particular:

- Does Asian Americans' lengthy life expectancy provide some insight as to why they live seven-and-a-half years longer than whites? Using data from the Centers for Disease Control and Prevention involving whites' and Asian Americans' deaths covering the years 2006 to 2010, a team of sociologists found that for all of the major causes of death, Asian Americans had a lower death rate than whites, with heart disease and cancer contributing the most to their advantage.

These findings suggest that an effective way to increase whites' longevity or, in fact, any group's, is to develop effective approaches for curtailing those deadly diseases. It could prove informative to learn if Asian Americans possess individual- or family-network health-related behaviors that support their advantage. Another topic to research might be a determination of details about their relationship to prominent diseases—whether they have been more adept at delaying their onset or have simply managed to live longer once they were affected by them (Acciai et al. 2015a; Acciai et al. 2015b).

- Why do Hispanics have a fairly lengthy life expectancy? Paola Scommegna, a veteran writer at the Population Reference Bureau, has noted that for over three decades, "demographers have probed why Hispanics' socioeconomic disadvantages are not linked to shorter lives, as they are for other generally nonaffluent racial and ethnic groups." This unusual pattern is known as the "Hispanic Health Paradox." Besides some indications that Hispanic immigrants to the US tend to be healthy, Scommegna found that relatively few are smokers (Scommegna 2017), with that finding impacting the first two diseases in the upcoming list. Using data primarily from the U.S. National Vital Statistics System, researchers have found that major contributors to Hispanics' longer life expectancy than non-Hispanic whites' included lower rates of major diseases and other prominent sources of death, including cancer (particularly lung cancer), chronic respiratory diseases, heart disease, unintentional injuries, suicide, and for men Parkinson's disease, and for women Alzheimer's disease (Arias et al. 2015; Fenelon 2016; Lariscy et al. 2016).

Unlike Hispanics, African Americans follow the dominant pattern, where a less affluent group has relatively low life expectancy.

- What are important findings involving Blacks' longevity? Relying on data from the U.S. National Vital Statistics System, investigators concluded that overall when compared to whites, Blacks have had higher rates of death for a wide variety of lethal conditions, including homicide, heart disease, diabetes, different types of cancer, stroke, and perinatal problems occurring to infants during or soon after birth (Cunningham et al. 2017; Kochanek et al. 2013).

Some results comparing Blacks' and whites' longevity have been startling. Examining the 500 largest American cities containing 66,000 or more residents, researchers from the Department of Health at the New York University School of Medicine found that Chicago had two neighborhoods with the largest gap in residents' expected longevity—30 years. In Streeterville, an attractive, affluent, largely white neighborhood, residents live on average to be 90 while only eight miles away in Englewood, a poor, rundown, violence-prone, primarily Black neighborhood with the kinds of life-threatening problems just listed, life expectancy is 60 (Lartey 2019; NYU University Langone Health NewsHub 2019; Schencker 2019). Commenting on that stark difference in longevity, Dr. Marc Gourevitch, the leading researcher in the NYU study, observed that "your zip code has as much to do with your health as your genetic code." He added, "Another way to look at that is that your zip code shouldn't determine whether you get to see your grandkids. And at some level, that's how I see and feel about these kinds of data. It's shocking" (Lartey 2019).

The following finding comparing Blacks and whites is hardly shocking but somewhat surprising. At age 80 throughout the nation, the life expectancy between Blacks and whites has disappeared, and then among the select number of individuals surviving into their nineties, African Americans have had a slight advantage over whites. A pair of psychologists wrote, "The survivors in the cohort of 90-year-old African Americans represent a unique group that seem to possess special characteristics that could provide insight into longevity." Preliminary research has suggested that certain genes in long-living Blacks have reacted with environmental conditions differently than they do in other racial groups (Whitfield and Thorpe 2017, 2).

Native Americans, the final group in the previous list of racial groups' longevity, have had nearly a four-year lower life expectancy than whites.

- American Indians and Alaska Natives have been persistently dying at higher rates than whites and other racial groups from various conditions, including heart disease, cancer, chronic liver disease and cirrhosis, suicide, unintentional injuries, chronic respiratory disease, assault/homicide, and diabetes (Indian Health Service 2019).

While Native Americans have the shortest life expectancy of the five groups reported, the gap separating them from the other racial groups has been declining. Margaret Moss, a member of the Rosebud Sioux tribe and an assistant dean at the University of Buffalo School of Nursing, is skeptical about that recently reported trend. She indicated that among her tribal members men average living to the late forties and women to the early fifties. Moss's impression is that the life-expectancy numbers get elevated by some individuals' suspect claims of Indian ancestry on their Census forms. "It's self-report. I'm not sure exactly where they are coming from," Moss said. "For instance, as we have seen on the news, people can say, 'Oh, I think my grandmother was Indian,' and then they click Indian, which can skew the numbers that are reported" (Lindsay 2018).

Besides seeking longevity, elderly people of color face the challenge of staying healthy. A large study of more than 230,000 people who completed the Medicare Health Outcomes Survey found that with key demographic factors controlled, elderly minority-group respondents, with the exception of Asian Americans, were more likely than non-Hispanic whites to report a variety of serious health-related issues, including poor mental health, extensive symptoms of disease and disability, and sensory limitations (Ng et al. 2015).

Good health tends to be very important to elderly people, and a study of nearly 2,000 women belonging to the major racial minorities and 80 years of age or older were no exception. When the researchers controlled for such factors as income, education, and social support, they found no significant differences in physical functioning among the racial groups. What they did find was that throughout the sample self-rated level of health was the only subjective factor consistently associated with quality of life. Participation in regular exercise tended to contribute to high levels of self-rated health (Cené et al. 2016).

At times elderly people of color can find that discrimination seriously threatens their quality of life. For instance, an experimental study of 80 elder-care facilities using testers found that compared to white applicants, Blacks were more likely to hear that there were no vacancies, that the waiting list was longer, or that certain health conditions such as incontinence made their acceptance problematic (Kenyon 2004).

Discussing health care, 53 elderly, primarily Black people at an urban senior center sometimes spoke positively about it but also provided criticisms and suggestions. Invariably these elderly patients wanted to be treated in a dignified manner that communicated effectively. A woman explained,

> No matter what we're not that damn friendly. Okay? That's the first thing. But I don't think they should be calling me honey child. You know. This is kind of condescending. I don't want that either. There must be a happy medium. Like, "Do you understand what I said? Do you really understand what I'm talking about?"
>
> *(Hansen et al. 2016)*

In some health-care settings, elderly minority-group members who have received discriminatory treatment can reach dangerous, even life-threatening conclusions about their medical care. For instance, at a center where staff members were working to improve the experience for Black women undergoing treatment for early-stage breast cancer, a nurse explained, "I had a patient tell me that she heard there is a cure for cancer and they are keeping it from patients." …. [The nurse added,] "I talked with her about how her care team did not want to see her or any patient suffer and we're here to do whatever is needed to care for her" (Hostetter and Klein 2018).

As the upcoming discussion indicates, racism is also a factor that comes into play in the course of environmental change.

Climate Change and Inequality

On August 16, 2020, the National Weather Service's automated weather station at Furnace Creek in Death Valley, California, recorded what appears to have been the hottest reading ever reliably registered on earth—129.9 Fahrenheit or 54.4 Celsius (*The Guardian* 2020). This reading emphasizes what is already well known—that global warming is an increasingly serious modern reality.

The Synthesis Report, a highly detailed study on climate change based on contributions from over 800 scientists, listed the many environmental problems modern nations face. The report indicated that dangers "are unevenly distributed between groups of people and between regions; risks are generally greater for disadvantaged people and communities everywhere" (Pachauri and Mayer 2014, 72). A UN document about The Synthesis Report added, "People who are socially, economically, culturally, politically, institutionally, or otherwise marginalized are especially vulnerable to climate change" (UN Environment Programme 2014). While poor countries with warm, dry climates producing shrinking crop yields will probably be among the first to experience a formidable impact (Goldenberg 2014), the US also contains some particularly vulnerable groups.

For instance, poor communities, which inevitably have limited resources, are likely to suffer considerably when environmental destruction occurs. A research team from the World Meteorological Organization concluded that because of progressive global warming an increase in intense (Category 4 and 5) hurricanes is likely to occur (Geophysical Fluid Dynamics Laboratory 2020).

In 2005 Hurricane Katrina hit New Orleans, the sixth poorest city in the nation with a 28-percent poverty rate, a condition which came into play as the storm unfolded (Shapiro and Sherman 2005). After the hurricane passed, more than 1 million residents, many of them poor, were shipped to nearby states where they had no family or friends, no job, and little sense of how to proceed with their lives. Some eventually felt satisfied with the relocation, but many preferred to return. Often, however, they could not.

What happened in New Orleans' Lower Ninth Ward occurred both elsewhere in the city and in other cities during numerous hurricanes. Because it was a poor area, the housing was generally old, badly built, or inadequately maintained. Katrina's impact was devastating, destroying massive numbers of homes in the area. Following the hurricane, the city established new safety standards increasing the cost of housing, and many poor families simply could not afford to return (White 2015).

The dire social-reproduction impact of race decisively influenced the relocation opportunities for whites and Blacks. Historically New Orleans has been a highly segregated city, with whites living along the river and on ridges while Blacks, including the more affluent, ended up with lower-quality housing in less desirable, less safe districts like the Lower Ninth Ward "below" the rest of the city in areas close to a poorly maintained shipping canal with walls that gave way during the storm, producing flooding that persisted for weeks.

The architects for the state-run Road Home program, which provided rebuilding grants to homeowners, developed a formula based on pre-storm home values and not rebuilding costs, providing whites much larger grants and making it more feasible for their owners to rebuild than their Black counterparts. Not surprisingly a local poll showed that among evacuated residents whites more often returned within a year of the hurricane—70 percent to 42 percent for African Americans (Reckdahl 2015).

PHOTO 6.2 Hurricane Katrina struck New Orleans, a racially segregated city, where whites tended to live in areas above the flooded districts while Blacks generally resided in lower-quality housing that was much more exposed to punishing winds and flooding. This photo, showing flood waters still ravaging homes, was taken nearly two weeks after the hurricane hit the city.

Source: Getty/ Helifilms Australia

Like many poor Blacks who formerly lived in the Lower Ninth Ward, Carol Young and her husband Michael wanted to return, but they lost both their house and Michael's job. Carol explained,

> Many days and nights I sit up in this apartment and I have cried. My whole life has been rooted up and I have been put somewhere else, somewhere I didn't ask to be at. You can mark my word; New Orleans is not coming back. It's a hard pill to swallow. It's like you're walking but your feet ain't going nowhere.
>
> *(Carlisle 2006)*

Native Americans is another racial minority that is particularly vulnerable to climate change and other environmental impacts. In Alaska, in particular, many Indians live close to the coast or to rivers, and as temperatures rise at well above the global average, a federal report indicated that flooding and erosion threaten 184 out of 213 (86 percent) of Native American villages. The inhabitants of the 31 most threatened villages qualify for relocation. In addition, traditional sources of food including salmon, trout, shellfish, and such marine animals as whales, walruses, seals, and ducks have been declining along with various plants traditionally used for medicines (National Congress of American Indians 2015; U.S. Climate Resilience Toolkit 2017).

Meanwhile in the Southwest, tribes experiencing climate change must deal with warmer temperatures, longer droughts, and plummeting water supplies. In the past, snow during the winter built snowpacks, masses of snow that produce natural reservoirs providing water during the drier months. However, as temperatures have risen, snowfall has reduced by two thirds since 1930, and the snowpacks have been diminishing, meaning less buildup of water.

Karletta Chief, a hydrologist (a specialist on the basic properties of water and its relationship with the environment) and a member of the Navaho tribe, indicated that recent loss of water had caused sand dunes to inundate many homes. For decades managing water has been a critical concern. Until she left for college, Chief never lived in a place where water came out of a faucet. For decades many Indians have needed to travel as much as 40 miles to fill huge drums that would provide water for several weeks (Gass 2015; Zielinski 2016).

In spite of the difficult life, most Navaho feel a commitment to keep up the struggle, believing that they are blessed to inhabit a special place. To strengthen their connection to the land, many bury a newborn child's umbilical cord nearby. Chief said, "Every day an individual wakes up praying, thankful to be living within the four sacred mountains ... I think that connection is resilient through time and space and climate" (Gass 2015).

While the two situations just described involving Native Americans and Blacks took place at selected locations, another impact of climate change has been much more widespread. As discussion in Chapter 4 indicated, government planners in the 1930s created maps of hundreds of American cities, redlining them for the alleged riskiness of investment. Neighborhoods containing people of color, particularly Blacks, usually received the lowest rating and as a result the least investment for federally backed loans and other credits, greatly limiting any hopes residents might have of improving their economic status. That disadvantage has carried into the present, with poor neighborhoods possessing limited parks and trees and an excess of heat-absorbing pavement, producing temperatures that are 5 degrees Fahrenheit higher in summer than in historically affluent districts. In such cities as Baltimore, Dallas, Denver, Miami, New York, and Portland, the summer temperatures in poor, largely Black neighborhoods can average as much as 20 degrees higher than in wealthier, primarily white areas (Plumer and Popovich 2020; Wilson 2020).

The preceding discussion suggests the persistent influence of racism, but its current impact pales in comparison to the effect produced in the course of the upcoming issue.

Black Lives Diminished

prison system

In 2017 there were slightly fewer than 1.5 million adult inmates in American prisons, with over 90 percent men. Blacks' imprisonment rate was almost six times greater than whites' and nearly double the rate for Hispanics. While African Americans represented 12 percent of the population, they were 33 percent of prisoners; whites were 64 percent of the nation's total but just 30 percent of all inmates; and Hispanics comprised 16 percent of American adults and 23 percent of prisoners (Gramlich 2019; Loesche 2017).

Dozens of studies have emphasized three conditions contributing to the skewed Black prison presence. One issue is that distinctly racist policies and practices contribute to the disparities. A prominent illustration involves drug crimes, with Blacks nearly four times more likely than whites to be arrested for drug offenses and two-and-a-half times as likely to be arrested for drug possession—in spite of the fact that the two groups use drugs at about the same rate. One of the issues involving drug arrests is who is arrested, with a study in New York City showing that police made the highly questionable choice to do more frisking of suspects in areas with a heavy concentration of Black residents than in those that are notably high in crime.

A second contributing factor, going hand in hand with the first, is implicit racism, with studies indicating that judges and the police often view people of color as threats to public safety. Furthermore the mass media continue to provide extensive coverage of crimes committed by people of color, particularly Black-on-white violent crimes (Nellis 2016; Simon 2016). In a national survey, the Pew Research Center found that Black adults are about five times more likely than whites to say that police have unfairly stopped them—44 vs. 9 percent. Fifty-nine percent of Black men compared to barely half the percentage of Black women—31 percent—make this claim (DeSilver et al. 2020).

A third factor, which is well documented in earlier chapters, is that African Americans often live in neighborhoods that are structurally at risk—that, in fact, about three fifths reside in segregated, poor areas with unstable families, low-quality schools, and high rates of crime, especially violent crime. Young Black males growing up in such areas are distinctly disadvantaged in developing the educational and interpersonal skills to do well in the job world and as a result become disproportionately vulnerable to criminal involvement as a source of income (Nellis 2016; Simon 2016).

Assessing the impact of these three factors, an observer can readily conclude that many young Black men end up facing an intersectional nightmare, where the combined impacts of race and social class promote a decidedly bleak future. Once several decades ago, I was meeting with Donald, a young African American man who had spent over ten years in prison. As our discussion drew toward a close, he said, "You know, Chris, you and your white friends grew up with college in your future. For me and my guys, our college was the slammer."

Throughout this chapter's discussion of the formidable challenges disadvantaged groups face, we have seen that they find that the barrage of social-reproduction conditions impacting their lives make a pleasant, productive life difficult. The last chapter addresses this reality, examining some means of combating those conditions and improving their prospects.

Key Terms in the Glossary

food insecure
implicit racism
implicit sexism

Discussion Topics

1. How does a poor neighborhood impact people differently from one that is not poor?
2. Do families that are food insecure have certain strategies that are particularly effective for obtaining food? Discuss.
3. Consider how implicit racism and implicit sexism affect health care. Provide specific examples from the text or elsewhere.
4. Is it fair or unreasonable to conclude that a gender bias exists in American health care?
5. Evaluate the following statement: Individuals who smoke or become obese simply lack the character and discipline to lead a healthy life.
6. In reading the section on longevity, did you find any of the observations about specific racial groups particularly interesting or surprising? Explain.
7. Focus on either neighborhoods or health care, describing what seem to be the most effective means of improving the prospect for some at-risk groups.
8. Discuss the challenges that disadvantaged groups need to face in the course of global warming. Be detailed, mentioning specific racial groups and the particular problems they will encounter.
9. Skim or reread the section about Blacks in prison. Then thinking about the issues raised concerning why Black men have such disproportionate presence in prison, research the topic. Drawing on the conclusions of the sources you find, write a paper focusing on the best ways to combat African American men's skewed incarceration rates.

Bibliography

Acciai, Francesco, Aggie J. Noah, and Glenn Firebaugh. 2015a. "Why Do Asian Americans Live So Much Longer than Other Ethnic Groups?" MedicalResearch.com. (July

20). https://medicalresearch.com/author-interviews/why-do-asian-americans-live-so-much-longer-than-other-ethnic-groups/15884/.

Acciai, Francesco, Aggie J. Noah, and Glenn Firebaugh. 2015b. "Pinpointing the Sources of the Asian Mortality Advantage in the United States." *Journal of Epidemiology and Community Health* 69 (October): 1006–1011.

American Public Media. 1988. "The American Underclass: Inner-City Ghettoes and the Norms of Citizenship." (April). http://americanradioworks.publicradio.org/features/blackspeech/wjwilson.html.

Arango, Tim. 2020. "Vans Full of Families Lined Up for Food." *The New York Times.* (September 4): A15–A19.

Arias, Elizabeth, Kenneth D. Kochanek, and Robert N. Anderson. 2015. "How Does Cause of Death Contribute to the Hispanic Mortality Advantage in the United States?" NCHS Data Brief. (November): 1–7.

Bauer, Laura. 2020. "About 14 Million Children in the US Are Not Getting Enough to Eat." Brookings. (July 9). https://www.brookings.edu/blog/up-front/2020/07/09/about-14-million-children-in-the-us-are-not-getting-enough-to-eat/.

Bosman, Julie, and Richard Fausset. 2020. "The Coronavirus Swamps Health Departments Already Crippled by Cuts." *The New York Times.* (March 14). https://lightlynews.com/2020/03/14/us/the-coronavirus-swamps-local-health-departments-already-crippled-by-cuts/.

Carlisle, Kristin. 2006. "It's Like You're Walking but Your Feet Ain't Going Nowhere." Shelterforce. (September 23). https://shelterforce.org/2006/09/23/its_like_youre_walking_but_your_feet_aint_going_nowhere/.

Cedars-Sinai. 2019. "Examining Gender Bias in Medical Care." https://www.cedars-sinai.org/research/news/cedars-science/2019/examining-gender-bias-in-medical-care.html.

Cené, Crystal W., Peggye Dilworth-Anderson, Iris Lang, Lorena Garcia, Liola Benevente, Milagros Rosal, Leslie Vaughn, Laura H. Coker, Gisele Corbie-Smith, and Mimi Kim. 2016. "Correlates of Successful Aging in Racial and Ethnic Minority Women Aged 80 and Older: Findings from the Women's Health Initiative." *The Journals of Gerontology Series A: Biological Sciences and Medical Sciences.* https://www.ncbi.nlm.nih.gov/pmc/articles/PMC5964968/.

Center for Endometriosis Care. 2020. "Excision of Endometriosis." (March). http://centerforendo.com/lapex-laparoscopic-excision-of-endometriosis.

Centers for Disease Control and Prevention. 2019. "Smoking & Tobacco Use among People of Low Socioeconomic Status." (November 25). https://www.cdc.gov/tobacco/disparities/low-ses/index.htm.

Centers for Disease Control and Prevention. 2020a. "Adult Obesity Facts." https://www.cdc.gov/obesity/data/adult.html.

Centers for Disease Control and Prevention. 2020b. "Infographic: Racial/Ethnic Disparities in Pregnancy-Related Deaths, 2007–2016." https://www.cdc.gov/reproductivehealth/maternal-mortality/disparities-pregnancy-related-deaths/infographic.html.

Chang, Alvin. 2018. "Living in a Poor Neighborhood Changes Everything about Your Life." *Vox.* (April 4). https://www.vox.com/2016/6/6/11852640/cartoon-poor-neighborhoods.

Chetty, Raj, and Nathaniel Hendren. 2015. "The Impacts of Neighborhoods on Intergenerational Mobility: Childhood Exposure Effects and County-Level Estimates." Harvard University and National Bureau of Economic Research. https://scholar.harvard.edu/files/hendren/files/nbhds_paper.pdf.

Chetty, Raj, Nathaniel Hendren, and Lawrence F. Katz. 2016. "The Effects of Exposure to Better Neighborhoods on Children: New Evidence from the Moving to Opportunity

Experiment." *American Economic Review* 106 (April): 855–902. https://scholar.harvard.edu/files/lkatz/files/chk_aer_mto_0416.pdf.

Chetty, Raj, Michael Stepner, and Sarah Abraham. 2016. "The Association between Income and Life Expectancy in the United States, 2001–2014." *Journal of the American Medical Association.* (April 26). https://jamanetwork.com/journals/jama/fullarticle/2513561?guestAccessKey=4023ce75-d0fb-44de-bb6c-8a10a30a6173.

Coleman-Jensen, Alisha, Matthew Rabbitt, Christian A. Gregory, and Anita Singh. 2019. "Household Food Security in the United States in 2018." United States Department of Agriculture. (September). https://www.ers.usda.gov/webdocs/publications/94849/err270_summary.pdf?v=963.1.

Cunningham, Timothy J., Janet B. Croft, Yong Liu, Hua Lu, Paul I. Eke, and Wayne H. Giles. 2017. "Vital Signs: Racial Disparities in Age-Specific Mortality among Blacks or African Americans — United States, 1999–2015." Centers for Disease Control and Prevention. https://www.cdc.gov/mmwr/volumes/66/wr/mm6617e1.htm.

D'Anna, Laura, Marissa Hansen, and Stephanie Sumstine. 2018. "Social Discrimination and Healthcare: A Multidimensional Framework of Experiences among a Low-Income Multi-Ethnic Sample." *Social Work in Public Health* 33. https://www.ncbi.nlm.nih.gov/pmc/articles/PMC6464629/.

DeSilver, Drew, Michael Lipka, and Dalia Fahma. 2020. "10 Things We Know about Race and Policing in the U.S." Pew Research Center. (June 3). https://www.pewresearch.org/fact-tank/2020/06/03/10-things-we-know-about-race-and-policing-in-the-u-s/.

Fenelon, Andrew. 2016. "Widening Life Expectancy Advantage of Hispanics in the United States: 1990–2010." *Journal of Immigrant and Minority Health* 17: 1130–1137.

Fielding-Singh, Priya. 2017. "A Taste of Inequality: Food's Symbolic Value across the Socioeconomic Spectrum." *Sociological Science* 4: 424–448. https://www.sociologicalscience.com/download/vol-4/august/SocSci_v4_424to448.pdf.

Gass, Henry. 2015. "Climate Change Turning Sacred Land against Navaho." *The Christian Science Monitor.* (June 19). https://www.csmonitor.com/Environment/2015/0619/Climate-change-turning-sacred-land-against-Navajo.

Geophysical Fluid Dynamics Laboratory. 2020. "Global Warming and Hurricanes." (February 5). https://www.gfdl.noaa.gov/global-warming-and-hurricanes/.

Goldenberg, Suzanne. 2014. "Climate Change: The Poor Will Suffer Most." *The Guardian.* (March 30). https://www.theguardian.com/environment/2014/mar/31/climate-change-poor-suffer-most-un-report.

Gramlich, John. 2019. "The Gap between the Number of Blacks and Whites in Prison Is Shrinking." Pew Research Center. (April 30). https://www.pewresearch.org/fact-tank/2019/04/30/shrinking-gap-between-number-of-blacks-and-whites-in-prison/.

Greenwood, Brad N., Seth Carnahan, and Laura Huang. 2018. "Patient–Physician Gender Concordance and Increased Mortality among Female Heart Attack Patients." Proceedings of the National Academy of Sciences. (August 21). https://www.pnas.org/content/115/34/8569.

The Guardian. 2020. "Death Valley Temperature Rises to 54.4 C—Possibly the Hottest Ever Recorded." (August 17). https://www.theguardian.com/us-news/2020/aug/17/death-valley-temperature-rises-to-544c-possibly-the-hottest-ever-reliably-recorded.

Gunja, Munira Z., Roosa Tikkanen, Shanoor Seervai, and Sara R. Collins. 2018. "What Is the Status of Women's Health and Health Care in the U.S. Compared to 10 Other Countries?" The Commonwealth Fund. (December 19). https://www.

commonwealthfund.org/publications/issue-briefs/2018/dec/womens-health-us-compared-ten-other-countries.

Hansen, Bryan, Nancy A. Hodgson, and Laura N. Gitlin. 2016. "It's a Matter of Trust: Older African Americans Speak about Their Health Care Encounters." National Center for Biotechnology Information. https://www.ncbi.nlm.nih.gov/pmc/articles/PMC4530080/.

Haroldson, Amber, Zachary Cordell, and Lauren Haldeman. 2015. "Analysis of Child Food Requests and Maternal Compliance in Low-Income Hispanic and Non-Hispanic Families." *Family & Consumer Sciences Research Journal* 44 (September): 37–50.

Harvard Heart Letter. 2009. "Women's Hearts Need Extra Attention." (April 1). https://web-a-ebscohost-com.scsu.idm.oclc.org/ehost/pdfviewer/pdfviewer?vid=3&sid=247db746-8277-4817-9ec3-94b46ec6104d%40sessionmgr4008.

Harvard Women's Health Watch. 2017. "What You May Not Know about Your Heart." (February). https://web-a-ebscohost-com.scsu.idm.oclc.org/ehost/pdfviewer/pdfviewer?vid=7&sid=247db746-8277-4817-9ec3-94b46ec6104d%40sessionmgr4008.

Hero, Joachim O., Alan M. Zaslavsky, and Robert J. Blendon. 2017. "The United States Leads Other Nations in Differences by Income in Perceptions of Health and Health Care." *Health Affairs* 36 (June). https://www.healthaffairs.org/doi/full/10.1377/hlthaff.2017.0006.

Hospitals & Health Networks. 2006. "U.S. Ranks Lowest of Six Affluent Nations in Patients' Opinions, Health Care Equity." (May). https://web-a-ebscohost-com.scsu.idm.oclc.org/ehost/pdfviewer/pdfviewer?vid=3&sid=9633aeb9-5b8c-4629-9448-d49e6cc47ae9%40sessionmgr4007.

Hostetter, Martha, and Sarah Klein. 2018. "In Focus: Reducing Racial Disparities in Health Care by Confronting Racism." The Commonwealth Fund. (September 27). https://www.commonwealthfund.org/publications/newsletter-article/2018/sep/focus-reducing-racial-disparities-health-care-confronting.

Indian Health Service. 2019. "Disparities." (October). https://www.ihs.gov/newsroom/factsheets/disparities/.

Isaacs, Katlin P., and Sharmila Choudhury. 2017. "The Growing Gap in Life Expectancy by Income: Recent Evidence and Implications for the Social Security Retirement Age." Congressional Research Service. https://fas.org/sgp/crs/misc/R44846.pdf.

Jackson, Aubrey L., Brian Soller, and Christopher R. Browning. 2017. "The Influence of Women's Neighborhood Resources on Perceptions of Social Disorder." *City & Community* 16 (June): 189–208.

Jarrett, Robin L., Ozge Sensoy Bahar, and Angela Odoms-Young. 2014. "'You Just Have to Build a Bridge and Get Over It': Low-Income African American Caregivers' Coping Strategies to Manage Inadequate Food Supplies." *Journal of Poverty* 18: 188–219.

Johnson, Carolyn Y. 2017. "America Is a Leader in Health Inequality." *The Washington Post.* (June 5). https://www.washingtonpost.com/news/wonk/wp/2017/06/05/america-is-a-world-leader-in-health-inequality/.

Kenyon, Nancy. 2004. "Racial Discrimination in Elder Care Facilities." *Human Rights* 31 (Spring): 18–19.

Khazan, Olga. 2018. "Being Black in America Can Be Hazardous to Your Health." *The Atlantic.* (July/August). https://www.theatlantic.com/magazine/archive/2018/07/being-black-in-america-can-be-hazardous-to-your-health/561740/.

Khullar, Dhruv, and Dave A. Chokshi. 2018. "Health, Income & Poverty: Where We Are & What Could Help." *Health Affairs.* (October). https://www.healthaffairs.org/do/10.1377/hpb20180817.901935/listitem/HPB_2017_RWJF_05_W.pdf.

Kling, Jeffrey R. 2008. "A Summary Overview of Moving to Opportunity: A Random Assignment Housing Mobility Study in Five U.S. Cities." Brookings. https://dares.travail-emploi.gouv.fr/IMG/pdf/Resume_J.Kling.pdf.

Kochanek, Kenneth D., Elizabeth Arias, and Robert N. Anderson. 2013. "How Did Cause of Death Contribute to Racial Differences in Life Expectancy in the United States in 2010?" NCHS Data Brief. (July): 1–7.

Lariscy, Joseph T., Claudia Nau, Glenn Firebaugh, and Robert A. Hummer. 2016. "Hispanic-White Differences in Lifespan Variability in the United States." *Demography* 53: 215–239.

Lartey, Jamiles. 2019. "'It's Totally Unfair:' Chicago: Where the Rich Live 30 Years Longer than the Poor." *The Guardian*. (June 23). https://www.theguardian.com/us-news/2019/jun/23/chicago-latest-news-life-expectancy-rich-poor-inequality.

Lindsay, Shelby. 2018. "Native Americans Close the Gap—Almost—on U.S. Life Expectancy." *Cronkite News*. (May 10). https://cronkitenews.azpbs.org/2018/05/10/native-americans-close-the-gap-almost-on-u-s-life-expectancy/.

Loesche, Dyfed. 2017. "The Prison Gender Gap." *Statista*. (October 23). https://www.statista.com/chart/11573/gender-of-inmates-in-us-federal-prisons-and-general-population/.

Martin, Nina, and Renee Montagne. 2017. "Nothing Protects Black Women from Dying in Pregnancy and Childbirth." *ProPublica*. (December 7). https://www.propublica.org/article/nothing-protects-black-women-from-dying-in-pregnancy-and-childbirth.

Mather, Mark, Paola Scommegna, and Lillian Kilduff. 2019. "Fact Sheet: Aging in the United States." Population Reference Bureau. (July 15). https://www.prb.org/aging-unitedstates-fact-sheet/.

Matthew, Dayna Bowen. 2015. *Just Medicine: A Cure for Racial Inequality in American Healthcare*. New York: NYU Press.

Miller, Kenneth. 2018. "How Healthcare Fails Women." *Prevention*. (July 2). https://www.prevention.com/health/a22022580/how-health-care-fails-women/.

National Congress of American Indians. 2015. "Climate Change." http://www.ncai.org/policy-issues/land-natural-resources/climate-change.

Nellis, Ashley. 2016. *The Color of Justice: Racial and Ethnic Disparity in State Prisons*. The Sentencing Project. https://www.sentencingproject.org/wp-content/uploads/2016/06/The-Color-of-Justice-Racial-and-Ethnic-Disparity-in-State-Prisons.pdf.

Ng, Judy H., Arlene S. Bierman, Marc N. Elliott, Rachel L. Wilson, Chengfei Xia, and Sarah Hudson Scholle. 2015. "Beyond Black and White: Race/Ethnicity and Health Status among Older Adults." National Center for Biotechnology Information. (June 19). https://www.ncbi.nlm.nih.gov/pmc/articles/PMC4474472/.

Norwood, Carolette R. 2018. "Mapping the Intersections of Violence on Black Women's Sexual Health within the Jim Crow Geographies of Cincinnati Neighborhoods." *Frontiers: A Journal of Women Studies* 39: 97–135.

NYU University Langone Health NewsHub. 2019. "Large Life Expectancy Gaps in U.S. Cities Linked to Racial & Ethnic Segregation by Neighborhood." (June 5). https://nyulangone.org/news/large-life-expectancy-gaps-us-cities-linked-racial-ethnic-segregation-neighborhood.

Odoms-Young, Angela M., Shannon N. Zenk, Allison Karpyn, Guadalupe Xochitl Ayala, and Joel Gittelsohn. 2012. "Obesity and the Food Environment among Minority Groups." *Current Obesity Reports* 1 (July): 141–151.

Pachauri, Rajendra K., and Leo Mayer. 2014. *Climate Change 2014: Synthesis Report*. https://www.ipcc.ch/site/assets/uploads/2018/02/SYR_AR5_FINAL_full.pdf.

Pampel, Fred C., Patrick M. Krueger, and Justin T. Denney. 2010. "Socioeconomic Disparities in Health Behaviors." *Annual Review of Sociology* 36 (August): 349–370.

Plumer, Brad, and Nadja Popovich. 2020. "Housing Policy Left Neighborhoods Sweltering." *The New York Times*. (April 24). https://www.nytimes.com/interactive/2020/08/24/climate/racism-redlining-cities-global-warming.html?referringSource=articleShare.

Reckdahl, Katy. 2015. "The Dark Side of Katrina Recovery." *Politico Magazine*. (August 31). https://www.politico.com/magazine/story/2015/08/katrina-inequality-race-new-orleans-213087.

Sabin, Janice A., and Anthony G. Greenwald. 2012. "The Influence of Implicit Bias on Treatment Recommendations for 4 Common Pediatric Conditions: Pain, Urinary Tract Infection, Attention Deficit Hyperactivity Disorder, and Asthma." *American Journal of Public Health*. https://www.ncbi.nlm.nih.gov/pmc/articles/PMC3483921/#!po=10.0000.

Sandel, Megan, and Renée Boynton-Jarrett. "Why Do Poor People Smoke More?" *CNN* (March 31). https://www.cnn.com/2014/03/26/opinion/sandel-poverty-smoking/index.html.

Schencker, Lisa. 2019. "Chicago's Lifespan Gap: Streeterville Residents Live to 90. Englewood Residents Die at 60. Study Finds It's the Largest Divide in the U.S." *Chicago Tribune*. (June 6). https://www.chicagotribune.com/business/ct-biz-chicago-has-largest-life-expectancy-gap-between-neighborhoods-20190605-story.html.

Scommegna, Paola. 2017. "New Studies Link Hispanics' Longer Life Expectancy to Migration Patterns, Less Smoking." Population Reference Bureau. https://www.prb.org/hispanics-life-expectancy-migration-patterns/.

Seervai, Shanoor. 2019. "How the U.S. Fails Women When It Comes to Health." The Commonwealth Fund. (January 24). https://www.commonwealthfund.org/publications/podcast/2019/jan/how-us-fails-women-when-it-comes-health.

Shapiro, Isaac, and Arloc Sherman. 2005. "Essential Facts about the Victims of Hurricane Katrina." Center on Budget and Policy Priorities. (September 19). https://www.cbpp.org/research/essential-facts-about-the-victims-of-hurricane-katrina.

Simon, Caroline. 2016. "There is a Stunning Gap between the Number of White and Black Inmates in America's Prisons." *Business Insider*. (June 16). https://www.businessinsider.com/study-finds-huge-racial-disparity-in-americas-prisons-2016-6.

Stanford School of Medicine. 2020. "Health History: Health and Longevity since the Mid-19th Century." https://geriatrics.stanford.edu/ethnomed/african_american/fund/health_history/longevity.html

Truesdale, Kimberly P., Donna M. Matheson, Meghan M. Jaka, Sarah McAleer, Evan C. Sommer, and Charlotte A. Pratt. 2019. "Baseline Diet Quality of Predominantly Minority Children and Adolescents from Households Characterized by Low Socioeconomic Status in the Childhood Obesity Prevention and Treatment Research (COPTR) Consortium." *BMC Nutrition*. (September). https://bmcnutr.biomedcentral.com/articles/10.1186/s40795-019-0302-y#Sec8.

UN Environment Programme. 2014. "Climate Change Threatens Irreversible and Dangerous Impacts, but Options Exist to Limit Its Effects." (November 2). https://www.unenvironment.org/news-and-stories/press-release/climate-change-threatens-irreversible-and-dangerous-impacts-options.

U.S. Climate Resilience Toolkit. 2017. "Climate Change Threatens Traditional Ways of Life." (September 25). https://toolkit.climate.gov/topics/tribal-nations.

White, Gilliam B. 2015. "A Long Road Home." *The Atlantic*. (August 3). https://www.theatlantic.com/business/archive/2015/08/hurricane-katrina-sandy-disaster-recovery-/400244/.

Whitfield, Keith E., and Ronald J. Thorpe, Jr. 2017. "Perspective: Longevity, Stress, Genes and African Americans." *Ethnicity and Disease* 27 (Winter): 1–2.

Wilson, Ben. 2020. "Urban Heat Management and the Legacy of Redlining." *Journal of the American Planning Association*. (May 22). https://www.tandfonline.com/doi/full/10.1080/01944363.2020.1759127.

Wilson, William Julius. 1996. *When Work Disappears: The World of the New Urban Poor*. New York: Vintage Books.

Woolf, Steven H., and Heidi Schoomaker. 2019. "Life Expectancy and Mortality Rates in the United States, 1959–2017." *The Journal of the American Medical Association*. (November 26): 1996–2016.

World Life Expectancy. 2018. "USA Health Rankings." https://www.worldlifeexpectancy.com/usa/life-expectancy-white.

Zielinski, Sarah. 2016. "How Will Native Americans in the Southwest Adapt to Serious Impacts of Climate Change?" *Smithsonian Magazine*. (February 22). https://www.smithsonianmag.com/science-nature/how-will-native-americans-southwest-adapt-serious-impacts-climate-change-180958172/.

7

INITIATIVES FOR IMPROVING IMPERILED PEOPLE'S LIVES

Twice in the history of the Gallup Poll, interviewers have asked a representative national sample of Americans whether or not they had the urge to participate in protests. In 1965 as the civil-rights movement was well underway and as protests against the Vietnam War were increasing, 10 percent of the respondents replied affirmatively. In 2018 with the growing influence of organizations like Black Lives Matter promoting social justice for African Americans and the Me Too campaign combating sexual harassment and assault of women, 36 percent of the sample indicated having felt the urge to participate in a public demonstration involving some issue.

Certain respondents' traits appeared noteworthy, particularly education and political ideology. Among individuals with a high-school education or less, 21 percent admitted they had felt the urge to protest while college graduates at 46 percent and post-graduates at 58 percent were over twice as likely to have felt the impulse. As far as political ideology was concerned, liberals at 60 percent were nearly three times more likely than conservatives at 21 percent to indicate support for protest (Reinhardt 2018). The Gallup Poll did not address the issue of age, but it is likely that young people, those in their teens and twenties, are more likely than their elders to support protest (Gringlas 2020; McNulty 2019).

While potential participants' traits will affect their willingness to engage in protests, the context in which individuals find themselves can promote their involvement. Protests have become an international reality, possessing certain shared similarities. With his organization's unrelentingly critical view of the political and economic scene, a reporter for the British newspaper *The Guardian* wrote,

The protests raging today and in the past months on the streets of cities around the world have varying triggers. But the fuel is familiar: ... stifled democracy and the bone-deep conviction that things can be different—even if the alternative is not always clear.

Later in the article he wrote, "Not all the protests are driven by economic complaints, but widening gulfs between the haves and have-nots are radicalising many young people in particular" (Safi 2019). The phrase in the previous quotations that seems to stand out is "the bone-deep conviction that things can be different." It emphasizes that regardless of protesters' personal traits, what fundamentally motivates them is how they feel.

Before the George Floyd killing led to greatly increased national attention to the social injustice Blacks have suffered, some professional athletes had already felt the bone-deep conviction that the world in which they were living could be different. In the US, players from the National Basketball Association (NBA) appeared to be leading the way. While the majority have been Black, some whites are included. In *The Players' Tribute*, an online publication that offers pro athletes a chance to present their views and experiences, thereby helping readers understand and combat discrimination and social inequality, Kyle Korver, a white NBA veteran, spelled out how he gradually began to appreciate that race relations could and should be different.

Korver described a couple of situations indicating how he automatically reacted and then later on reassessed his feelings and responses. One instance took place in a game against the Oklahoma Thunder during which Russell Westbrook, a prominent Black player, got into an exchange with a fan. When after the game a reporter asked Korver about his reaction to Westbrook's response he said, "I told him I hadn't seen it—and added something like, 'But you know Russ. He gets into it with the crowd a lot'" [italics removed].

Afterwards, however, it came out that the fan had said something ugly to Westbrook, who asserted that the comment was racially charged. The president of the Utah Jazz, Korver's team, set up a closed-door meeting, and at that time a number of the Black players described similar experiences they had endured. Korver indicated that everyone was upset. He was embarrassed about his kneejerk comments after the game. Clearly, perhaps for the first time, Korver was starting to examine the implicit racism that festered in both the NBA setting and in his own psyche.

Black players were sick and tired of such incidents. Discussion was lengthy, and when the meeting ended the participants appeared to believe that while it had been a positive step, nobody felt satisfied.

After the incident Korver realized that even though he had failed to appreciate it, his race gave him a singular privilege that his Black colleagues lacked—the option to get into the issue of race and defend players of color in pro ball or "I can also fade into the crowd, and my face can blend in with the faces of those hecklers, any time I want."

Fading into the crowd, however, seemed to be a decidedly negative option, and Korver listed some of the realities he now felt it was necessary to address: to learn much more about the history of racism, to listen carefully to what people of color have to say, and to develop a better grasp of the contributions protest activities like those in which Black Lives Matter engages make to promoting racial equality (Korver 2019).

The last topic is one of two that receives extensive attention in the last major section of the chapter. Meanwhile several other persistent problems have also had a destructive effect on the three categories of people examined in this book. Discussion focuses on the tax structure, jobs for disadvantaged people, and the promotion of universal health care—all current problem-ridden issues where significant reforms could vastly improve many people's lives.

American Taxation and Its Injustices

In Chapter 1 detailed information indicates that following the Tax Cuts and Job Acts of 2017, top corporate personnel and other wealthy individuals had unprecedented access to lower tax rates and increased tax loopholes. The richest 1 percent of Americans possess almost 40 percent of the nation's wealth but pay only 20 percent of all taxes (Linden 2019). For those privileged few, the upshot has been a massive increase in wealth, but for Americans generally, particularly poor families, many of which belong to racial minorities, social programs that could significantly improve their standard of living are severely curtailed. *[margin note: who pays the taxes]*

A study of 21 affluent nations demonstrated the contribution tax revenues could make to the lives of their most disadvantaged residents. The evidence indicated that overall the greater a country's percentage expenditure of GDP (gross domestic product) for cash aid and various essential benefits, the lower the child-poverty rate. For example, Denmark provided 20.9 percent of GDP and had a 2.9 percent child-poverty rate while the US supplied 12 percent of GDP for those types of assistance and produced a 20.2 percent child-poverty rate (Wilson and Schneider 2018). Table 7.1 provides data on the topic from ten nations, with Denmark and the US representing the lowest and the highest child-poverty rates respectively.

International survey data indicate that generally the greater the percentage of its GDP that a nation provides for social expenditure, the lower its child-poverty rate. Other factors, however, can come into play. For instance, Spain has a higher child-poverty rate than the US, in spite of contributing a larger percentage of its GDP to social programs. *[margin note: 26.]*

One critical area where the US has been less supportive of poor children than other affluent countries involves the funding of public education. To begin, the American system can hardly be faulted for overall cheapness; among 36 wealthy nations, it ranks second in expenditure in US dollars per student (National Center for Education Statistics 2019). Besides, as Chapter 1 noted, local cities and towns serve as prominent participants in the funding process. Inevitably families

TABLE 7.1 Selected Affluent Nations' Relationship between Expenditure on Social Programs and Child Poverty[1]

Nation	Social expenditure as % of GDP	Child-poverty rate
Denmark	20.9%	2.9%
Sweden	19.4%	9.2%
Finland	19.1%	3.6%
Norway	17.5%	7.2%
Netherlands	17.1%	10.3%
Great Britain	15.5%	11.5%
Germany	14.9%	9.5%
Iceland	14%	7.2%
Canada	12.4%	15%
United States	12%	20.2%

Source: Wilson and Schneider 2018.

Note: International survey data indicate that generally the greater the percentage of its GDP that a nation provides for social expenditure, the lower its child-poverty rate. Other factors, however, can come into play. For instance, Spain has a higher child-poverty rate than the US, in spite of contributing a larger percentage of its GDP to social programs.

[1] In this table children belong in the child-poverty category when they live in households receiving less than half of the nation's household-size-adjusted median income.

wealthy areas → better schools

living in wealthier areas possess higher quality schools; those with badly funded programs, particularly residents of poor districts, have markedly less effective ones. It means that even in richer states less affluent students will suffer educationally, thereby significantly curtailing their job and income prospects.

Connecticut is a case in point. A journalist wrote,

> This is one of the wealthiest states in the union. But thousands of children here attend schools that are among the worst in the country. While students in higher-income towns such as Greenwich and Darien have easy access to guidance counselors, school psychologists, personal laptops, and up-to-date textbooks, those in high-poverty areas like Bridgeport and New Britain don't. Such districts tend to have more students in need of extra help, and yet they have fewer guidance counselors, tutors, and psychologists, lower-paid teachers, more dilapidated facilities and bigger class sizes than wealthier districts.
>
> *(Semuels 2016)*

Some countries do better—much better. For example, a study of 36 wealthy nations revealed that Japan provides highly equitable school funding. The Organisation for Economic Co-operation and Development (OECD), to which all of these countries belong, found in two assessments that the socioeconomic background of students in Japan accounted for less than 10 percent of the factors determining scores in OECD standardized tests—well below the average for all the OECD countries and barely half the 17 percent for their American counterparts (OECD 2015, 1; OECD 2020; Semuels 2017). John Mock, an anthropologist at Temple University's Japan campus, said, "In Japan, you may have poor areas, but you don't have poor schools." Public schools in Japan have a graduation rate of nearly 97 percent. "It's one of the few [education] systems that does well for almost any student," an OECD official who works on education and skills development explained. "Disadvantage is really seen as a collective responsibility" (Semuels 2017).

Besides the equitable education produced for children of all socioeconomic backgrounds, public-schooling in Japan has other outstanding qualities. The belief is that teaching is the key to successful education. As a result even though the nation allots a smaller portion of the GDP for schooling than many other OECD countries and expenditure for buildings and administrative staff is decidedly modest, the value placed on education means that teachers are paid above the OECD average, and their entrance exams are very challenging (National Center on Education and the Economy 2020).

In Japanese schools an emphasis exists on helping students learn to think effectively. A former teacher noted, "They really focus on problem-solving, which means the ability to attack problems they had never seen before" (Semuels 2017). When a school is low-performing, educators have developed the practice of bringing in high-performing teachers from other schools and encouraging them with substantial income bonuses. Throughout the country, though, OECD test results have indicated

PHOTO 7.1 The Japanese system of education not only requires equal funding for all students but also emphasizes the ability to think effectively, starting when children are very young.
Source: Shutterstock/ Tom Wang

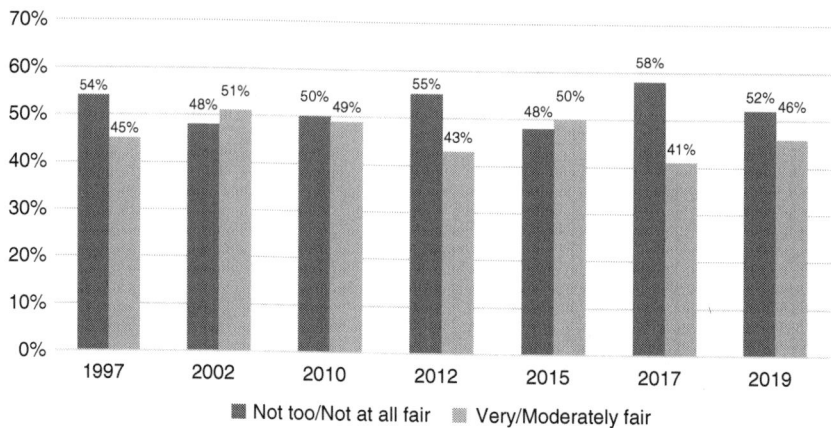

FIGURE 7.1 Americans' Evaluation of the Federal Tax System[1]
Source: Pew Research Center 2019.
Note: Over more than two decades, Americans have displayed fairly similar percentages of those who feel the federal tax system is not fair and those who believe it is fair. Overall those supporting the not-fair options have represented a slight majority.
[1] National random samples of Americans 18 and older conducted seven times between 1997 and 2019.

that students in Japan achieve well above average national scores for science, reading, and mathematics (National Center on Education and the Economy 2020; OECD 2015, 1, 8). As far as all students' chances for success are concerned, public education in Japan appears to be ground-breaking, providing other countries a model for a system that is both thoughtfully conceived and successful for most students.

In contrast, one might wonder how Americans feel about a federal taxation system that provides minimal support for poor children's education and their general well-being while handsomely rewarding wealthy individuals. Figure 7.1 indicates that in the course of more than a decade the public's evaluation of the system has been split, with slightly more people critical than supportive. Furthermore, while in recent years, many Americans have become actively involved in selected social issues, few efforts have mobilized to alter the federal taxation system.

Just as the US funding of programs to help poor children are underfunded compared to those in other wealthy countries, financial support for unemployed people tends to be less than in most other affluent nations.

Disadvantaged People's Paths to Jobs

When Americans receiving average- or below-average pay face unemployment, they must deal with one of the least generous insurance systems in the industrialized world. While the weekly payments are about average for affluent countries, the benefits are short-lived, typically six months or even less while many wealthier nations provide support for a year or even longer (Burtless 2018).

The people most vulnerable to unemployment are individuals with limited education. The National Household Education Survey, which obtained a representative sample of Americans aged 25 to 64 in the workforce, found that the less schooling people have, the more likely they are unemployed or involuntarily working part time or temporarily. In 2019 19 percent of individuals with less than high-school completion were unemployed compared to 13 percent who had finished high school and just 5 percent with a bachelor's degree (U.S. Department of Education 2019).

A small study of staff members at a One-Stop Career Center for unemployed or underemployed individuals indicated the relevance of education—that the nation's shift from a manufacturing emphasis to one stressing information and services has often left many of them without the schooling and skills necessary for much of the modern job market. Others encountered such specific barriers as a drug problem, alcoholism, or an abusive husband.

One-Stop staff members found that since their clients were often disoriented by the world in which they found themselves, it was a useful starting point to hear their personal stories. An agency employee explained, "The majority of those that utilize the One-Stop have gone through a significant loss, which is apparent in their overall emotional state including depression, anxiety, anger, and despair."

Clients showed significant differences in their willingness or capacity to move toward reemployment. Another One-Stop staffer said, "Sometimes they know the next step and most of the time they don't. That is why there is so much fear, depression, and anxiety. They want to move on but don't know how. We help by setting goals and show them the steps to get to those goals."

Staff members realized that hearing clients' stories was very useful. One of them said, "Listening to the stories lets them know we care. Their stories have value for them. By listening, it helps them move through their experiences. It also lets them know that they are not alone." A colleague pointed out that the clients were eager to tell their stories, knowing that upon hearing them the One-Stop staffers planned to help them get back into the workforce (Russell 2011, 57).

In telling their stories, however, unemployed or underemployed workers are unlikely to address a potentially important issue, one that again emphasizes the role of education in job seeking. Academic degrees and certificates in broad fields like information technology and health care often suggest to hiring staff that applicants have **soft skills**, the attributes that prove essential for effective interaction on many jobs, involving such traits as communication abilities, flexibility, teamwork capacities, reliability, and problem-solving knowledge.

Social reproduction comes into play here, with individuals possessing soft skills most likely developing them not only from schooling but also from their families and social networks. While modern employers often cite the importance of soft skills in their hiring choices, many entry-level jobs involving industries like retail or food service do not have any widely recognized competencies that job candidates can demonstrate to show they possess these abilities. In fact, elusive as this issue proves to be, many applicants are largely unaware of its importance (Deming 2020; Hossain and Terwelp 2015).

Unlike job candidates with limited soft-skill qualifications, some unemployed people seeking fairly low-paying positions need little assistance to reenter the job world. Rose was an African American mother of four children living in Detroit and working at a part-time, low-wage job. However, she had a cosmetology license and would have been able to increase her income appreciably if she could obtain barber shears and several other tools. Rose explained, "I'm a mother of 4 working ... [parttime], but the job has reduced my hours dramatically. These tools will let [me] work independently & help me provide for my family" (Kashner 2017). Valerie, a family advocate at Starfish Family Services, knew Rose well, having hired her as a child-care worker. Valerie enthusiastically vouched for Rose, and through her job she had the connections to help Rose obtain the tools she needed (Benevolent 2014; Kashner 2017; Thomas et al. 2019).

As in the case of employment, many disadvantaged Americans find themselves at risk for health care.

The Prospect of Improving American Health Care

Martin Makary, a surgeon and a professor of health policy, has studied the American health-care system and concluded that the system can readily overwhelm not only low-income people but also many in the middle class. Makary said,

> Half of Americans have less than $400 in savings and live paycheck to paycheck. And the reality is, things are fine when you are wealthy, but when you live paycheck to paycheck, a medical bill can be catastrophic. It can wipe out a college savings. It can mean a family doesn't have money for food; it can mean a single mom can't afford day care.
>
> *(Wehrwein 2019)*

Experts' estimates indicate that because of less access to health care and lower quality of care, African Americans and Latinos have 30 to 40 percent less effective health outcomes than whites, resulting not only in increased illness and shorter life expectancy but also about $60 billion a year in lost productivity. It is notable that among racial minorities middle-class individuals report more unsatisfactory medical treatment than whites. In fact, in the case of young Blacks who are advancing through the job ranks, discriminatory health care largely accounts for the differences in self-rated health between them and whites (Colen et al. 2018; Pearl 2015).

Furthermore the American health-care system appears particularly deficient when compared to those in other affluent nations. The Commonwealth Fund examined health care in Australia, Canada, Germany, the Netherlands, New Zealand, the United Kingdom, and the United States and found that the US ranked first in one respect—namely, expense. However, it was last "on measures of quality, efficiency, access to care, equity, and the ability to lead long, healthy, and productive lives" (The Commonwealth Fund 2020). It is an evaluation that produces little or no confidence in the current system and strongly suggests the need to improve it drastically.

In contrast, European countries have developed several different kinds of health-care systems, which have distinct similarities. Throughout the continent the federal governments generally commit to making sure that everyone in the nation has access to health care and that obtaining that care will not hurt them financially. The chief source of funding is taxes collected from employers and the public. (Booth 2019; Rook 2018).

The US system is more complicated and less supportive, with principal funding coming from several sources, including private health-insurance companies, employers, and government programs like Medicare and Medicaid. A journalist specializing in health care wrote, "The system we have right now places America's health system on an island on its own, away from its peers on the global stage" (Booth 2019).

While European governments generally exert considerable control over the health-care system, some of these nations also maintain private health insurance, which purchasers can use for selected dental or vision care, elective surgery, private hospital rooms, and other benefits.

Interested parties might wonder whether European programs have any disadvantages compared to US health care. A frequent criticism involves the time patients must wait to obtain medical care for nonemergency conditions. An expert on health-care systems concluded, "They may have to wait a few days to see a doctor, but they also don't have many out-of-pocket costs associated with their healthcare — and when they do, it's *substantially* [author's italics] less than what Americans pay" (Rook 2018).

The focus now shifts to two social movements that in recent years have become increasingly significant topics of both interest and debate throughout the nation.

Major Contemporary Mobilizations for Change

The following section contains two principal parts, each of which focuses on the past and present efforts to reduce the oppressions their respective groups have historically suffered. Social movements play a substantial part in the discussion.

A social movement is an organized, collective activity undertaken by people to promote or resist social change (Doob 2000, 575). Like social movements generally, these two are loosely organized, composed of individuals continuously vulnerable to and often supporting social change. In recent years both social movements have expanded, receiving extensive public attention in the process.

*Social movements →
black lives matter*

In 2013 three Black women founded Black Lives Matter following the highly publicized killing of a young Black man. The rapidly growing Black Lives Matter initiative contains about 40 chapters in the US and Canada dedicated to reducing discrimination and violence against African Americans and other people of color (Black Lives Matter 2020a, 2020b).

Black activist Tarana Burke, a victim of sexual assault herself, founded the Me Too initiative in an effort to provide, impoverished, young women of color who were victims of sexual assault empathy and support following their ordeal and has spent over two decades establishing programs on their behalf. When Me Too activities suddenly received extensive attention in the media, the most publicized victims became white women who had suffered sexual abuse from prominent white men. Over time Me Too has supported various legal, financial, and educational means to oppose and eventually eliminate sexual harassment (Brockes 2018; North 2017; North 2019).

Sarah J. Jackson, a professor of communications studies who has examined disadvantaged groups' use of social and mass media to reduce the inequalities they suffer, indicated that in the case of sexually oppressed women Me Too is "a campaign" and "women's rights" the movement. One might add that in a similar vein Black Lives Matter is a campaign attached to the Black rights social movement. Campaigns, in short, are initiatives to accomplish specific goals within a larger social movement.

Jackson noted, "And I would say #MeToo is one indication of the sort of conversations that need to happen." She added that since the Me Too campaign has clearly stated the need to attack the sexual oppression of women, the next step involves the global expansion of that conversation (Seales 2018). To recruit new members and to promote communication among them, both the Me Too and Black Lives Matter campaigns rely heavily on Twitter and other messaging services.

Jackson's distinction about campaigns and social movements seems useful and well worth employing in the upcoming section. However, journalists, activists, and others in the public arena often do not make such a clear distinction. In particular, from 2017 onward, the events involving the two campaigns have been so impactful and received such extensive media attention that when many Americans refer to either one of them, the campaign is synonymous with the social movement, often using the term "movement" in referring to either the Black Lives Matter or the Me Too campaigns.

A light-hearted warning: Because of the widespread and growing interest in and support for these two renowned social movements, it seems difficult, if not impossible, to discuss them briefly.

The Black Rights Movement: From the Civil-Rights Era to Black Lives Matter

This issue appeared as a massive presence in 2020, but it has roots in what became known as "the civil-rights movement," a collective effort by Blacks and their allies to oppose racial segregation and discrimination. It has had a lengthy history, with some scholars contending that its analysis should extend back in time to the late nineteenth century. However, most people engaged in the topic consider that it became a significant issue in the 1950s and the 1960s. What distinguishes that time period is that during it the protests in which activists engaged began to produce significant legal reforms (Schmidt 2016).

A century after the end of slavery southern states remained highly segregated, with Jim Crow laws barring African Americans from "classrooms and bathrooms, from theaters and train cars, from juries and legislatures" In addition, they faced disenfranchisement and often risked the prospect of lethal violence (Anti-Defamation League 2020).

Then in December 1955, the first mass action of the modern Black rights movement occurred. Rosa Parks, a Black seamstress, was arrested for refusing to give up her seat on a bus to a white passenger, and the civil-rights movement was underway, with Blacks the major participants in both leadership and activist roles. The arrest led to the Montgomery Bus Boycott, which served for Black activists as a model for hundreds of nonviolent protests including "sit ins" at segregated lunch counters and "freedom rides" with Black and white riders taking buses from northern cities to southern destinations, where Black activists defied established laws at each stop by entering legally segregated areas. As the freedom rides persisted, local whites, often with police support, did what the protesters wanted—reacted violently with beatings and hundreds of arrests and brought national attention to the freedom rides. Eventually the activists gained a victory when the Interstate Commerce Commission pressured by the Kennedy administration ordered the integration of all interstate buses, trains, and airports (Constitutional Rights Foundation 2020).

During the civil-rights era, legal actions seeking to secure equal rights for racial minorities played an increasingly important role. The leadoff occurred in 1954 when the Supreme Court made segregated schools illegal, declaring that state laws supporting separate schools for Blacks and whites were unconstitutional. Then in the 1960s, the protests prompted important legislation. The sweeping Civil Rights Act of 1964 prohibited racial discrimination in all public places and also stated that discrimination in employment because of race, color, sex, religion, or national origin was illegal. The following year the Voting Rights Act of 1965 ended racial discrimination in voting throughout the country, establishing the right throughout the nation, most notably denied in the South, for all people of color to vote. In addition, the Civil Rights Act of 1968, widely referred to as the "Fair Housing Act," was a follow-up to the earlier Civil Rights Act, expanding its prohibition of housing discrimination by offering important detail on the subject—in particular, that it was strictly illegal to discriminate in the sale, rental, or financing of housing because of race, religion, or national origin (Anti-Defamation League 2020).

An outcome of the civil-rights protests was that Martin Luther King, Jr., a local minister, emerged as a leader during the Montgomery Bus Boycott. In 1963 more than 200,000 people joined the March on Washington for Jobs and Freedom and gathered in front of the Lincoln Memorial, where King delivered one of the most famous speeches in American history—what became known as his "I have a dream" address in which he shared images that suggested the death of racism and victory for racial equality (King Institute, Stanford University 2020).

Clarence B. Jones, King's legal counsel, was present at the speech. He had heard him speak many times, but at the March on Washington "there was something kind of mystical. He had transformed. Oh my God, something had taken over his body. It was spell-binding," Jones said, not in the content, "but it's the way he spoke and the intensity of how he felt" (Waxman 2020).

During the civil-rights era, King and Malcolm X and to a lesser extent others like Bayard Rustin and James Farmer were often considered charismatic in Max Weber's sense of the term, meaning they were perceived as leaders displaying extraordinary qualities, exceeding normal human capacities. Charismatic leadership is inspired behavior, not relying on established rules or laws, and is revolutionary, arising at times when many people seek changes in the social order (Gerth and Mills 1946, 295–96). For several decades, however, some expert observers have considered the claims about charismatic leadership overstated—that, as a prominent historian concluded, while King was unquestionably influential, the civil-rights movement would have developed much as it did without his presence (Carson 1987, 451–52). It is an interesting issue that is too complicated for lengthy analysis here.

What is unquestionable is that a half-century later a very different type of leadership became prominent in the struggle to curtail and eliminate discrimination and violence against Blacks and other racial minorities. In 2013 three Black women, Alicia Garza, Patrisse Cullors, and Opal Tometi, founded Black Lives Matter following the acquittal of the mixed-race man who shot and killed Trayvon Martin, an unarmed 17-year-old Black youth (Black Lives Matter 2020b). Spokespeople for the organization indicated that their "mission is to eradicate white supremacy and build local power to intervene in violence inflicted on Black communities by the state and vigilantes" (Black Lives Matter 2020a). Unlike the civil-rights movement of earlier decades, Black Lives Matter downplays charismatic leadership, indicating that the campaign possesses a number of both female and male leaders who are "low ego, high impact" individuals that produce a "leader-full" structure (Copeland 2016, 6–7).

For modern activists the setting in which they operate has changed significantly from the civil-rights era. Social media have become major players, with their contribution increasing over time. At the fifth anniversary of the founding of Black Lives Matter in May 2018, a survey by the Pew Research Center found that the hashtag #BlackLivesMatter had appeared almost 30 million times on Twitter, an average of over 17,000 times a day.

The rising popularity of the #BlackLivesMatter hashtag along with others such as those for #MeToo and #environmentaljustice has promoted discussion and debate about the use of social media for political involvement and social activism.

A Pew survey conducted with a representative sample of Americans 18 years and older found that nearly 70 percent of the respondents believed that these sites were both somewhat to very important for accomplishing such goals as getting politicians to pay attention to issues and producing effective social movements supporting societal changes. In addition, over 60 percent of respondents indicated that social-media sites provided disadvantaged groups opportunities for expression, with Blacks endorsing this position more strongly than whites. The majority of the American public, however, has some doubts about social media, indicating that at times they give participants an unrealistic sense of the influence they can wield (Anderson et al. 2018). Unquestionably, though, as the upcoming discussion indicates they have played a significant role in the growth of both the Black Lives Matter and the Me Too campaigns.

As the spring of 2020 approached, some observers were aware of the existence of certain unsettling conditions throughout American society. In his theory of collective behavior, which concerns activities occurring under conditions that are both unstructured and unstable, sociologist Neil J. Smelser (1962, 15–17) examined factors that mobilize social movements, including the contribution that structural strain makes.

Structural strain involves conditions in the society producing tension and pressure for people, perhaps encouraging them to reject normal behavioral norms. By 2020 those conditions, which affected racial minorities more harshly than whites, included widespread unemployment, the persistent occurrence of police violence, and a terrifying pandemic that magnified existing health and financial inequalities. A journalist noted that starting nearly three months before George Floyd's death in May 2020, COVID-19 caused many

> Americans … [to be] living in a state of hypervigilance and anxiety, coping with feelings of uncertainty, fear and vulnerability — things many Black Americans experience on a regular basis. Information about how to avoid the virus was distressingly sparse and confusing as local and federal officials sparred about the severity of the pandemic and how best to contain it.
>
> *(Goldberg 2020)*

The coronavirus crisis was particularly acute for Blacks and Hispanics, who became sick and died at higher rates than whites and also were more likely because of widespread stay-at-home measures to lose their jobs (Stewart 2020).

For many Blacks a potent source of structural strain has been the unrelenting awareness that police violence toward Blacks has been extensive, with Black deaths at their hands considerably higher proportionately than it has been for whites. The data on the topic are decisive. In 2019, for example, when adjusted for their proportion of the population, Blacks were about 2.5 times as likely as whites to be killed by police (Roper 2020; Statista 2020)—a reality they widely recognized and one leading to widespread anger and fear.

In addition, through the opening decades of the twenty-first century, many mass media and social media have urged a renewed campaign to curtail discrimination and violence against Blacks and other people of color, emphasizing that social justice for those groups unquestionably must become an immediate priority.

In Smelser's theory the latter development would involve "the growth and spread of a generalized belief," promoted by structural strain and providing critical support for the expansion of an emerging social movement.

Smelser indicated that as a social movement emerges, a so-called "precipitating factor" setting it off eventually occurs. In the 1960s when Smelser was writing, that conclusion made sense—a single factor or incident. The twenty-first century is different, with the impact of television greatly increased along with a steadily increasing role for social media. Nowadays with the potential for both types of media covering and publicizing events, it seems sensible to suggest a minute but significant change in Smelser's terminology, referring now to "precipitating factors" (Smelser 1962, 15–16).

In the social movement promoting Blacks' social justice, a number of precipitating factors are readily apparent. Widespread mass-media coverage along with frequent input from smart phones provide not only information but sometimes pictures and sounds publicizing events that display contempt for African Americans' lives. Prominent examples include Eric Garner in a police officer's chokehold on the sidewalk saying 11 times before dying "I can't breathe" (Border and Shepardson 2019); Colin Kaepernick, a pro quarterback, taking a controversial knee during the playing of the national anthem at football games to protest the unrelenting occurrence of police brutality and racism and in retaliation finding that in the ensuing years no team owner would hire him (Haislop 2020).

Because of its importance and the attention received, a third precipitating event requires lengthier commentary. In 2016 Kimberlé Crenshaw, the law professor who created the concept of intersectionality, and several other associates started the #SayHerName campaign, focusing on police murders of Black women. Four years later the campaign became identified with one celebrated murder which occurred when police broke into health-care worker Breonna Taylor's apartment and shot her eight times, soon prompting protesters to call on people to "Say Her Name" in recognition of the reality that police violence against Black women has been underpublicized (Romano 2020). Between 2015 and 2020, American police killed 48 Black women, with murder charges occurring in only two cases. Like Taylor, the majority of the Black women were unarmed. In fact, an earlier study of a racially diverse sample of over 1,700 fatal encounters involving police indicated that Black women were the only race/gender combination where the majority of the members killed were unarmed (African American Policy Forum 2020; Gupta 2020; Johnson et al. 2018).

While the impact of the three events just mentioned on subsequent developments in the Black Lives Matter campaign has been unquestionable, a single precipitating factor has produced the greatest impact, and some background about it seems appropriate. On May 25, 2020 in Minneapolis, over two months after Breonna Taylor's death, George Floyd bought a pack of cigarettes at a convenience store, paying for it with a $20 bill. A store employee claimed the bill was counterfeit and demanded that Floyd return the cigarettes. When he refused, the man called the police, who showed up within 10 minutes and found Floyd sitting in a car parked around the corner.

One of the two officers drew his gun and forced Floyd out of the car. He was handcuffed and when led toward a squad car resisted being put into it, falling to the ground. A few minutes later, two more officers arrived, and the policemen made one more attempt to get Floyd into the squad car. Once again, he fell to the ground, still handcuffed and lying face down. At that moment several witnesses began shooting video of the incident on their smart phones, and soon the story went viral, showing the gruesome detail of four white policemen gathered around a helpless Black man.

While the other officers restrained Floyd, Officer Derek Chauvin put a knee between his head and neck, holding it in place for eight minutes and 46 seconds until his victim died. During that time Floyd, repeatedly using Garner's last words, said "I can't breathe," begged "please, please, please," and called for his mother (BBC News 2020). Meanwhile Chauvin seemed relaxed, unconcerned. Rashad Robinson, the president of Color of Change, a prominent nonprofit group promoting social justice for Blacks and other people of color, said, "The police officer is looking into the camera as he's pushing the life out of him." According to Robinson, the "stark cruelty" of the video captivated viewers (Wortham 2020).

It was a horrifying incident but as a precipitating factor unparalleled, prompting analysts to speculate about how much greater the impact on the mobilization of the Black Lives Matter turned out to be than it would have been without smart phones shooting and sending videos and exchanging messages.

In the subsequent days and weeks, an unprecedented reaction to the death occurred. On the third day following it, 8 million tweets tagged with #BlackLivesMatter were posted compared to December 4, 2014, nearly five months after Eric Garner's well-publicized killing, when Black Lives Matter tweets peaked at 146,000 (Wortham 2020).

A national survey conducted shortly before George Floyd's killing indicated that 43 percent of a national sample of Americans strongly or somewhat supported the Black Lives Matter campaign. About a week after his death, that figure shot up to 67 percent, with Blacks showing the greatest support followed by Hispanics, Asians, and whites in that order. While ranked the least supportive of the four groups, whites at 60 percent showed a majority of their members backing the campaign (Horowitz and Livingston 2020; Parker et al. 2020).

Soon after Floyd's death, activists gathered in all 50 states and at least 600 American cities "to march, chant, host vigils, and congregate in massive groups"

PHOTO 7.2 Like this peaceful protest in Coral Springs, Florida, that occurred during the pandemic, activists in hundreds of other American cities carried signs that often read "Black Lives Matter" and sometimes said "I can't breathe," haunting words which both George Floyd and Eric Garner uttered shortly before their deaths.

Source: Shutterstock/ YES Market Media

(Colarossi 2020). The demonstrations quickly went global, with hundreds of protests in Australia, Canada, Europe, and South America (Colarossi 2020; *The Economist* 2020; The New York Times 2020).

American demonstrations drew people from wide-ranging backgrounds—diverse in race, social class, and age. Most of the daytime protests were peaceful, but especially at night extensive arson, looting, and vandalism occurred, destroying large numbers of buildings, including businesses (Dettmer 2020; Rosen 2020). In at least 140 cities during demonstrations (Robertson et al. 2020), accusations of police brutality arose, describing "punching, kicking, gassing, pepper-spraying and driving vehicles at often peaceful protesters in states across the country." Thousands of people were arrested, and unknown numbers of protesters and police were injured (Gabbatt 2020).

In dozens of cities including New York City, Chicago, Los Angeles, and Atlanta, activists rode bicycles, appropriately a longtime symbol of individual freedom and equal opportunity, and sometimes found themselves confronting police on bikes (Rosen 2020).

Besides the public demonstrations following George Floyd's death, many other significant statements or actions occurred. A host of testimonials, some covered by media and others not, from racially diverse activists, athletes, business people, and members of many other occupations emphasized the importance of promoting social justice for Blacks and other people of color, sometimes indicating the speaker's or writer's intention to make an individual or group commitment to the expanding social movement, such as a financial donation or some specific promise to help others, particularly children. In addition, the public heard or read about individuals' voluntary confessions involving their own past racist statements or actions or their accusations about other people's race-related misdeeds. Finally, individuals and organizations have removed or demanded the removal of statues of prominent men supporting racist causes or views and also called for the removal of all Confederate flags or other Confederate insignia.

A week after the George Floyd killing, a national survey of over a 1,000 adults aged 18 and older found that 73 percent, nearly three quarters of the respondents, indicated that in response to Floyd's death, they supported peaceful protests and demonstrations—an impressive increase from the general support for protest cited in the Gallup Poll survey in this chapter's opening. Eighty-six percent of Democrats and 59 percent of Republicans subscribed to this point of view, meaning that a majority of members belonging to both political parties supported it (Ipsos 2020).

At this writing it is much too early to draw any conclusions about the long-term impact of the social movement for Blacks' rights. As one writer surveying the scene two weeks after Floyd's death declared, "Ladies and gentleman, this is what you call uncharted territory" (Pilkington 2020). Meanwhile the modern women's movement has expanded and changed.

The Growing Mobilization of Women's Rights: From Winning the Vote to the Me Too Campaign

In 1792 in her book *The Vindication of the Rights of Women*, English writer Mary Wollstonecraft acknowledged the fact that men generally viewed women as inferior beings. She stated:

> My own sex, I hope, will excuse me, if I treat them like rational creatures, instead of ... viewing them as if they were in a state of perpetual childhood, unable to stand alone.... I wish to persuade women to endeavor to acquire strength, both of mind and body, and to convince them that the soft phrases, susceptibility of heart, delicacy of sentiment, and refinement of taste, are almost synonymous with epithets of weakness.
>
> *(Wollstonecraft 1980, 459)*

In the nineteenth century, Wollstonecraft's writings were influential, with other spokespeople for increased women's rights echoing similar themes. For instance, in 1848, at the first women's rights convention in Seneca Falls, NY, Elizabeth

Cady Stanton indicated in her keynote address that the participants were "assembled to protest against a form of government, existing without the consent of the governed ... [and] to declare our right to be free as man is free, to be represented in the government which we are taxed to support" (Van Burkleo 2001, 112).

Before industrialization the family was a production unit, with women's role acknowledged in keeping their members fed, clothed, and in good health while they were legally designated "perpetual minors." In the early 1800s, a respected church member used to regularly beat his wife. Commenting on her neighbors, Emily Collins wrote,

> Now this wife, surrounded by six or seven children ... was obliged to spin and weave cloth for all the garments of the family, ... to milk, ... to make butter and cheese, and do all the cooking, washing, making and mending, ... and, with the pains of maternity forced upon her every eighteen months, was whipped by her pious husband "because she scolded."
>
> *(Calhoun, Vol. 2, 1960, 92–93)*

Harshly but accurately, sociologists John and Letha Scanzoni labelled the standard pre-industrial couple arrangement "owner–property marriage." As essentially a type of property, women faced two formidable power-denying conditions—they were not allowed to visualize a sense of themselves as independent of their husbands and, in addition, in virtually all matters the right to make decisions was a foregone conclusion, with wives inevitably deferring to their husbands (Scanzoni and Scanzoni 1988, 245).

Eventually, however, times began to change. In the twentieth century as industrialization expanded, consumer expectations increased, and to meet their families' growing sense of need a greater proportion of women entered the workforce.

In the course of about a century extending from the late 1860s to the 1960s, several factors reduced the resistance to women entering what had traditionally been men's work world. First, in 1869 the National Woman Suffrage Association launched a campaign for a universal-suffrage amendment to the US Constitution. Remaining strong until 1920 when the passage of the Nineteenth Amendment permitted women the right to vote, this campaign also provided support for women's right to work in previously all-male jobs. For instance, in her well-known *Women and Economics*, the activist Charlotte Perkins Gilman expressed anger at the common practice of systematically keeping homemakers out of the work world, and she turned to the early feminist movement as a force for altering the situation. Yes, she agreed, women should get the vote, but more important was equal participation in the economy. Gilman declared:

> The women's movement ... should be hailed by every right-thinking man and woman as the best birth of our country. The banner advanced proclaims

"equality before the law," women's share in political freedom; but the main line of progress is and has been toward economic equality and freedom.

(Gilman 1973, 587)

Second, the two world wars made it necessary to bring many women into essential but vacated jobs, primarily into factory and farm labor during World War I and into factory and office positions in World War II. While most of these jobs returned to men after the wars, stereotypes of women as constitutionally unable to do such work proved unjustified, and within several decades their numbers in the workforce sharply increased (Khan Academy 2020; National Archives 2016; National World War I Museum and Memorial 2020).

Finally, in the second half of the twentieth century, a growing proportion of married women began combining homemaking and a second career. The fact that they had already served as housewives made it impossible to level the traditional insult that they turned to work outside the home because they could not catch a man (Matthaei 1982, 290–91). Between the middle 1950s and the middle 1970s, several studies compared the two categories of wives. Investigation found that married women in the workforce when compared to housewives of the same age, education, and social class were similar in both current and previous psychiatric symptoms and diagnosis and in their behavior as wives.

However, one decisive difference between the two sets of women emerged. The researchers wrote, "The housewives are considerably more disinterested in and bored with their housework than the working wives are with their paid employment" (Newberry et al. 1979, 289). Inevitably over time many of the employed housewives publicized the upside of having a job outside the home.

During this era a growing number of women became involved in seeking to improve women's rights. In 1965 as noted earlier, the U.S. Equal Employment Opportunity Commission (EEOC) received the mandate to enforce Title VII's prohibition against gender discrimination on the job. As a reference in Chapter 5 indicated, Title VII is a potentially powerful tool for annihilating work discrimination, but in 1965 what now seems like a mind-boggling majority of the EEOC commissioners voted in favor of segregated job advertisements for women and men.

The following year at a conference on the status of women Betty Friedan, a well-known feminist writer, made a significant contribution. Friedan had observed the EEOC's failure to oppose job discrimination and also that the two EEOC commissioners who voted against segregated job advertisements along with a prominent EEOC attorney privately agreed that like Blacks, women needed a powerful organization acting on behalf of their rights. On the last day of the conference, Friedan invited 15 to 20 women to her hotel room to discuss possible strategies. With a space between the letters, she wordlessly wrote the acronym "N O W," on a paper napkin. A participant, who recalled the meeting, said,

Catherine Conroy pulled out a five-dollar bill from her wallet and, in her usual terse style, invited us to "put your money down and sign your name." NOW [the National Organization of Women] was a reality and I think we all felt somehow we had participated in a significant beginning.

(NOW 2011)

Four months later 300 women and men had become charter members of the organization, but ultimately while just 30 were actively involved, they still got the organization off the ground.

Modern NOW activists have described their organization and its goals with the following statement:

NOW is an intersectional, multi-issue, multi-strategy organization that takes a holistic approach to women's rights. Our official priorities are winning economic equality and securing it with an amendment to the U.S. Constitution that will guarantee equal rights for women; championing abortion rights, reproductive justice along with other women's health issues; opposing racism; fighting discrimination based on sexual orientation or gender identity in all areas, including employment, housing, health services, and child custody; and ending violence against all women, no matter race, age, or socio-economic class.

(NOW 2020)

To address this formidable agenda, NOW members have used "both traditional and nontraditional means … NOW activists do extensive electoral and lobbying work and bring lawsuits. We also organize mass marches, rallies, pickets, [and] non-violent civil disobedience" (NOW 2020).

In the decade following NOW's creation, a number of new organizations formed, each involved in its own campaign battling for selected legal and social changes promoting women's equal rights. Prominent organizations included:

- The National Women's Political Caucus, a group seeking to increase women's participation as voters, delegates at party conventions, and both elected and nonelected officeholders at all levels of government
- The Coalition of Labor Union Women created by union women in 41 states and 58 unions to increase women's involvement in both unions and political activities, with the particular intention of addressing women's needs
- Women Employed formed particularly to support non-union office workers to gain both respect and equality
- Built by Girls, which is dedicated to increasing women in the STEM fields by hosting events and helping female students obtain internships at tech companies; in engineering in particular, Girls Who Code focuses on closing the gender gap in computer science, finding itself on track in 2018 to achieving gender parity in that field by 2027

- The National Abortion Rights Action League, which initially focused on repealing anti-abortion laws and then in 1973 following the landmark *Roe v. Wade* decision making abortions legal throughout the country, battling against laws and regulations limiting abortion access (Avila 2018; Lewis 2019).

From the 1970s onward, NOW has remained active. The organization has taken a significant role in addressing the issues of sexual harassment and violence. In particular, in 1995 NOW planned the first mass demonstration focusing on violence against women, drawing a quarter-million activists to the Mall in Washington, DC (NOW 2020).

Just two years later as actress Ashley Judd's career was taking off, she was invited to a meeting with Harvey Weinstein, the head of Miramax, a major producer and distributor of films and television shows. Astonished and repulsed by Weinstein's persistent efforts to coerce her into bed, Judd managed to escape. Later she recalled feeling "panicky, trapped," and deeply intimidated by the realization that this powerful man had the clout to destroy her career. At that moment Judd asked herself, "How do I get out of the room as fast as possible without alienating Harvey Weinstein?" (Kantor and Twohey 2017).

A few minutes after leaving Weinsten, Judd told her father about the incident and soon afterwards many other people. However, it was not until 20 years later that she truly went public when a reporter from *The New York Times* interviewed her. Judd was the first of many women, including a number of stars, to go on record about Weinstein's sexual misconduct (Zacharek et al. 2017).

Following the Judd statement, investigators for *The New York Times* found that undisclosed accusations against Weinstein extended back almost three decades and that he had made settlements with eight women, including two former assistants, an actress, and an Italian model (Kantor and Twohey 2017). A screenwriter told Ashley Judd that "Weinstein's behavior was an open secret passed around on the whisper network that had been furrowing through Hollywood for years" (Zacharek et al. 2017).

Shortly after Judd went public, Weinstein gave a statement to *The New York Times* in which he said, "I appreciate the way I've behaved with colleagues in the past has caused a lot of pain, and I sincerely apologize for it. Though I'm trying to do better, I know I have a long way to go" (Kantor and Twohey 2017). It was too late. Major forces were mobilizing against him.

Like Black Lives Matter, the Me Too campaign became prominent in a social setting containing the supportive social conditions Neil Smelser (1962, 15–17) described in his theory of collective behavior. Structural strain associated with sexual harassment and assault has been prevalent in the work world, persistently oppressing women in various job settings as Chapter 5 indicated. A team of journalists writing in *Time* indicated that as a result many women have felt "a very real and potent sense of unrest."

Under such stressful conditions, many women have embraced the growth and spread of a generalized belief condemning sexual harassment and assault. Because of so much attention to the Weinstein case, that belief seemed to have surfaced suddenly, but, as the journalists noted, "it has actually been simmering for years, decades, centuries." They declared,

> Women have had it with bosses and co-workers who not only cross boundaries but don't even seem to know that boundaries exist. They've had it with the fear of retaliation, of being blackballed, of being fired from a job they can't afford to lose. They've had it with the code of going along to get along.
>
> *(Zacharek et al. 2017)*

Then along came Judd—the initial precipitating factor, with others following. The journalists wrote, "Emboldened by Judd, ... a host of other prominent accusers, women everywhere ... [began] to speak out about the inappropriate, abusive and in some cases illegal behavior they've faced." The team of reporters labeled them "the silence breakers" (Zacharek et al. 2017).

Several days after Judd's interview, actress Alyssa Milano sent a tweet that racheted up readers' response, "all revolving [as a journalist wrote] around two words: 'Me too'" (Chen 2017). Within the next 24 hours, she had received over a half-million replies using the hashtag #MeToo. During that same day, other social media were also active. For instance, *Facebook* provided statistics indicating that 4.7 million users made 12 million posts involving the Me Too issue.

In the subsequent year, over 19 million tweets included the hashtag #MeToo, that is more than 55,000 a day, and according to a media-analytics company, during that time period, that hashtag received more American journalists' references than the term sexual harassment. Furthermore in the days following Milano's tweet, the issue went viral, with 85 countries having at least 1,000 #MeToo tweets (Anderson and Toor 2018; *The Economist* 2017; Park 2018).

Over a three-year period, the Me Too campaign produced various distinct impacts:

- An increasing number of Americans have begun to examine the use of power in gender relations more extensively. An analysis of the tweets on the Me Too issue following Harvey Weinstein's public exposure provided some insight into the content of the exchanges that occurred on social media.

Prominent topics in the tweets included the individual's personal account of sexual harassment or violence, references to the entertainment industry or celebrities, and comments about the relationship of sexual abuse to politics and politicians (Anderson and Toor 2018).

For victims these communications could be very helpful, proving to them, according to a journalist, that "they were not alone. And people who had never had to think about sexual harassment before suddenly saw how much it had affected their coworkers, children, parents, and friends" (North 2019).

- To feed what clearly was becoming a major campaign, an outpouring of not only social and mass media material developed but a host of books soon followed—for instance, Linda Hirshman's *Reckoning: The Epic Battle against Sexual Abuse and Harassment* describing the roots of the Me Too movement and others providing detail about well-known men's downfall, along with a number covering the sexual-abuse scandals in politics and sports (Helmore 2019).

- Investigation into the most prominent cases involving sexual misconduct revealed that when reaching a settlement with a victim the men often included a nondisclosure agreement that prohibited the awarded victim from disclosing any details about their behavior. For instance, Weinstein's lawyers compelled a former assistant to sign such an agreement, indicating that she would tell nobody, including family members, that their client had frequently exposed himself to her and that she was required to take dictation while he bathed.

Obviously nondisclosure agreements are a very effective means of keeping past illegal or immoral behavior secret, readily allowing individuals to carry on with other victims. Once this reality became known, the legislatures in three heavily populated states acted quickly. Within a year of the Weinstein case going public, California, New Jersey, and New York had passed laws prohibiting nondisclosure agreements in situations involving sexual harassment or assault as well as sex discrimination, and other states have begun to produce similar legislation.

- Additional new laws involving sexual abuse are now in the offing. Currently self-employed individuals like actors and Uber drivers are not eligible for federal protection, and neither are child or farm workers in businesses with fewer than 15 employees. The only sexually aggrieved people who can approach the U.S. Equal Employment Opportunity Commission (EEOC) with an issue are those working for organizations with at least 15 workers. However, it is hardly clear sailing for these individuals. The process they face is long and places a number of deadlines on the time frame in which to file a complaint (Campbell 2018; North 2019).

Some recourse is already apparent, and in the future it is likely to become more prevalent. In at least eight states, a victim can file a claim in a state agency and sue for protection for discriminatory treatment under current civil-rights laws. Furthermore some initiatives are underway to obtain federal protection. For example, a sexually harassed domestic worker with seven children from a state without protections led over 200 domestic and farm workers to Capitol Hill, where they met with 60 lawmakers to discuss the need to repeal the exemption of selected workers under the current federal law (Campbell 2018).

- While since 2017 sexually abused women have had an unprecedented opportunity to strike back against their oppressors, many have lacked the money for such a legal battle. Some organizations have offered assistance, among them the TIME'S UP Legal Defense Fund, an initiative produced by women in Hollywood, who were already focused on sexual harassment. In about a year, the group received over 4,000 requests for help and raised over $24 million to help women sexually harassed on the job who are pursuing legal action against sexual predators (Faut and Driscoll 2019; North 2019).

While many of the requests came from women in low-paid positions and about one third were from women of color, the victims overall displayed diverse personal traits. Describing the program, a pair of writers explained,

> In the past year and a half, we've heard ... stories of sexual harassment from actresses and fast food workers, from paramedics and Ph.D. students, from fish packers and legislators. We've heard stories of sexual harassment at work from a 15-year-old girl at her first job at McDonalds, ... from a new mother trying to pump in privacy, and from a grandmother, working towards retirement.
>
> *(Faut and Driscoll 2019)*

A Tentative Look Ahead

I find myself wondering about the future coexistence of these two campaigns. Notably at one time, Alicia Garza, a co-founder of Black Lives Matter and a victim of sexual assault, paid tribute to Tarana Burke, the African American activist who started Me Too in 2007 to assist survivors of sexual assaults in disadvantaged communities without any rape-crisis centers. Many Me Too supporters are unaware of how their campaign started.

Catherine Rottenberg, a professor of American studies and an author on modern feminism, noted that it is only when "powerful, wealthy, and mostly white women" initiate lawsuits that important, influential men lose their positions. Rottenberg added, "This raises the absolutely crucial question of when and where claims of sexual harassment and assault are heard and whose voices count" (Rottenberg 2018). Yes, inevitably as our society moves into the future, some groups will continue to be more advantaged than others, and it will be critical for the overall success of this campaign that advocates supporting disadvantaged victims will continue the hard fight, playing a prominent role.

All in all, it seems inevitable that the pair of established social movements as well as the recent campaigns emerging from them will persist, undoubtedly remaining influential, encouraging activists and sometimes producing abrupt changes as the following examples suggest.

About three months after George Floyd's death, two women's professional softball teams began what was supposed to be a seven-game series in Florida. During the game and unbeknownst to the players, the general manager of Scrap Yard Fast Pitch, one of the participating teams, contacted President Trump, who had frequently been critical of Colin Kaepernick's kneeling during the national anthem, and proudly tweeted "Everyone standing for the FLAG!"

After the game the players learned what had happened. "It was a shock," said Cat Osterman, a renowned pitcher. "An actual, genuine speechless shock took over our locker room." Immediately the players started discussing the issue, readily concluding that the most troubling fact about the post was that without consulting the players, the general manager had spoken for all of them and that her tweet suggested the players opposed the Black Lives Matter campaign.

The team had two Black players, and the other 16 were white. After the discussion Kelsey Stewart, a Black player, said that the general manager's tweet revealed that she "didn't care about my or Kiki's [the other Black player's] life." Stewart was pleased to see that her white teammates "got very, very angry" and participated energetically in the exchanges.

Until that moment few if any of the players had been activists. However, living in the context of the two developing social movements, they well might have been on the cusp of activism. Now the entire team acted quickly and decisively, quitting Scrap Yard even though they knew it was one of very few organizations sponsoring top-tier professional softball teams. "We're not going to tolerate that in our sport," Osterman said. "It wasn't as hard as everyone thinks it was, because we knew it was the right thing to do" (Weiner 2020, B10).

During the era of the Black Lives Matter campaign, the motivation for organizational changes vary. Consider pro football's Washington Redskins and the lengthy debate about changing its name. For decades many activists had condemned "Redskins" as a racist slur, but Daniel Snyder, the team's principal owner, refused to change it, remaining outspokenly defiant on the subject. In 2013 Snyder inflamed the debate by telling a reporter, "We'll never change the name. It's that simple. NEVER. You can use caps."

However, about a month after George Floyd's death, Snyder agreed to change the name. Did he, like the Scrap Yard team members, suddenly realize it was the right thing to do, in this instance appreciating that Native Americans' lives really mattered? NO. In large part the impetus came from FedEx, which had been paying $8 million a year for the naming rights to the team's stadium. Its legal counsel informed an official for the team that unless a name change occurred, that lucrative deal was off (Belson and Draper 2020).

Whether it involves the two celebrated social movements featured in the preceding section or some other issue affecting disadvantaged groups, the prospect of changes and the struggles that accompany them will continue.

Conclusion: Can We Do Better?

It does appear that in the wake of the coronavirus and the two campaigns just discussed, the people of this nation, at least many of them, might have become more attuned to the reality that some of their fellow citizens, the ones seriously at risk, have lived their lives affected by at least one of the three scourges featured in this book—poverty, racism, or sexism.

What follows is a brief proposal of the kind of positive response that can be made to such an awakening—in this instance involving what appears to have been a useful and productive teamwork between investigators and practitioners. First, a team of researchers gathered detailed information about the specific disadvantages a certain group of people suffered. Second, staff members in organizations which could provide the individuals assistance received the study results and with that information were able to work with their clients to meet the various economic, psychological, or social challenges they faced. The data for this collaboration are from the U.S. Census Bureau involving children either born in the US between 1978 and 1983 or similarly aged children who have parents who were legal immigrants (Chetty et al. 2018, 12).

In this case study, a distinguished team of researchers found that among the major racial groups Black males stand out as having depressed economic advancement—lower rates of upward mobility and higher rates of downward mobility than their white peers, with variations in wages and employment rates producing the differences. Among women, however, there were no differences.

The research team realized that they needed to take a hard look at possible programs, only engaging in measures that had previously proved successful. Certain widely supported programs proved ineffective, providing invaluable information about options to avoid. For instance, the investigators examined cash-transfer programs and minimum-wage increases that could offer instant relief, but they did not stimulate upward mobility. In addition, programs that reduced residential segregation or facilitated Black and white children attending the same schools without achieving racial segregation within either neighborhoods or schools left the gap between Black and white male employment rates largely intact.

An important finding, already addressed in Chapter 6, was that the childhood neighborhood environment affects adults' earning capacity. The research suggested that Black boys have been more likely to become successful economically when growing up in areas with half of their fathers in the home and less than a 10 percent poverty rate in the neighborhood. However, barely 4 percent of Black boys' childhood years occur in such areas compared to 62.5 percent of their white counterparts (Chetty et al. 2018, 40–42).

The team concluded "our results suggest that efforts that cut *within* neighborhoods and schools and improve environments for specific racial subgroups, such as [B]lack boys, may be more effective in reducing the [B]lack–white gap"—for instance, mentoring programs for Black children, organized local efforts to reduce whites' racial bias, and exercises that promote improving social interaction among racial groups within a neighborhood or community (Chetty et al. 2018, 42).

So the researchers discovered potentially precious information that could improve many Black males' life chances. What's the most productive next step for effectively extending such a coordinated approach to a variety of at-risk groups? An enlightened, mobilized citizenry would support a nation-wide cooperative effort that would use valuable information obtained to address the kinds of destructive conditions just mentioned, urging a renewal of competent, caring national, state, and local leadership encouraging and supporting a host of economic, political, and social advances. It is a cooperative venture that could produce exciting, life-enhancing results.

Key Terms in the Glossary

social movement
soft skills

Discussion Topics

1. How do you feel about pro athletes' participation in protests involving racial or gender issues? What is your personal preference about taking part in such protests?

2. Would you leave the federal tax system the way it is, or would you make changes? If you support changes, indicate why.

3. Focus on two or three soft skills and illustrate how they are essential for workers in specific types of jobs.

4. Consider whether or not the American health-care system compares favorably to affluent nations' systems in its support for disadvantaged groups. If you are critical of the American system, what would you advocate as the most important changes to make?

5. Using material from this chapters and a variety of other sources, produce a paper which carefully and thoroughly discusses a potentially effective effort to alleviate prominent risks and challenges that one of the groups discussed in this book must constantly confront.

6. Would the Black Lives Matter campaign have had such an international impact if it had originated in another country? Discuss the factor(s) coming into play.

7. What positive results is the Me Too campaign likely to bring? In the future are wealthy white women likely to continue to be the chief beneficiaries of lawsuits involving sexual misconduct?

8. A highly respected professional coach who emphasizes the need to address the fact that social injustice for Blacks and other people of color is widespread in our society indicated that the production of more informative textbooks would represent a significant advance. Comment on his suggestion.

Bibliography

African American Policy Forum. 2020. "#SayHerName Campaign." https://aapf.org/sayhername.

Anderson, Monica and Skye Toor. 2018. "How Social Media Users Have Discussed Sexual Harassment since #MeToo Went Viral." Pew Research Center. (October 11). https://www.pewresearch.org/fact-tank/2018/10/11/how-social-media-users-have-discussed-sexual-harassment-since-metoo-went-viral/.

Anderson, Monica, Skye Toor, Lee Rainie, and Aaron Smith. 2018. "Activism in the Social Media Age." Pew Research Center. (July 11). https://www.pewresearch.org/internet/2018/07/11/activism-in-the-social-media-age.

Anti-Defamation League. 2020. "Civil Rights Movement." https://www.adl.org/education/resources/backgrounders/civil-rights-movement.

Avila, Theresa. 2018. "10 Women's Rights Organizations You Can Support This Election Season (and Always)." girlboss. (October 25). https://www.girlboss.com/identity/womens-rights-organizations.

BBC News. 2020. "George Floyd: What Happened in the Final Moments of His Life." (May 30). https://www.bbc.com/news/world-us-canada-52861726.

Belson, Ken, and Kevin Draper. 2020. "Redskins to Drop Name, Yielding to Pressure from Sponsors and Activists." *The New York Times*. (July 13). https://www.nytimes.com/2020/07/13/sports/football/washington-redskins-new-name.html.

Benevolent. 2014. "Rose from Inkster, MI." (December 24). http://www.benevolent.net/need.html?needId=902.

Black Lives Matter. 2020a. "About Black Lives Matter." https://blacklivesmatter.com/about/.

Black Lives Matter. 2020b. "Our Co-founders." https://blacklivesmatter.com/our-co-founders/.

Booth, Stephanie. 2019. "Medicare for All: What Is It and How It Will Work." (September 11). healthline. https://www.healthline.com/health/what-medicare-for-all-would-look-like-in-america#1.

Border, Gabriella and David Shepardson. 2019. "No Federal Charges for New York Policeman in 2014 'I Can't Breathe' Death." Reuters. https://www.reuters.com/article/us-usa-police-garner/us-wont-charge-new-york-police-officers-in-2014-i-cant-breathe-death-idUSKCN1UB1IG.

Brockes, Emma. 2018. "#MeToo Founder Tarana Burke: You Have to Use Your Privilege to Serve Other People." *The Guardian.* (January 15). https://www.theguardian.com/world/2018/jan/15/me-too-founder-tarana-burke-women-sexual-assault.

Burtless, Gary. 2018. "When the Next Recession Hits, Will Unemployment Benefits Be Generous Enough?" Brookings. (November 28). https://www.brookings.edu/opinions/when-the-next-recession-hits-will-unemployment-benefits-be-generous-enough/.

Calhoun, Arthur W. 1960. *A Social History of the American Family.* Vol. 2. New York: Barnes and Noble.

Campbell, Alexia Fernández. 2018. "Housekeepers and Nannies Have No Protection from Sexual Harassment under Federal Law." *Vox.* (April 26). https://www.vox.com/2018/4/26/17275708/housekeepers-nannies-sexual-harassment-laws.

Carson, Clayborn. 1987. "Martin Luther King, Jr: Charismatic Leadership in a Mass Struggle." *Journal of American History* 74 (September): 448–454.

Chen, Joyce. 2017. "Alyssa Milano Wants Her 'Me Too' Campaign to Elevate Harvey Weinstein Discussion." *Rolling Stone.* (October 17). https://www.rollingstone.com/movies/movie-news/alyssa-milano-wants-her-me-too-campaign-to-elevate-harvey-weinstein-discussion-123610/.

Chetty, Raj, Nathaniel Hendren, Maggie R. Jones, and Sonya R. Porter. 2018. "Race and Economic Opportunity in the United States: An Intergenerational Perspective." Harvard University. http://www.equality-of-opportunity.org/assets/documents/race_paper.pdf.

Colarossi, Natalie. 2020. "Stunning Photos and Videos Show the Protests against Police Brutality from the Skies." *Insider.* (June 8). https://www.insider.com/black-lives-matter-protests-aerial-footage-photos-2020-6.

Colen, Cynthia G., David M. Ramey, Elizabeth C. Cooksey, and David R. Williams. 2018. "Racial Disparities in Health among Nonpoor African Americans and Hispanics: The Role of Acute and Chronic Discrimination." *Social Science & Medicine* 199 (February): 167–180.

The Commonwealth Fund. 2020. "*U.S. Ranks Last among Seven Countries on Health System Performance Measures.*" https://www.commonwealthfund.org/publications/newsletter-article/us-ranks-last-among-seven-countries-health-system-performance.

Constitutional Rights Foundation. 2020. "Social Protests." https://www.crf-usa.org/black-history-month/social-protests.

Copeland, Phillipe. 2016. "Let's Get Free: Social Work and the Movement for Black Lives." *Journal of Forensic Social Work* 5 (January): 3–19.

Deming, David D. 2020. "The Value of Soft Skills in the Labor Market." National Bureau of Economic Research. https://www.nber.org/reporter/2017number4/deming.html.

Dettmer, Jamie. 2020. "Who's Behind the Violence at George Floyd Protests in US?" VOA. (June 4). https://www.voanews.com/usa/whos-behind-violence-george-floyd-protests-us.

Doob, Christopher Bates. 2000. *Sociology: An Introduction,* 6th ed. New York: Harcourt Press.

The Economist. 2018. "After a Year of #MeToo, American Opinion Has Shifted against Victims." (October 15). https://www.economist.com/graphic-detail/2018/10/15/after-a-year-of-metoo-american-opinion-has-shifted-against-victims.

The Economist. 2020. How George Floyd's Death Reverberates around the World." (June 8). https://www.economist.com/international/2020/06/08/how-george-floyds-death-reverberates-around-the-world.

Faut, Nicole, and Ellie Driscoll. 2019. "TIME'S UP Legal Defense Fund—Helping to Break the Cycle of Silence and Isolation." (March 26). https://www.impactfund.org/social-justice-blog/timesup.

Gabbatt, Adam. 2020. "Protests about Police Brutality Are Met with Wave of Police Brutality across the US." *The Guardian.* (June 6). https://www.theguardian.com/us-news/2020/jun/06/police-violence-protests-us-george-floyd.

Gerth, Hans, and C. Wright Mills. 1946. *From Max Weber: Essays in Sociology.* New York: Oxford University Press.

Gilman, Charlotte Perkins. 1973. "Excerpts from *Women and Economics,*" pp. 572–598 in Alice S. Rossi (ed.), *The Feminist Papers.* New York: Bantam Books. Originally published in Boston, MA: Small, Maynard. 1898.

Goldberg, Michelle. 2020. "America is a Tinderbox." *The New York Times.* (May 29). https://www.nytimes.com/2020/05/29/opinion/george-floyd- protests-minneapolis.html.

Gringlas, Sam. 2020. "Young Activists Pour Energy into Protests, but What about the Elections?" *npr.* (June 14). https://www.npr.org/2020/06/14/876101226/young-activists-pour-energy-into-protests-but-what-about-the-election.

Gupta, Alisha Haridasani. 2020. "Since 2015: 48 Black Women Killed by the Police. And Only 2 Charges." *The New York Times.* (September 24). https://www.nytimes.com/2020/09/24/us/breonna-taylor-grand-jury-black-women.html.

Haislop, Tadd. 2020. "Colin Kaepernick Kneeling Timeline: How Protests during the National Anthem Started a Movement in the NFL." *Sporting News.* (June 9). https://www.sportingnews.com/us/nfl/news/colin-kaepernick-kneeling-protests-timeline/xktu6ka4diva1s5jxaylrcsse.

Helmore, Edward. 2019. "#MeToo: After Weinstein and Epstein, an 'Unprecedented' Wave of Books." *The Guardian.* (September 14). https://www.theguardian.com/us-news/2019/sep/13/metoo-the-unprecedented-movement-that-launched-a-wave-of-books.

Horowitz, Juliana Menasce, and Gretchen Livingston. 2020. "How Americans View the Black Lives Matter Movement." Pew Research Center. (July 8). https://www.pewresearch.org/fact-tank/2016/07/08/how-americans-view-the-black-lives-matter-movement/.

Hossain, Farhana, and Emily Terwelp. 2015. "Increasing Employment Opportunities for Disadvantaged Young Adults." Manpower Demonstration Research Corporation. (February). https://www.mdrc.org/publication/increasing-employment-opportunities-disadvantaged-young-adults.

Ipsos. 2020. "Reuters/Ipsos Poll: Civil Unrest in the Wake of George Floyd's Killing." https://www.ipsos.com/en-us/news-polls/reuters-ipsos-civil-unrest-george-floyd-2020- 06-02.

Johnson, Odis, Jr., Keon Gilbert, and Habiba Ibrahim. 2018. "Race, Gender, and The Contexts of Unarmed Fatal Interactions with Police." Washington University in St. Louis. https://cpb-us-w2.wpmucdn.com/sites.wustl.edu/dist/b/1205/files/2018/02/Race-Gender-and-Unarmed-1y9md6e.pdf.

Kantor, Jodi, and Megan Twohey. 2017. "Harvey Weinstein Paid Off Sexual Harassment Accusers for Decades." *The New York Times.* (October 5). https://www.nytimes.com/2017/10/05/us/harvey-weinstein-harassment-allegations.html.

Kashner, Megan. 2017. "Underemployment, Poverty and the New Normal in America." *HuffPost.* (December 6). https://www.huffpost.com/entry/underemployment-poverty-a_b_5831064.

Khan Academy. 2020. "American Women and World War II." https://www.khanacademy.org/humanities/us-history/rise-to-world-power/us-wwii/a/american-women-and-world-war-ii.

King Institute, Stanford University. 2020. "'I Have a Dream' Address Delivered at the March on Washington for Jobs and Freedom." https://kinginstitute.stanford.edu/king-papers/documents/i-have-dream-address-delivered-march-washington-jobs-and-freedom.

Korver, Kyle. 2019. "Privileged." *The Players' Tribune*. (April 8). https://www.theplayerstribune.com/en-us/articles/kyle-korver-utah-jazz-nba.

Lewis, Jone Johnson. 2019. "Feminist Organizations of the 1970s." ThoughtCo. (February 21). https://www.thoughtco.com/top-feminist-organizations-of-the-1970s-3528928.

Linden, Michael. 2019. "What Could the US Afford If It Raised Billionaires' Taxes? We Do the Math." *The Guardian*. (December 13). https://www.theguardian.com/us-news/2019/dec/13/billionaires-taxes-inequality-one-percent.

McNulty, Jennifer. 2019. "Youth Activism Is on the Rise around the Globe, and Adults Should Pay Attention, Author Says." University of California, Santa Cruz. (September 17). https://news.ucsc.edu/2019/09/taft-youth.html.

Matthaei, Julie A. 1982. *An Economic History of Women in America: Women's Work, the Sexual Division of Labor, and the Development of Capitalism*. New York: Schocken Books.

National Archives. 2016. "Women in the Workforce during World War II." (August 15). https://www.archives.gov/education/lessons/wwii-women.html.

National Center for Education Statistics. 2019. "A Letter from the Commissioner of the National Center for Education Statistics." (May). https://nces.ed.gov/programs/coe/commissioner.asp.

National Center on Education and the Economy. 2020. "Japan: Governance and Accountability." http://ncee.org/what-we-do/center-on-international-education-benchmarking/top-performing-countries/japan-overview/japan-system-and-school-organization/.

National World War I Museum and Memorial. 2020. "Women in World War I." https://www.theworldwar.org/learn/women.

Newberry, Phyllis M., Myrna M. Weisman, and Jerome K. Myers. 1979. "Working Wives and Housewives: Do They Differ in Mental Status and Social Adjustment?" *American Journal of Orthopsychiatry* 49 (April): 282–291.

The New York Times. 2020. "Minneapolis to Band Use of Chokeholds by Police." https://www.nytimes.com/2020/06/05/us/george-floyd-protests.html.

North, Anna. 2017. "For Every Harvey Weinstein, There's a Hundred More Men in the Neighborhood Doing the Exact Same Thing." *Vox*. (October 28). https://www.vox.com/2017/10/28/16563668/me-too-tarana-burke-harvey-weinstein-harassment-assault.

North, Anna. 2019. "7 Positive Changes That Have Come from the #MeToo Movement." *Vox*. (October 4). https://www.vox.com/identities/2019/10/4/20852639/me-too-movement-sexual-harassment-law-2019.

NOW. 2011. "Founding." (July). https://now.org/about/history/founding-2/.

NOW. 2020. "Who We Are." https://now.org/about/who-we-are/.

OECD. 2015. "Japan: Programme for International Student Assessment (PISA). Results from PISA 2015." https://www.oecd.org/pisa/PISA-2015-Japan.pdf.

OECD. 2020. "Japan." (May 12). https://gpseducation.oecd.org/CountryProfile?primaryCountry=JPN&treshold=10&topic=PI.

Park, Andrea. 2017. "#MeToo Reaches 85 Countries with 1.7M Tweets." CBS News. (October 24). https://www.cbsnews.com/news/metoo-reaches-85-countries-with-1-7-million-tweets/.

Parker, Kim, Juliana Menasce Horowitz, and Monica Anderson. 2020. "Amid Protests, Majorities across Racial and Ethnic Groups Express Support for the Black Lives Matter Movement." Pew Research Center. (June 12). https://www.pewsocialtrends.org/2020/06/12/amid-protests-majorities-across-racial-and-ethnic-groups-express-support-for-the-black-lives-matter-movement/.

Pearl, Robert. 2015. "Why Health Care Is Different If You're Black, Latino or Poor." Forbes. (March 5). https://www.forbes.com/sites/robertpearl/2015/03/05/healthcare-black-latino-poor/#650e42837869.

Pew Research Center. 2019. "Widest Partisan Gap in Views of Fairness of Tax System in at Least Two Decades." (April 4). https://www.people-press.org/2019/04/04/growing-partisan-divide-over-fairness-of-the-nations-tax-system/pp_2019-04-04_taxes_0-01/.

Pilkington, Ed. 2020. "After 15 Days of Antiracist Protests ... What Happens Next?" The Guardian. (June 10). https://www.theguardian.com/us-news/2020/jun/10/george-floyd-protests-what-happens-next.

Reinhardt, R.J. 2018. "One in Three Americans Have Felt the Urge to Protest." Gallup Poll. (August 24). https://news.gallup.com/poll/241634/one-three-americans-felt-urge-protest.aspx.

Robertson, Campbell, Rick Rojas, and Kate Taylor. 2020. "After George Floyd's Death, Toll Rises in Protests across the Country." The New York Times. (June 1). https://www.nytimes.com/2020/06/01/us/george-floyd-unrest-toll.html.

Romano, Aja. 2020. "'Arrest the Cops Who Killed Breonna Taylor': The Power and the Peril of a Catchphrase." Vox. (August 10). https://www.vox.com/21327268/breonna-taylor-say-her-name-meme-hashtag.

Rook, David. 2018. "How Does Healthcare in Europe Work?" G.P. Griffin Group. https://www.griffinbenefits.com/employeebenefitsblog/how-does-healthcare-in-europe-work.

Roper, Willem. 2020. "Black Americans 2.5X More Likely than Whites to Be Killed by Police." (June 2). https://www.statista.com/chart/21872/map-of-police-violence-against-black-americans/.

Rosen, Jody. 2020. "The Bicycle as a Vehicle of Protest." The New Yorker. (June 10). https://www.newyorker.com/culture/cultural-comment/the-bicycle-as-a-vehicle-of-protest.

Rottenberg, Catherine. 2018. "Can #MeToo Go beyond White Neoliberal Feminism?" Aljazeera. (December 17). https://www.aljazeera.com/indepth/opinion/metoo-white-neoliberal-feminism-171213064156855.html.

Russell, Jessica C. 2011. "The Use of Narratives to Contextualize the Experiences and Needs of Unemployed, Underemployed, and Displaced Workers." Journal of Employment Counseling 48 (June): 50–62.

Safi, Michael. 2019. "Protests Rage around the World—but What Comes Next?" The Guardian. (October 25). https://www.theguardian.com/world/2019/oct/25/protests-rage-around-the-world-hong-kong-lebanon-chile-catalonia-iraq.

Scanzoni, John and Letha Scanzoni. 1988. Men, Women, and Change, 3rd ed. New York: McGraw-Hill.

Schmidt, Christopher W. 2016. "Legal History and the Problem of the Long Civil Rights Movement." Law & Society Inquiry 41 (Fall): 1081–1107.

Seales, Rebecca. 2018. "What Has #MeToo Actually Changed?" BBC News. (May 12). https://www.bbc.com/news/world-44045291.

Semuels, Alana. 2016. "Good School, Rich School; Bad School, Poor School: The Inequality at the Heart of America's Education System." The Atlantic. (August 25). https://www.theatlantic.com/business/archive/2016/08/property-taxes-and-unequal-schools/497333/.

Semuels, Alana. 2017. "Japan Might Be What Equality in Education Looks Like." The Atlantic. (August 2). https://www.theatlantic.com/business/archive/2017/08/japan-equal-education-school-cost/535611/.

Smelser, Neil J. 1962. Theory of Collective Behavior. New York: The Free Press.

Statista. 2020. "Number of People Shot to Death by the Police in the United States 2017 to 2020, by Race." https://www.statista.com/statistics/585152/people-shot-to-death-by-us-police-by-race/.

Stewart, Emily. 2020. "George Floyd's Killing Has Opened the Wounds of Centuries of American Racism." *Vox.* (June 3). https://www.vox.com/identities/2020/5/30/21275694/george-floyd-protests-minneapolis-atlanta-new-york-brooklyn-cnn.

Thomas, Melvin, Hayward Derrick Horton, and Loren Henderson. 2019. "Working but Poor: Racial Differences in Underemployment and Economic Hardship." American Sociological Association. (January): 1–13.

U.S. Department of Education. 2019. "Relationship between Educational Attainment and Labor Underutilization." (April). https://nces.ed.gov/pubs2019/2019039.pdf.

Van Burkleo, Susan F. 2001. *Belonging to the World. Women's Rights and American Constitutional Culture.* New York: Oxford University Press.

Waxman, Olivia B. 2020. "'He had Transformed:' What It Was like to Watch Martin Luther King Jr. Give the 'I Have a Dream' Speech." *Time.* (January 9). https://time.com/5379364/martin-luther-king-dream-speech-anniversary/.

Wehrwein, Peter. 2019. "'Broken American Health Care: Good People, Bad System, and the Health Powers of the Disruptors." *Managed Care.* (August 5). https://www.managedcaremag.com/archives/2019/8/broken-american-health-care-good-people-bad-system-and-health-powers-disruptors.

Weiner, Natalie. 2020. "Team's Tweet to President Leads Players to Quit Series." *The New York Times.* (June 25): B10.

White, Gilliam B. 2015. "A Long Road Home." *The Atlantic.* (August 3). https://www.theatlantic.com/business/archive/2015/08/hurricane-katrina-sandy-disaster-recovery-/400244/.

Wilson, Valerie, and Jessica Schneider. 2018. "Countries Investing More in Social Programs Have Less Child Poverty." Economic Policy Institute. (June 1). https://www.epi.org/publication/countries-investing-more-in-social-programs-have-less-child-poverty/.

Wollstonecraft, Mary. 1980. "A Vindication of the Rights of Women," pp. 457–463 in Sheila Ruth (ed.), *Issues in Feminism.* Boston, MA: Houghton Mifflin. Originally published in 1792.

Wortham, Nenna. 2020. "A 'Glorious Poetic Rage.'". *The New York Times.* (June 5). https://www.nytimes.com/2020/06/05/sunday-review/black-lives-matter-protests-floyd.html.

Zacharek, Stephanie, Eliana Dockterman, and Haley Sweetland Edwards. 2017. "The Silence Breakers." *Time.* (December 18). https://time.com/time-person-of-the-year-2017-silence-breakers/.

GLOSSARY

affirmative action a policy that seeks to improve the educational or occupational opportunities for candidates historically limited by their race, gender, religion, disability, age, or national origin

apprenticeship a worker's on-the-job training accompanied by classroom instruction for which the individual receives wages and also an industry-recognized credential after one to six years on the job

colorblind racism whites' assertion that they are living in a world where racial privilege no longer exists while their behavior supports structures and practices perpetuating racial advantage

conflict theory a perspective contending that the struggle for wealth, power, and prestige in society should be the central concern of sociology

disconnected youth teens and young adults between the ages of 16 and 24 who are neither in school nor working, often resulting in a high-risk, stressful limbo

doing gender a process influenced by the prevailing norms involving the construction and performance of gender while also possessing the potential to resist or ignore those norms

food insecure possessing insufficient funds and other resources to provide food for active, healthy, hunger-free living

hidden curriculum the important but unofficial messages about values, beliefs, and behavior that teachers and administrators can implicitly communicate to students

high-stakes testing the use of standardized tests as the basis for accountability, with decisions about students' admission, grade promotion, and graduation as well as teachers' and administrators' salaries and promotion based on students' test scores

ideology the complex of values and beliefs that support a society's social-stratification systems and their distribution of wealth, income, and power

implicit racism the unconscious, biased perceptions of and behavior toward members of a racial group

implicit sexism men's unconscious, biased perceptions of and behavior toward women

intersectionality the recognition that an individual's oppressions, limitations, and opportunities often result from the combined impact of two or more influential statuses—in particular, gender, race, social class, age, job, parent role, and sexual preference

Jim Crow era the century extending from Reconstruction to the 1960s during which laws and customs mandated a castelike separation of Blacks and whites, featuring Blacks' subordination and oppression

microaggressions disrespectful behavior, whether intended or not, that indicates the person initiating the action considers the other individual an inferior

mortality rate a measure of the number of deaths in a specific population over a designated time span

pedagogy of poverty a set of ineffective even destructive teaching practices in poor schools often imposed on their students

racially restrictive covenant a contract among property owners prohibiting specified minorities from buying, leasing, or occupying property in their locale

racial socialization the process during which parents or others teach children the values, norms, beliefs, and behavior considered appropriate for their racial or ethnic group

racism the belief that real or imagined traits of one race establish its superiority over another or others

redlining the discriminatory practice of refusing to provide mortgage loans or property insurance or only providing them at accelerated rates for reasons not associated with any conventional assessment of risk

risk the probability of an unwanted outcome involving exposure to loss or injury

risk factor an element in a situation that increases the probability of a certain outcome, usually an unpleasant one such as a disease or some other negative condition

separate–but–equal standard a legal doctrine establishing segregated services and facilities for Blacks and whites

sexism beliefs asserting that real or imagined differences between women and men establish the superiority of men

social class a large category of similarly ranked people located in a hierarchy and distinguished from the other categories by such traits as education, occupation, income, and wealth

social movement an organized, collective activity undertaken by people to promote or resist social change

social reproduction the process by which people belonging to certain categories, such as social classes, have differing access to the valuable resources that influence the transmission of inequality from one generation to the next

soft skills the attributes that prove essential for effective interaction on many jobs, involving such traits as communication abilities, flexibility, teamwork capacities, reliability, and problem-solving knowledge

stereotype a set of distinctly negative traits that prejudiced people apply to the members of a group against whom they are prejudiced

tracking a process where educators evaluate students and then place them in programs with a curriculum that allegedly is appropriate for their abilities

urban war zone a poor, crime-, and gang-ridden district numerically dominated by people of color in which deteriorated, violent, even war-like conditions and underfunded, largely ineffective schools promote inferior academic performance, including irregular attendance and disruptive or noncompliant classroom behavior

INDEX

Concepts that are boldfaced are defined in the book, often on the first page listed in the index and also in the end-of-text glossary.